Behavioral Approaches to Alcoholism

NIAAA-RUCAS
ALCOHOLISM TREATMENT SERIES

Edited by
Ernest P. Noble, Ph.D., M.D.
Sponsored by
The National Institute on Alcohol Abuse and Alcoholism
and
The Rutgers University Center of Alcohol Studies

This series, jointly sponsored by the National Institute on Alcohol Abuse and Alcoholism and the Rutgers University Center of Alcohol Studies, makes available to the therapeutic and allied professions the best and most systematic current knowledge on helping, treating and rehabilitating those affected by alcoholism, alcohol addiction, problem drinking or drinking problems. Each volume in this series represents the views of its authors, and does not necessarily reflect the stands of the sponsoring institutions.

No. 1.   Selection of Treatment for Alcoholics. Edited by E. Mansell Pattison.*

No. 2.   Behavioral Approaches to Alcoholism. Edited by G. Alan Marlatt and Peter E. Nathan.

No. 3.   Alcoholism Rehabilitation; Methods and Experiences of Private Rehabilitation Centers. Edited by Vincent Groupé.*

No. 4.   Interfaces between Alcoholism and Mental Health. Edited by Earl X. Freed.*

* In press.

Behavioral Approaches to Alcoholism

Edited by

G. ALAN MARLATT AND PETER E. NATHAN

PUBLICATIONS DIVISION
RUTGERS CENTER OF ALCOHOL STUDIES
NEW BRUNSWICK, NEW JERSEY

Library of Congress catalog card number: 77-620035
ISBN: 911290-48-6   ISSN: 0147-0515

MANUFACTURED IN THE UNITED STATES OF AMERICA

CONTENTS

CONTRIBUTORS

GLENN R. CADDY, Ph.D., Associate Professor and Director, Addiction Research and Treatment Center, Old Dominion University, Norfolk, Virginia.

DON CAHALAN, Ph.D., Professor of Behavioral Sciences in Residence and Director of the Social Research Group, School of Public Health, University of California, Berkeley, California.

DAVID M. LAWSON, Ph.D., Assistant Professor, Department of Psychology, University of British Columbia, Vancouver.

G. ALAN MARLATT, Ph.D., Professor of Psychology, University of Washington, Seattle, Washington.

PETER M. MILLER, Ph.D., Director, Department of Behavioral Medicine, Hilton Head Hospital, Hilton Head Island, South Carolina.

PETER E. NATHAN, Ph.D., Professor of Psychology and Director of the Alcohol Behavior Research Laboratory, Rutgers University, New Brunswick, New Jersey.

JOHN B. REID, Ph.D., Research Scientist, Oregon Social Learning Center (a branch of the Wright Institute), Eugene, Oregon.

LINDA C. SOBELL, Ph.D., Director of Alcohol Programs, Dede Wallace Center, Nashville, Tennessee.

MARK B. SOBELL, Ph.D., Associate Professor of Psychology and Director of Graduate Research and Training on Alcohol Dependence, Vanderbilt University, Nashville, Tennessee.

G. TERENCE WILSON, Ph.D., Professor of Psychology and Co-Director of the Alcohol Behavior Research Laboratory, Rutgers University, New Brunswick, New Jersey.

Preface

During the summer of 1975 the Alcoholism and Drug Abuse Institute of the University of Washington sponsored a 2-day conference in Seattle entitled "Behavioral Approaches to Alcoholism and Drug Dependencies." The conference, which attracted a wide audience, brought together a group of nationally known researchers who reported on their work in this rapidly growing field. Apart from previous symposia sponsored by the American Psychological Association and the Association for the Advancement of Behavior Therapy, the Seattle conference was the first national meeting devoted specifically to behavioral approaches to alcoholism and other drug dependencies.

The present volume goes far beyond a presentation of the proceedings of this conference. Each presenter whose work appears in this book was asked to prepare an original chapter outlining developments in and current status of his or her own area of expertise. As such, the material in this volume represents a comprehensive overview of recent research dealing with behavioral approaches to alcoholism, with a critical review of past research significant to the understanding of contemporary issues in the field. We believe that this book represents a scholarly review of the "state of the art" in this area of research.

In addition to the book's 12 chapters, Peter Nathan provides introductory commentaries for each of its three main sections. In addition, at the end of the volume, Alan Marlatt takes a brief "look to the future" and attempts to predict the most important trends for potential research developments in this field.

Many individuals helped make this book possible. We would like to thank the members of the Program Committee of the University of Washington Alcoholism and Drug Abuse Conference, Albert Carlin and Roger Roffman, who worked with Alan Marlatt in planning the conference program. Marc Schuckit, the Director of the Alcoholism and Drug Abuse Institute, is thanked for his opening remarks and introductory comments at the start of the

viii BEHAVIORAL APPROACHES TO ALCOHOLISM

conference. Roberta Lewandowski, of the office of Short Courses and Conferences at the University of Washington, helped make the conference an organizational success. Most of all, however, we extend our sincere thanks to the individuals who contributed the chapters for this book.

G.A.M.
P.E.N.
March 1977

BEHAVIORAL THEORY, BEHAVIORAL THEORIES OF ALCOHOLISM, AND SCOPE OF THE PROBLEM

This section, an overview of what will follow, begins with a brief chapter by Nathan designed to provide a succinct orientation to behavioral theory and practice, sufficient, we hope, to permit the reader who is not conversant with that approach to read, understand and appreciate the rest of the book. The same chapter then deals with the specific application of behavioral theory to the question of the etiology of alcoholism.

The second chapter selectively views the dimensions of the alcoholism problem in the United States. Although various estimates of the extent and severity of alcoholism have been provided through the years, the work of Cahalan and his colleagues stands among the best designed and, for that reason, among the most accurate of these efforts. That Cahalan also traces some of the diverse etiological factors relevant to alcoholism in this country adds greatly to the significance of his findings and to his chapter in this book.

Behavioral Theory and Behavioral Theories of Alcoholism[1]

Peter E. Nathan

THE ADJECTIVE "BEHAVIORAL" coming before words like "theory," "assessment" and "treatment" means different things to different people—some negative, some positive. To some it implies objectivity; to others it denotes single-minded attention to the observable aspects of behavior without due regard for such components as thinking and feeling. To some clinicians behavioral treatment means thought and mind control, often by the use of aversive techniques, e.g., electric shock. To others the phrase "behavioral treatment" connotes the use of reward tokens to shape behavior, usually schizophrenic behavior, without further involving the patient in any planning for his or her future.

When used in the phrase "behavioral theory," behavioral means above all that the theory is designed from its inception to be open to empirical investigation, which will ultimately permit assessment of its validity—its accuracy—by means of scientific study. More than anything else, the word used in this context means a respect for data and evidence above inference, hypothesis or speculation. Accordingly, the ultimate test of any behavioral theory—of behavior, etiology or intervention—rests on the extent to which it can be investigated by accepted scientific methods.

Because of their respect for the ultimate test of empirical investigation, behavioral theorists evolve theories that do not posit cause or influence from entities that cannot be measured and hence must be only inferred. It is for this reason that behavioral theories of alcoholism assume that at least some of the manifold varieties of alcoholism are acquired and maintained, at least in part, via identifi-

[1] Preparation of this chapter was facilitated by grant No. AA00259 from the National Institute on Alcohol Abuse and Alcoholism.

able, recognizable, known mechanisms of learning. The most popular position in this regard is that stress and anxiety have been acquired and are maintained by alcoholics in greater than normal quantities and intensities, and that alcoholics have learned that drinking alcohol reduces these unpleasant emotions—that alcohol is a learned means of reducing conditioned (learned) anxiety.

Behavioral theories of alcoholism treatment, discussed in Section III, turn this coin over and assume that alcoholism, acquired and maintained by known mechanisms of learning, can be modified, perhaps eliminated, by judicious application of techniques derived from these very principles of learning. In other words, the behavioral theory of alcoholism is consistent in the manner in which it relates etiology and treatment.

Unfortunately, to date, behavioral views of the etiology of alcoholism have not been overwhelmingly supported by research results. Most of these theories are variations on a basic theme, first developed in the animal laboratory (68, 69), that drinking is a learned means of reducing conditioned anxiety. Most variations on this basic theme derive from disagreement over the precise mechanisms responsible for the presence of the conditioned anxiety. Franks (100) offered a detailed historical treatment of this body of research and the resultant conflict over its interpretation.

The hypothesis that drinking is a reinforced behavior derives from the assumption that alcohol reduces high levels of anxiety in most or all alcoholics. However, a study comparing the behavior of alcoholics and matched nonalcoholics during a period of experimental intoxication (224) indicated that alcohol actually increases levels of anxiety and depression in alcoholics, though only after an initial 12- to 24-hour period of drinking during which anxiety levels often decrease modestly; Mello and Mendelson drew similar conclusions from their series of programmed drinking studies of alcoholics (190, 195). Nathan as well as Mello and Mendelson point to what seems to be a "state-dependent" phenomenon to explain alcohol's apparent ability to increase anxiety and depression in alcoholics during lengthy drinking bouts. These researchers agree that being drunk seems to arouse in an alcoholic many memories that had been forgotten or suppressed since the previous drinking episode. Because these memories are often concerned with events that took place during prior drinking periods, and since distressing things often happen to alcoholics when they drink, the memories for the most part are unpleasant and anxiety-provoking. Memories of family confrontations, loss of jobs, arrests, and humiliations figure especially large in the remembrances of drinking alcoholics.

An excellent review of the literature on tension reduction and alcohol in animals was published by Cappell and Herman in 1972 (50), and research on the relationship in humans was carefully reviewed by Mello (189). Both of these research areas were recently reviewed by Cappell (49). These reviews conclude that the simple tension-reduction model of alcoholism has proved to be insufficient to account for continued drinking by alcoholics. In an effort to extend the behavioral view of etiology beyond this model, Miller and Eisler (205) suggest that "social learning theory," a more complex and inclusive theory of behavior, is useful for understanding the development and maintenance of excessive drinking by alcoholics. Their explication of this view, excerpted here, probably now represents the view of the majority of behavioral researchers:

"Within a social-learning framework, alcohol and drug abuse are viewed as socially acquired, learned behavior patterns maintained by numerous antecedent cues and consequent reinforcers that may be of a psychological, sociological, or physiological nature. Such factors as reduction in anxiety, increased social recognition and peer approval, enhanced ability to exhibit more varied, spontaneous social behavior, or the avoidance of physiological withdrawal symptoms may maintain substance abuse" (205, p. 5).

In other words, Miller and Eisler adopted the consensus viewpoint among social learning theorists that almost no acquired human behavior is so simple that it is always learned according to a single learning mechanism. Instead, drinking by nonalcoholics as well as alcoholics must be explained in terms of such additional learning mechanisms as imitation or modeling (e.g., watching a parent drink and acquiring a few of that parent's drinking behaviors), operant conditioning (e.g., drinking immoderately because a peer group reinforces immoderate drinking), and classic conditioning (drinking because it reduces conditioned anxiety, at least on a short-term basis). Typically, a person's approach to drinking is shaped by all of these learning mechanisms, each expressed in manifold individual terms.

2

Implications of American Drinking Practices and Attitudes for Prevention and Treatment of Alcoholism

Don Cahalan

THIS CHAPTER summarizes some of the principal findings of 15 years of research into American drinking practices and problems measured by surveying the general adult population. Although the primary purpose of these studies was to describe in detail, for general scientific purposes, what people do and say about drinking, the findings do have important implications for prevention and treatment of alcoholism.

Our findings on American behavior and attitudes reveal consistent patterns, although interpretation of the meanings or implications of these findings is open to vigorous debate because of their controversial nature. However, so that the reader can interpret the perspectives from which I arrive at my interpretations of our research findings, I should make it clear that I came into the field of alcohol studies as a survey research specialist with a background in many types of social–psychological studies of human behavior, rather than as a clinical specialist in alcoholism. Thus I am drawing conclusions from more of an inductive or data-oriented perspective than from a particular ideological perspective.

The series of studies reviewed here were begun under the direction of Wendell Lipscomb, Ira Cisin and Genevieve Knupfer in the California Department of Public Health in 1960, starting with a series of Bay Area–Northern California community studies. Professor Cisin developed a parallel series of national surveys at The George Washington University in 1962, where I joined him in 1964. In 1968 the two series of studies were consolidated under my direction, and since 1971 our work has been conducted under the auspices of the School of Public Health at the University of California in Berkeley. In all, we conducted a dozen Bay Area community surveys and five national surveys. I limit my discussion to some of the findings from the national surveys, particularly those reported in our three books, *American Drinking Practices* (43), *Problem Drinkers* (41) and *Problem Drinking Among American Men* (46).

BACKGROUND ON GENERAL-POPULATION SURVEYS

Our general-population surveys were supported by the National Institute on Alcohol Abuse and Alcoholism (NIAAA) and its predecessors because they concurred with the idea expressed by Selden Bacon (8), Ira Cisin (61) and Jim Fox of the National Institute of Mental Health, that we must study the general population —rather than merely the clinical alcoholic—if we are to understand the processes by which people get into and out of drinking problems or "alcoholism." The alcoholics seen in clinics by and large are an overrepresentation of society's chronic failures, so it is little wonder that clinicians and physicians whose observations of the workings of alcoholism are confined primarily to clinical cases tend to have a much more pessimistic perspective on the prognosis for alcoholics than is warranted by the facts concerning drinking behavior and problems in the general population, where problems typically tend to be an "off and on" affair. In my opinion, the pessimism of many medical practitioners and clinical workers is further magnified by ideological factors, particularly the classic Jellinekian conception (138) of the "alcoholic" as suffering from a distinct disease syndrome in which the patient has a host of physical, mental and social liabilities which develop in a classic, orderly fashion and which imply a poor prognosis for full recovery. The "problem drinkers" in our general-population surveys do not fit the classic disease model of consistent addictive craving accompanied by steady drinking, but for that matter neither do a good many alcoholics in clinics, as Mello and Mendelson's controlled clinical observations (193) pointed out.

Our program of community and national surveys passed through three distinct phases. During the first few years descriptions of drinking practices and attitudes about drinking were emphasized (43, 61, 153). Then there were a number of studies concentrating on specific problems related to drinking (41, 46, 63, 152). The current, final stage concentrates on analysis of longitudinal data on drinking behavior and problems among persons interviewed two or more times over a span of years. Each survey was a strictly controlled (scientifically randomized) probability sampling of the general population aged 21 or older, with a high rate of completed interviews with persons selected for sampling plus other quality controls, thereby making it appropriate to project the findings against the total population from which the samples were drawn.

DRINKING BEHAVIOR AND ATTITUDES TOWARD DRINKING

Our early national surveys, as well as those of others (8, 118, 121, 170, 220, 290), consistently reflect the conflict in values between groups (and within individuals) concerning drinking. Much ambivalence is found among the general public as to whether alcoholism is an illness or a moral or social problem, whether alcohol does more harm than good, and what might be done to alleviate alcohol problems. Consistent with this, the 1971 Harris survey (170) found that a large proportion of adults throughout the United States were very poorly informed about the effects of alcohol and how to cope with overdoses. The general lack of knowledge and the ambivalent attitudes toward drinking found in our national surveys are consistent with our national heritage, especially the classic conflict between the Protestant-ethic values and the hard-drinking behavior of a large number of our citizenry, from the time of the frontiersman to the age of the suburban cocktail circuit.

Our first national survey in 1964 found that most adults drank at least once a year—68% of the total population: 77% of the men and 50% of the women (43). Although 12% were arbitrarily defined as "heavy drinkers," the population was quite evenly divided between the 47% who did not drink as often as once a month and the 53% who drank once a month or more.

The highlights of the first national survey are shown in Chart 1. The highest proportion of heavier drinkers are among those about age 45; of lower social status; living in large cities and in the Middle Atlantic, New England and Pacific areas; and of Irish, British or Latin-American extraction. However, the groups with the highest proportion of drinkers were not the groups with the most heavy drinkers. For example, although Jews and Episcopalians had the lowest proportions of abstainers, they also had extremely low ratios of heavy or problem drinkers. Abstainers were more likely to be older persons of below-average income, from the South or rural areas, of native-born parentage, and from conservative Protestant denominations.

CHART 1.—*Demographic Characteristics of Drinkers and Heavy Drinkers*[a]

Most Likely to be Drinkers	*Among Drinkers, Most Likely to be Heavy Drinkers*
Men under 45 years of age	Men aged 45 to 49
Men and women of high social status	Those of low social status
Professional, business and other white-collar workers	Operatives; service workers
College graduates	Men who completed high school but not college
Single men	Single, divorced or separated men and women
Residents of the Middle Atlantic, New England, East North Central, and Pacific areas	Residents of Middle Atlantic, New England and Pacific areas
Residents of suburban cities, towns	Residents of largest cities
Those whose fathers were born in Ireland or Italy (age-adjusted findings)	Those whose fathers were born in Ireland, Latin America or the Caribbean, or the United Kingdom (age-adjusted)
Jews, Episcopalians	Protestants of no specific denomination, Catholics, those without religious affiliation

[a] Adapted from Cahalan et al. (43, *Chart 3*).

Even though most people drank at least a little, and relatively few (9%) of all drinkers said they worried at all about their *own* drinking, there is ambivalence about use of alcohol. This became evident when three-fourths of all respondents (and even a majority of men heavy drinkers) said they thought "drinking does more harm than good." Alcohol appeared to be a greater threat to those of lower economic and social status, possibly because they are more vulnerable and economically insecure than those of higher status.

NATIONAL SURVEYS OF DRINKING PROBLEMS

We have now completed four nationwide surveys on the prevalence of specific drinking problems. The first (41) was a follow-up in 1967 of a subsample of 1359 of the respondents in the 1964–65 survey of drinking practices. The second was conducted in 1969 with a sample of 978 men in the high-risk group (aged 21–59). In the third study[1] in 1973, 725 of the 1969 sample of men were reinterviewed to measure changes in drinking behavior and problems over a 4-year span. An additional national follow-up was completed in 1974 of 900 men and women who were first interviewed during the 1964–65 survey and again during the 1967 survey; the data from this 3-wave survey are now being analyzed.

All these studies of drinking problems emphasize that what we want to measure is the prevalence of specific types of problems (or potential problems) associated with alcohol, rather than "alcoholism," however defined. We followed the definition that "problem drinking is a repetitive use of beverage alcohol causing physical, psychological, or social harm to the drinker or to others" (70, *p. 38*). This is similar to Knupfer's more general definition that "a problem—any problem—connected fairly closely with drinking constitutes a drinking problem" (152, *p. 974*). Our national drinking-problem surveys were patterned closely after the 1964 San Francisco study conducted by Knupfer and her colleagues (63, 152), and we also drew from the work of the earlier Iowa surveys of Mulford and Miller (219) and the Washington Heights survey of Bailey et al. (10).

As with Knupfer's survey (152), our national surveys covered a number of actual, objective problems as well as several potential problems (such as drinking enough to constitute a potential health problem); we tabulated the various problems separately, as well as in certain combinations. We took into account three types of variables in scoring responses on a dozen specific types of problems: (*1*) the severity of problems in terms of frequency and the presumed gravity of the problem; (*2*) the certainty or reliability of measurement (in terms of the number of items used in assessing the problem); and (*3*) the time when the problems occurred, i.e., within the past 3 years or more than 3 years ago. The types of problems or potential problems covered in the 1967 survey were as follows:

(*1*) *Frequent Intoxication.* A high score is attained by drinking a maximum of five or more drinks at least once a week, or eight or more on one of the two most recent drinking occasions and twice during the last year, or currently getting "high" or "tight" at least once a week.

(*2*) *Binge Drinking.* This potential problem is defined as being

---

[1] CAHALAN, D., and ROIZEN, R. Changes in drinking problems in a national sample of men. Presented at the North American Congress on Alcohol and Drug Problems, San Francisco, December 1974.

intoxicated for at least several days at a time or for two days on more than one occasion.

(3) *Symptomatic Drinking.* This potential problem refers to signs of what Jellinek defined as "gamma alcoholism" (138, *p. 37*), including signs of physical dependence and loss of control (e.g., drinking to get rid of a hangover, having difficulty in stopping drinking, having blackouts or lapses of memory, skipping meals while on drinking bouts, drinking very rapidly for quicker effect, or sneaking drinks). Positive responses on three or more of seven items are required for a high score.

(4) *Psychological Dependence.* This potential problem includes drinking to relieve depression or nervousness or to escape from problems of everyday living. A high score is attained if the respondent rates at least one of five psychological effects of alcohol as being "very helpful" or "very important," plus two others as "fairly helpful" or "fairly important."

(5) *Problems with Spouse or Relatives.* These include the spouse's leaving or threatening to leave the respondent or being concerned over his drinking, the spouse's or relative's asking the respondent to cut down on his drinking, or the respondent's judging his drinking as having had a harmful effect on his home life. (High scores are assigned to respondents whose spouse is angry or threatening to leave because of the respondent's drinking, and to those who reported any two of the following: spouse expressed concern; spouse or relative said respondent should cut down; or respondent rated drinking as harmful to his marriage or home life.)

(6) *Problems with Friends or Neighbors.* A high score was given for two or more of the following: friends indicated respondent should cut down on drinking; neighbors so indicated; or respondent believed his drinking had had a harmful effect on his friendships and social life.

(7) *Job Problems.* A high score was given for any one of the following: having lost a job or nearly lost one because of drinking; having people at work suggest he cut down on drinking; or rating drinking as harmful to his work and employment opportunities.

(8) *Problems with Law, Police, Accidents.* A high score was given to persons who had had trouble with the police over drinking regardless of whether driving was involved, and to those whose drinking had contributed to a personal-injury accident. (In later versions of our scoring, problems with police were scored separately from personal-injury accidents.)

(9) *Health.* A high score was based on a respondent's reporting

that drinking had been harmful to his health and that a physician had advised him to cut down.

(10) *Financial Problems.* A high score was given to respondents who reported that drinking had had a harmful effect on their financial status.

(11) *Belligerence Associated with Drinking.* This measure, which encompassed feeling aggressive or cross after drinking and getting into a fight or heated argument, was included as a potential problem so that in the future it would be possible to test the hypothesis that belligerence is often followed by an increase in interpersonal problems.

Table 1 summarizes the prevalence of each of the 11 types of actual or potential problems in terms of occurrence during the last 3 years. At the bottom of the table is an over-all "current problems score," in which each problem is given equal weight (except for health, financial and belligerence problems, which were given a lesser weight because they included very few items). A high over-all current problems score could be attained only by having problems in 2 or more areas, of which at least 1 was rated severe; problems in 3 or more areas, of which 2 or more were at least moderately severe; moderate to severe problems in 5 or more areas; or slight problems in 7 or more areas.

TABLE 1.—*Prevalence of Drinking-Related Problems (None, Moderate, High) During the Previous 3 Years Among Men and Women, in Per Cent*[a]

	MEN (N =751)			WOMEN (N = 608)		
	None	*Moderate*	*High*	*None*	*Moderate*	*High*
Index of frequent intoxication[b]	83	3	14	97	1	2
Binge drinking	97	0	3	100	0	*
Symptomatic drinking[c]	84	8	8	93	4	3
Psychological dependence	61	31	8	85	12	3
Problems with current spouse or relatives	84	8	8	96	3	1
Problems with friends or neighbors	93	5	2	97	3	*
Job problems	94	3	3	98	2	1
Problems with police or accidents	99	0	1	99	0	1
Health[d]	88	6	6	93	4	4
Financial problems	91	6	3	98	2	1
Belligerence associated with drinking	88	8	4	93	5	3
Current problems score[e]	57	28	15	79	17	4

[a] Data from Cahalan (41, *Table 1*).
[b] Components: frequency and amount-per-occasion, and frequency of getting "high" or "tight."
[c] Positive responses to such items as difficulty stopping drinking, blackouts, sneaking drinks.
[d] Physician told respondent to cut down drinking.
[e] Eleven problems combined. High score = 7 + of a maximum of 58.
* Less than 0.5%.

The most frequent problems for men were frequent intoxication, symptomatic drinking, psychological dependence, and problems with one's spouse or other relative. Four per cent of the women achieved high scores on health problems—more than achieved high scores in any other category. Fifteen per cent of the men and 4% of the women (9% of the total) were rather arbitrarily classified in the high-problems category. However, Table 1 clearly shows that selection of the cut-off point has an enormous effect on results: One can conclude that the adult population has a high rate of problem drinking since 43% of the men and 21% of the women (31% of the total) had one or more of the problems to some degree during the preceding 3 years; or one can emphasize the relatively low rate of problems by noting that "only" 15% of the men and 4% of the women were classified as being in the severe- or frequent-problems category.

We next concentrated on measuring drinking problems among men aged 21–59 because we found this to be the group with the highest rate of drinking problems in general. In analyzing this group, we combined data from the 1967 and 1969 surveys to get a larger total for this high-risk group.

Table 2 shows, first, that the general rate of problems is almost invariably much higher among those 21–24 years of age than among older men, and that the current over-all problems score is about twice as high among the youngest age group (21–24 years) than among the next oldest (25–29) group (which also rated next in problem ratings). This concentration of drinking problems among men aged 21–24 is dramatically at variance with data on the age of the average clinical alcoholic, which is around 42. However, this pronounced age trend is borne out in all our studies of the general population. It is also true in studies Cisin and I directed of the armed forces. Table 3 summarizes findings of separate studies we conducted in the Army and Navy (42, 44). In both services young enlisted men and officers had consistently higher levels of interpersonal problems related to drinking than older men.

These findings for age groups are consistent with a great turnover or change in problem-drinking status over time. We also found that roughly 50% more men aged 21–59 reported a current problem (last 3 years) than reported ever having had a problem in the same area (46, *p. 31*). Our first national study on drinking problems also found that a substantial proportion changed their problem-drinking status over a 3-year period (41, *pp. 114–115*). We obtained similar results in later studies, discussed below. Such find-

TABLE 2.—*Percentage of Men with Higher Severity Levels of Drinking Problems, by Age*[a]

	AGE								
	21–24 (N = 147)	25–29 (N = 204)	30–34 (N = 186)	35–39 (N = 216)	40–44 (N = 226)	45–49 (N = 201)	50–54 (N = 199)	55–59 (N = 182)	Total (N = 1561)
Heavy intake	7	7	5	7	6	3	5	6	6
Binge drinking	10	3	3	3	1	2	4	2	3
Psychological dependence	5	4	4	4	4	5	4	3	4
Loss of control	12	5	4	5	7	5	4	4	6
Symptomatic drinking	26	11	8	7	6	10	9	3	9
Belligerence	15	12	10	8	7	8	6	2	8
Problems with wife	19	17	15	10	9	9	11	6	12
Problems with friends or neighbors	15	5	7	5	4	4	6	4	6
Problems on job	10	4	3	5	5	5	6	2	5
Police problems	10	4	2	2	2	2	4	1	3
Health or injuries from drinking	8	4	5	6	4	6	8	6	6
Finances	11	4	6	4	3	2	4	3	4
Current over-all problems score 7+	40	22	20	21	17	17	17	11	20

[a] Data from Cahalan and Room (46, Table 2).

TABLE 3.—*Percentage of Men with High Consequences Score, by Age*

Age (years)	Civilians[a]		Naval Officers[b]		Army Officers[a]		Naval Enlisted[b]		Army Enlisted[a]	
	N	%	N	%	N	%	N	%	N	%
17–20			3		6		788	46	1007	53
21–24	130	34	368	16	709	21	1167	43	1942	42
25–29	117	17	1095	18	1408	16	624	32	898	37
30–34	122	19	733	18	832	19	523	30	625	30
35–39	124	15	686	19	681	16	457	29	573	26
40–44	133	18	569	21	408	14	116	24	316	25
45–49	114	13	230	22	130	12	31	10	81	20
50+	238	16	73	8	130	12	6		43	7

[a] Data from Cahalan et al. (44, *Table 3*).
[b] Data from Cahalan and Cisin (42, *Tables 33 and 34*).

ings cast doubt on the usefulness of the characterization of drinking careers in terms of irreversible progressive deterioration. These age-group findings, in addition to the retrospective reports of heavy drinkers about their early drinking (43), indicate that most of those who are problem drinkers in their forties formed their drinking habits 20 or more years earlier—which emphasizes the vital importance of early casefinding and prevention.

Table 4 supports our earlier findings that low-socioeconomic-status groups have a higher than average proportion of abstainers, but

TABLE 4.—*Drinking Problems Typology by Index of Social Position Among Men Aged 21–59, in Per Cent*[a]

Social Position	N	Non-drinker[b]	Drank, No Problems[c]	Potential Problems Only[d]	Heavy Intake or Binge, No Conse-sequences[e]	High Conse-quences[f]
Low	281	19	22	19	14	26
Lower middle	411	17	38	19	10	17
Upper middle	401	14	39	24	15	8
High	468	11	47	22	11	9
Total	1561	15	38	21	12	14

[a] Adapted from Cahalan and Room (46, *Table 22*).
[b] Nondrinker: did not drink during last 3 years.
[c] Drank, no problems: has been a drinker within the last 3 years, but not in groups d–f.
[d] Potential problems only: not in groups e or f but a problem of at least minimal severity in any problem area.
[e] Intake or binge: not in group f, but at least minimal severity intake or binge problems.
[f] High consequences score of 3+: tangible consequences, i.e., social consequences, health or injury problems associated with drinking, financial problems.

that among these same groups, the subgroup of those who do drink
tends to display a higher than average proportion of heavy drinkers.
This five-category typology of drinking problems shows that those
of lowest status have a higher absolute rate of drinking problems
than other persons, and that the ratio of consequences of drinking
to heavy intake or binge drinking is also higher among those of
lower status. In simple terms: more of the poor tend to get into
trouble over their drinking—out of proportion to the number who
drink heavily.

We classified regions of the country into "wetter" and "dryer" in
terms of past voting or survey findings on prohibition sentiment.
The "dryer" areas had a higher proportion of men aged 21–59 with
interpersonal problems related to drinking (relative to their rate of
heavy intake without interpersonal consequences) than was true for
men in "wetter" areas (Table 5). In other words, it is more difficult
to avoid drinking problems if one drinks in a traditionally "dryer"

TABLE 5.—*Current Problems Typology*[a] *by Region, in Per Cent*[b]

	N	Non-drinker	Drank, No Problems	Potential Problems Only	Heavy Intake or Binge, No Consequences	High Consequences
Dryer Regions						
South Atlantic	156	28	30	19	12	12
East South Central	113	29	30	16	5	20
West South Central	188	23	40	17	5	14
West North Central	134	10	47	17	12	14
Mountain	61	21	33	26	3	16
Total	652	22	37	18	8	15
Wetter Regions						
New England	89	7	43	33	11	7
Middle Atlantic	288	7	39	20	19	15
East North Central	353	13	41	22	13	12
Pacific	179	10	32	27	14	16
Total	909	10	39	23	15	13

[a] Defined in Table 4 footnotes.
[b] Adapted from Cahalan and Room (46, *Table 17*).

area. One implication is that efforts to minimize drinking problems could be more efficient if they took into account local cultural traditions; this is one indication that no single national prevention program will fit all regions.

Among ethnoreligious groups (Table 6), most Jewish men drink at least a little, but relatively few drink heavily or have drinking

TABLE 6.—*Current Problems Typology by Ethnoreligious Categories, in Per Cent*[a]

	N	Non-drinker	Drank, No Problems	Potential Problems Only	Heavy Intake or Binge, No Consequences	High (3+) Consequences Score
British						
Catholic	34	12	35	27	18	9
Liberal Protestant	48	13	31	38	8	10
Conservative Prot.	204	20	39	22	3	16
Irish						
Catholic	77	4	33	27	16	21
Conservative Prot.	74	27	46	15	3	10
German						
Catholic	76	7	40	21	22	11
Liberal Protestant	86	12	47	24	9	8
Conservative Prot.	120	22	42	21	7	9
Italian						
Catholic	64	5	52	14	23	6
Latin American						
Catholic	42	10	10	21	17	43
Jewish	40	8	60	25	5	3
Negro						
Conservative Prot.	97	18	23	16	13	31
Eastern European						
Catholic	71	6	38	21	21	14
Other Ethnicity						
Catholic	114	7	42	26	11	13
Liberal Protestant	56	5	43	18	23	11
Conservative Prot.	158	34	35	15	8	8

[a] Adapted from Cahalan and Room (46, *Table* 27). Categories with small numbers are omitted from the table. Ethnicity is defined by religion for Jews, by race for Negroes, and by "country most ancestors come from" for the remainder.

problems. Most Catholics and liberal Protestants ("liberal" in terms of their churches' stands on drinking) do drink, and a higher than average proportion have problems caused by their drinking; moreover, conservative Protestants (denominations favoring abstinence) show a higher proportion of abstainers but also a relatively high ratio of consequences in relation to heavy intake or binge drinking. These findings agree with those of Gusfield (118) concerning the history of connections between religious affiliation and attitudes toward alcohol. We could derive considerable benefit from studying such ethnoreligious differences more intensively: It might well be that if we fully understood how most American Jews manage to avoid drinking problems even though most drink and also live in urbanized areas where the rates of drinking problems are high, we might be able to institute more effective programs to inculcate moderate drinking habits and attitudes among the U.S. population as a whole.

A multivariate analysis of 51 variables is summarized in Table 7, which shows that drinking attitudes and environment are the variables most highly correlated with high drinking-problem scores, and that none of the psychologically oriented personality scales showed a very high relationship with drinking problems. This is consistent with the findings that the problem drinker does not represent a unique personality type (6, 246, 285).

With regard to this multivariate analysis, some people argue that "of course" one would expect there to be a correlation between favorable attitudes toward drinking and one's heavy drinking, but that the attitudes might be the effect rather than the cause of heavy drinking. However, a simplified two-stage study of respondents in the first national survey who were reinterviewed in 1967 found that favorable attitudes toward drinking preceded heavy or "escape" drinking behavior more often than those attitudes followed the behavior. My conclusion is that although certain personality traits (e.g., a tendency toward undercontrol and low self-esteem) may contribute to drinking problems if the person's attitudes toward alcohol are favorable and if he lives in an environment permissive toward heavy drinking, the environmental and attitudinal influences are of paramount importance in determining which of today's heavy drinkers are the problem drinkers of tomorrow. One obvious implication is that psychotherapy is not likely to be very effective with problem drinking if no effort is made to change the person's environment and his attitude toward drinking.

TABLE 7.—*Multiple Regression of Drinking Attitudes and Behavior (in Addition to 30 Demographic and 18 Intervening Variables) Against a Current Problems Score of 7 +* [a]

Step No.		Multiple R[b]	Partial Correlation	Pearson r
1.	Drinking by significant others	.26	.15	.26
2.	Tolerance of deviance	.33	.13	.22
3.	Own attitude toward drinking	.37	.18	.26
4.	Index of social position	.41	.11	.16
5.	Black	.42	.09	.15
6.	Nonhelpfulness of others	.43	.06	.16
7.	Central cities of SMSA[c]	.44	.04	.16
8.	Sedatives	.44	.05	.13
9.	Alienation summary	.45	.05	.19
10.	Health self-rating	.45	.04	.16
11.	Northeast regions (1, 2, 5)	.45	−.04	−.01
12.	Latin American/Caribbean ancestry	.45	.03	.10
13.	Moved within last 10 years	.45	.06	.05
14.	Age (10-year groups)	.46	−.05	−.13
15.	Somatization summary	.46	.04	.12
16.	Social controls	.46	.04	.08
17.	Childhood disjunction	.46	.03	.14
18.	Subjective anxiety	.46	.04	.11
19.	Does not belong to any organizations	.46	.03	.09
20.	Attends religious services seldom or never	.46	.04	.10

[a] Combined 1967 and 1969 surveys, 1561 men aged 21–59. From Cahalan and Room (45, *Table* 9).

[b] The cumulative multiple R for 51 variables (counting all categories including dummy variables) was .47 (22% of the variance). The 31 variables not shown above included social activities, smoking cigarettes, others' attitudes toward appropriate limits for respondent's drinking, impulsivity score, adult disjunction, use of stimulants, and various subgroups of categories represented above (e.g., regions, urbanization, religious affiliations).

[c] Standard Metropolitan Statistical Areas.

CHANGES IN DRINKING-PROBLEM STATUS OVER SEVERAL YEARS

The final stage in our 15-year series of surveys was to assess the correlates of change in drinking practices and problems over time. Longitudinal studies are crucial to the study of cause–effect relationships because only by studying individuals at two or more points in time is it possible to determine the events and states of mind that precede later events. Although the earlier national and community surveys in this series retrospectively uncovered indications of frequent changes in drinking-problem status over time, it was not until we conducted follow-up studies that we could conclusively measure the correlates of changes in drinking behavior and problems.

A San Francisco probability sample of men aged 21–59, initially interviewed in 1967 and reinterviewed in 1972, provided our first measure of detailed changes over several years. Table 8 shows the magnitude of changes in drinking-problem status over 4 years in the men who had specified problems at time 1. The traditional expecta-

TABLE 8.—*Drinking Problems at Time 1 (1967) by Selected Outcomes at Time 2 (1972), in Per Cent*[a]

Time 1 Problems or Potential Problems	N	Remission Of Problem by Time 2	Heavy Intake at Time 2	Binge Drinking at Time 2	One or More Drinking Problems at Time 2[b]
Binge drinking	29	59	48	41	55
Symptomatic drinking	21	51	62	38	76
Psychological dependence	42	50	48	14	48
Loss of control	18	78	67	17	78
Police problems	13	77	23	38	61
Problems with relatives or friends	23	61	56	35	70
Accidents	10	80	50	20	50
Financial problems	98	63	42	13	50
Problems with wife	25	52	52	20	64
Job problems	24	96	37	21	50

[a] Adapted from Clark and Cahalan (64, *Table 4*).

[b] Problems here include only the following current (time 2) problems (at the level of severity specified in Table 2): police problems, job problems, spouse problems, other interpersonal problems, accidents and financial problems.

tion, following Jellinek's models, is that alcoholics accumulate an increasing number of problems over time, with the "early symptoms" of progressive alcoholism not being replaced by later symptoms but added to the problems that already exist.[2] The San Francisco findings are at variance with the conventional expectation, however, because there was little "snowballing" of problems in more areas of the person's life with the passage of time. Table 8

[2] ROOM, R. Assumptions and implications of disease concepts of alcoholism. Presented at the 29th International Congress on Alcoholism and Drug Dependence, Sydney, Australia, February 1970.

shows that for each problem at time 1 the proportion of men who no longer had that problem at time 2 was high, ranging from 50% to 96%. However, people with a specific drinking problem at time 1 tended to have some type of problem at time 2, although not necessarily the same problem. Furthermore, those with specific problems at time 1 tended to have high rates of heavy intake or binge drinking at time 2.

We conclude from this study that continuity of specific problems over time is rather low, but that the probability of future involvement in some alcohol problems (although not necessarily the same ones) is increased if one develops alcohol-related problems. Thus the "progressive disease" concept of problem drinking is open to question. However, the fact that those who have drinking problems at one time tend to have drinking problems of varying kinds subsequently may imply that environmental factors play a considerable part in determining the type of alcohol-related problems that occur.

A national probability sample measuring change over 4 years was also conducted as part of the same series. In this survey 725 men aged 21–59 were first interviewed in 1969 and again 4 years later. Table 9 bears out the San Francisco findings of a high turnover in drinking problems. Approximately the same proportion shifted into

TABLE 9.—*Turnover in Summary Drinking Problem Scales, 1969–1973:*
National Sample of Men Aged 21–59 (N = 725)[a]

| | Turnover Proportions[b] | | | | Turnover Statistics[b] | |
High Problems Level	No/ No	No/ Yes	Yes/ No	Yes/ Yes	r	Changer Ratio
1+ drinking problems	58.8	9.1	12.6	19.6	.49	.53
3+ drinking problems	82.2	6.3	6.5	5.0	.36	.72
Social consequences summary scale	81.7	6.3	6.3	5.7	.40	.69
Tangible consequences summary scale	76.7	6.5	7.6	9.2	.48	.61
Problematic intake summary scale	80.6	6.5	6.1	6.9	.45	.65
Subjective problems summary scale	82.3	6.8	6.9	4.0	.29	.77

[a] Data from Cahalan D. and Roizen, R. Changes in drinking problems in a national sample of men. (Table 5b.) Presented at the North American Congress on Alcohol and Drug Problems, San Francisco, December 1974.

[b] *No/No:* proportion reporting problem at neither time 1 nor time 2. *No/Yes:* proportion reporting problem at time 2 but not at time 1. *Yes/No:* proportion reporting problem at time 1 but not at time 2. *Yes/Yes:* proportion reporting problem at time 1 and time 2. *r:* Pearson product-moment correlation coefficient. *Changer ratio:* proportion of (No/Yes + Yes/No) ÷ (No/Yes + Yes/No + Yes/Yes).

or out of a drinking-problem status as stayed there. For example, at the 3+ (three or more) problems level the changer ratio is high (.72), whereas the correlation of having the same specific problem at times 1 and 2 is relatively low (.36). The same tendency toward high turnover was found in each of the indices of change, as well as in measures of individual problems, which are not shown here.

Our analysis of the longitudinal data is still in progress: We have just completed another national follow-up survey that provides a sample large enough to permit us an even more detailed study of changes in drinking problems. However, we already have sufficient evidence to conclude that the "symptom" or "prodromal" status of specific drinking problems as a predictor of later, more serious problems has been considerably overrated, since our general-population change data suggest that an "early warning" prediction based on such "symptoms" yields a substantial number of false positives who never get into serious trouble. We believe that the high rates of turnover in drinking problems will be found to be highly associated with specific environmental circumstances and life events, and we are now conducting an intensive analysis of the impact of life events or environmental circumstances on changes in drinking problems.

IMPLICATIONS FOR PREVENTION OR MINIMIZATION OF ALCOHOL PROBLEMS

Americans have permissive attitudes toward occasional intoxication and heavy drinking, but at the same time there is widespread guilt or ambivalence about drinking. Such equivocal attitudes indicate an atmosphere in which Americans are quick to pay lip service to the need for moderation in drinking but are reluctant to endorse preventive measures that might limit the ready availability of alcohol. A poll of California adults we commissioned last fall with the sponsorship of the California Office of Alcohol Program Management is reasonably representative of the general American attitude toward alternative prevention measures. We found[3] that a large proportion of Californians (about 90%) would endorse a more active role by federal, state and local governments in providing treatment of people with drinking problems and in being more restrictive in keeping drunken drivers off the road. Moreover, about two-thirds

[3] CAHALAN, D., ROIZEN, R. and ROOM, R. Attitudes on alcohol problem prevention measures; a statewide California survey. Presented at the North American Congress on Alcohol and Drug Problems, San Francisco, December 1974.

would endorse measures to protect people from the consequences of their overindulgence by requiring that new cars have devices to prevent intoxicated persons from starting their cars, and the same number would provide more recreation as a possible substitute for drinking. Lastly, the same large majority would favor making arrangements for police to take people home if they had had so much to drink they were unable to drive safely. However, substantial majorities said they would be against measures to restrict the general availability of alcohol by such devices as prohibiting the sale of all alcoholic beverages (88% against), rationing alcohol so that everybody could buy only a modest amount each month (73% against) and making drinking more expensive by increasing alcohol taxes (57% against).

Our surveys showed that the highest incidence of drinking problems occurs in persons under 25 years of age, and other studies indicate that heavy drinking is on the increase among American youth. These findings certainly argue for placing a high priority on programs that discourage the development of heavy-drinking behavior among young people. However, because of the general public's evasive attitude toward taking personal responsibility for prevention of drinking problems, I think there is a great danger of our foisting the responsibility for preventive work on the school system, which is the traditional dumping ground for everything we are unwilling to teach our children in our homes or neighborhoods. We could take the responsibility ourselves primarily by setting the good example of moderation in our own drinking and serving of alcoholic beverages.

In addition to passing our responsibility on to the schools, another popular form of educational substitute activity is the advertising campaign—advocacy through television and radio—a method that has been rather vigorously pushed by the NIAAA. Although such campaigns may do little harm and may even do some good by sensitizing a large number of people to alcohol-related problems, it is naive to expect that such short-lived campaigns can do much to change deep-seated attitudes and behavior concerning drinking. The media-advertising approach is effective in switching consumer purchasing from one product to another that is nearly identical, but this is completely different from asking people to give up their long-established drinking habits without guaranteeing any immediate short-term gains. I am convinced that unless media campaigns are planned so they are closely linked to people-to-people grass-roots programs that obtain widespread personal commitment to set an example of moderation, the campaign will be of little consequence—especially since any campaign for moderation in drinking must compete with the many millions of dollars poured into advertising by the alcoholic beverage industry.

In view of the general climate of lip service to prevention of alcohol problems but an unwillingness to do anything about it except to pass the problem on to the schools and advertising media, I think it unlikely there will be much done to reduce alcohol problems at present. A genuine social movement toward moderation that enlists the energies and hopes of large numbers of people on the grass-roots level is necessary. The Temperance Movement was indeed such a genuine social movement: It gained widespread support among rank and file Americans for many generations because the movement filled a need. Although I am against the return of Prohibition—because of its apparent unworkability in its later stages and the class divisiveness and cynicism it brought about—I believe deeply that only a large-scale social movement would provide the person-to-person evangelizing that could crystallize the social norms which would enforce moderate drinking behavior on an informal but effective peer-pressure basis.

There are two indicators which make me believe such a social movement toward moderation might be possible. One is that an overwhelmingly large proportion of Americans pay at least lip service to the concept of moderation, and many feel guilty or uneasy about their own or others' heavy drinking. Another indicator of the possibility of stimulating a social movement toward moderation is the existence of several cultural groups within the U.S. with a consistent record of moderation in the use of alcohol—particularly the Jews and Chinese, among whom most individuals drink but relatively few have drinking problems. We should study these groups to determine exactly how they manage to maintain their record of moderation even when immersed in a heavy-drinking society. I believe that their moderation is directly related to setting a good parental and peer-group example at home and in other social situations.

It may take us many years to bring about an atmosphere of moderation. However, we will never attain our goal until we face up to the necessity for people to organize a grass-roots movement, setting a good example for moderation in their own drinking rather than self-indulgently passing the responsibility on to the school system, the communications media, or governmental agencies.

IMPLICATIONS OF DRINKING SURVEYS FOR TREATMENT OF DRINKING PROBLEMS

The paramount importance of early case-finding in treating persons with drinking problems is clear from all our surveys, which have consistently found that the average person with severe alcohol-related problems has worked up to a ripened problem-drinker status through many years of heavy drinking. We know of no "instant alcoholics." It seems that anyone with an ounce of common sense should know from observation—to say nothing of the vast fund of available research—that anyone in his family or among his friends who repeatedly drinks more than what is appropriate for the occasion is heading for deep-seated trouble, be he 16 or 60. However, because of our combination of guilt feelings about our own drinking, an unwillingness to alienate anyone by seeming to be a busybody or a bluenose, and believing a stereotyped description that "alcoholics" are born and not made, few of us are willing to exert social influence against inappropriate drinking behavior. Even if we want to exert influence, generally few of us know how to go about it gracefully yet effectively. Accordingly, I urge that we focus more attention on how to influence those around us toward moderate drinking, which includes *not* drinking as a viable option. Again, we should study how the Jews and the Chinese manage to maintain moderate drinking patterns, and how certain other groups in America have failed to promote moderation.

All our surveys clearly show that if we hope to make a dent in improving the treatment of alcoholics, we must work much harder to change the values and attitudes of problem drinkers. We consistently found that those with severe drinking problems are preoccupied with what alcohol will do for them; and although they tend to be ambivalent about alcohol, they have the attitude that their lives would be empty without it. Many of the chapters in this book recognize that attitudes toward alcohol play a paramount role in the future behavior of the problem drinker, but too many of us are hoping for some magical treatment that ultimately "cures" the alcoholic without requiring a basic change in his values and attitudes. Although as yet we have seen no fully controlled studies on the effects of attitude change on drinking behavior, I am certain that unless we keep those with drinking problems locked up, we cannot expect them to remain moderate drinkers or abstainers without changing their attitudes about the importance of alcohol in their lives. No matter how much we try to tinker with their personalities or their environments, they will find a thousand reasons to revert to their drinking habits—unless and until they learn that alcohol is worth less to them (short-term and long-term) than other considerations in life.

Additional evidence of the importance of attitudes in changing drinking behavior is clear from the findings of the recent study (247) on the presumed effectiveness of federally funded alcoholism treatment centers. This study found that if the client stayed in treatment as long as 18 months his chances of showing improvement were approximately 70%, no matter what specific treatment methods were used. However, the "catch" is to get the client to remain in treatment long enough to improve his health and his values concerning alcohol; a very large proportion of persons referred to treatment agencies "fall by the wayside" owing to lack of motivation—which I think must be attributed largely to being unwilling or unable to modify their attitudes about the importance of alcohol in their lives.

For years we have been convinced from our survey findings that there is a vital need for more effective long-term follow-up in reinforcing and restoring the appropriate social and economic supports for persons with recurrent drinking problems. Our society will get nowhere as long as we seek inexpensive, easy shortcuts in rebuilding the self-esteem and interpersonal support systems that problem drinkers need so badly. It will not be easy or inexpensive to integrate realistic preventive measures and longer-term reeducation of chronic problem drinkers; but such an integration will be far less costly and more humane in the long run than the patchwork of specialized (and special-interest) treatment programs and panaceas that now prevail throughout the country.

BEHAVIORAL OBSERVATION AND ASSESSMENT OF DRINKING BY ALCOHOLICS

Each of the three chapters in this section is designed to provide specifics of a different "piece" of the behavioral approach to the assessment of drinking behavior and alcoholism. Chapter 3, by Nathan and Lawson, gives an extended overview of behavioral methods of assessment in laboratory settings, including the use of operant indices of the relative reinforcement value of alcohol and other reinforcers to alcoholics as well as ad libitum measures of drinking at experimental bars and on experimental wards. The place of "taste-test" assessment procedures is also considered, though the specifics of these important methods are detailed later by Marlatt (Chapter 4). Nathan and Lawson's chapter also reviews behavioral assessment approaches to measuring drinking behavior in the natural environment, supplementing an intensive review of one such approach by Reid (Chapter 5).

The second chapter in the section (Chapter 4) describes the development and current status of Marlatt's promising taste-test assessment method, an analogue drinking situation that permits measurement of alcohol consumption in a disguised drinking situation. The significance of the taste test as a means of illuminating variables of etiological importance to the clinician is stressed in the chapter, as is use of the method as a measure of therapy outcome.

Chapter 5, by Reid, is devoted to a detailed description of his innovative approach to naturalistic observation of drinking and interpersonal behavior by bar patrons; the chapter also offers an extensive review of prior efforts to assess drinking in naturalistic settings.

3

Overview of Behavioral Efforts to Assess Alcoholics and Their Alcoholism[1]

Peter E. Nathan and David M. Lawson

MANY BEHAVIORAL RESEARCHERS believe that behavioral assessment instruments and procedures for use specifically with alcoholics were developed because of the unreliability of alcoholics' reports of their own drinking (284). Moreover, traditional personality assessment methods used to supplement self-report data have failed to permit specification of a given alcoholic's precise pattern of maladaptive drinking for treatment-planning purposes (100); these instruments are also inappropriate for the pre- and posttreatment assessments necessary to all behavioral treatment efforts (205).[2]

BEHAVIORAL ASSESSMENT IN THE LABORATORY

Recent years have witnessed the development of three distinct kinds of behavioral measures of drinking in laboratory settings. The first of these enabled Mello and Mendelson (190, 191, 195) and Nathan and co-workers (224, 225) to evolve objective operant indices of the relative reinforcement value of alcohol, money and socialization to the men alcoholics they studied in the laboratory. Among their findings were that (1) alcohol is profoundly reinforcing for men alcoholics during times of drinking; (2) many men alcoholics demonstrate a biphasic pattern of drinking (a week-long "spree" followed by a much more lengthy period of "maintenance" drinking); and (3) many men alcoholics choose to drink in isolation even when socialization is freely available. The latter observation,

---

[1] Preparation of this chapter was facilitated by NIAAA grant No. AA00259 to the first author.
[2] MILLER, P. M. and HERSEN, M. A quantitative measurement system for alcoholism treatment and research. Presented at the meeting of the Association for Advancement of Behavior Therapy, December 1972.

however, has been questioned by Bigelow[3] and Griffiths and co-workers (117), who report that most of their men alcoholic subjects were significantly more sociable on drinking days than on days they were not permitted to drink. As a result of these and other more recent studies, the nature of the effects of alcohol on interpersonal behavior remains an open question. To this end, we now believe that a person's prior learning of socialization skills probably plays a large role in determining how alcohol and alcoholism affect his interpersonal behavior. In other words, it is clear that not all alcoholics are social isolates, anymore than all social drinkers become more friendly and uninhibited after a few drinks.

Tracey and Nathan (289) recently reported on the behavior of women alcoholics in an experimental laboratory setting similar to those used previously by Mello and Mendelson and by Nathan. The results of this study bring into question the extent to which the earlier findings on drinking patterns and isolation of men alcoholics are relevant to alcoholism among women. The four women alcoholics in Nathan's study demonstrated a singular (rather than biphasic) pattern of alcohol consumption: they remained "maintenance" drinkers throughout the period programmed for drinking. Further, they drank more during periods of socialization than during isolation. On the other hand, because the women subjects were probably somewhat better integrated and in somewhat more comfortable economic circumstances than the earlier men alcoholics, a strict comparison between the two sets of subjects is not warranted. Nonetheless, these data are in accord with a prevailing view that women alcoholics remain more involved with society than men alcoholics at every stage of their alcoholism.

Alcoholic subjects in another recent operant study of alcoholism were more inclined than nonalcoholics to work to obtain alcohol in the presence of interpersonal stress (211). This study, which directly addressed the etiological role of stress in alcoholism, illustrates another use for operant assessment techniques: comparative studies of the effects of systematic environmental manipulation on drinking.

Operant assessment methods have also been employed to predict or assess the efficacy of behavioral-change procedures. In the only study thus far exploring this promising application of behavioral assessment methods, Miller and colleagues (209) found that pretreat-

[3] BIGELOW, G. Experimental analysis of human drug self-administration. Presented at the meeting of the Eastern Psychological Association, May 1973.

ment operant work rates of 20 men alcoholics to earn alcohol were predictive of their subsequent response to an 8-week behavioral-treatment regimen. The 10 alcoholics adjudged to be treatment successes produced fewer operant responses (handswitch presses) to earn points to buy beverage alcohol before treatment than the 10 matched alcoholics who were treatment failures. The potential of this method—and others currently being developed—to predict the chances of an individual alcoholic benefiting from behavioral treatment before it begins is very encouraging.

A second behavioral assessment approach dates from the mid-1960s, when drinking at experimental bars established within laboratory settings first permitted objective, reliable and continuous observation of drinking behavior by alcoholics and nonalcoholics. One of these experimental bars (Nathan's at Boston City Hospital) dispensed beverage alcohol only when subjects "paid" with operant tokens. Others dispensed alcohol freely, up to liberal limits, as part of a specific measurement system. From one such experimental bar, Schaefer and co-workers (256) observed differences between alcoholic and nonalcoholic subjects in drinking practices: Alcoholics chose to gulp straight drinks without ice, whereas nonalcoholics preferred mixed drinks with ice, which they sipped. Williams and Brown (306), employing a similar experimental bar setting, recently replicated the assessment study in New Zealand, reporting that North American and New Zealand alcoholics apparently drink in very similar ways.

For the most part, however, free-drinking assessment methods have been used less often to gather normative drinking data than to assess or predict treatment efficacy. The Fixed-Interval Drinking Decision (FIDD) assessment and treatment model developed by Gottheil and his colleagues (113, 114) at the Coatesville (Pennsylvania) Veterans Administration Hospital, for example, is an ad libitum drinking environment used for predictive purposes. The 6-week FIDD program includes a predrinking orientation week, a subsequent 4-week period during which fixed amounts of alcohol are available at hourly intervals from 9 AM through 9 PM on weekdays only, and a postdrinking week. When data on drinking patterns during the 4-week FIDD drinking period were compared with posttreatment drinking behavior, it was found that drinking during the program predicted subsequent posthospital drinking more reliably than the patients' past drinking behavior or their expressed desire to stop drinking. Patients who did no drinking during the 4-week drinking period more often maintained abstinence after leaving the program than did patients who began to drink and then stopped or those who drank throughout the entire program (112, 115, 265).

The "probe" sessions inserted three times during the 17-session behavioral treatment program designed by Sobell and Sobell and described later in this book also represent a free-drinking environment that was used as a measure of therapeutic progress. These probe sessions allowed subjects to drink their choice of alcoholic beverages in the absence of the electrical aversion contingencies which were operative during preceding and succeeding treatment sessions. Surprisingly, these assessment sessions showed that the aversive conditioning procedures that had been imposed during prior treatment sessions had no effect on drinking, which was heavy during the probe sessions, even though the Sobells reported very positive outcome data at 1- and 2-year follow-up sessions. One must conclude either that the probe data did not reflect a positive therapeutic change that was taking place or that they were correctly reflecting an absence of therapeutic change during treatment that occurred only after active treatment had ceased.

Researchers at the Alcohol Behavior Research Laboratory at Rutgers University have also employed interposed free-drinking periods to assess behavioral treatment efficacy before, during and immediately after periods of experimental treatment. Silverstein and colleagues (264) employed an A-B-A assessment strategy in their study of variables determining the ability of alcoholics to discriminate their own blood alcohol concentrations (BACs) and then to maintain them at moderate levels. (Caddy discusses this study in Chapter 8.) Wilson and co-workers (312) used a similar evaluative design to assess the efficacy of aversive conditioning as a treatment for alcoholism (see Chapter 7), and Steffen and colleagues (282) chose the same design to investigate the extent to which biofeedback of frontalis muscle action potential influences the impact of relaxation training on subsequent drinking by alcoholics.

The final laboratory assessment procedures discussed here are the "taste tests" developed by Marlatt and, independently and contemporaneously, by Miller. Both assessment methods require subjects to "taste" several alcoholic beverages in order to rate their taste dimensions. Although presented as a way to determine how people respond to the taste and smell of the beverages being "tested," the real purpose of taste tests is to measure alcohol consumption surreptitiously. These methods, like the operant and free-drinking assessment procedures reviewed above, have been used to examine various environmental influences on drinking by alcoholics and nonalcoholics, and to measure changes in rates of drinking after behavioral treatment. We do not review these methods further here since Marlatt, developer of one of these techniques, describes his procedure, as well as that of Miller, in Chapter 4.

BEHAVIORAL ASSESSMENT IN THE NATURAL ENVIRONMENT

In contrast to the assessment techniques just discussed—all of which were designed to reflect the impact of environmental determinants on alcoholic drinking, as well as experimental behavioral treatments to modify it—most assessment of alcoholic drinking in the real world continues to be distinctly nonbehavioral. Such measures range from multipurpose psychological tests, e.g., the Minnesota Multiphasic Personality Inventory (MMPI) and the California Psychological Inventory, to those specifically designed for use with alcoholics, e.g., the Alcadd Test. These assessment measures typically suffer from the same serious problems of reliability, validity and utility as personality tests used for other purposes.

Three recent efforts to develop and refine innovative behavioral assessment methods for long-term follow-up of behavioral treatment are worthy of brief mention here. The Sobells' intensive follow-up of their comprehensive individual behavioral treatment of 70 alcoholic patients comprises the first of these advances. Two methodological advances characterized this follow-up. The first was the novel way in which outcome data were organized around the concept of drinking disposition. The second was the intensive nature of the follow-up: Almost 100% of the original subjects participated in the follow-up. M. Sobell and L. Sobell spell out the details of these methodological advances in Chapters 10 and 11.

A second recent contribution to behavioral assessment, Marlatt's Drinking Profile (181), is a 19-page questionnaire designed to be completed during a standardized interview and to yield a thorough behavioral profile of drinking preferences, rates, patterns and settings along with motivational and reinforcement factors associated with the drinking. In this way the Drinking Profile provides all the data necessary for a complete behavioral assessment of an individual's drinking problem. Readministration of the questionnaire during follow-up may be useful for assessing long-term treatment effects.

The recent development of technology to capture drinking and associated interpersonal behaviors continuously, reliably and unobtrusively in naturalistic field settings constitutes a third advance in methodology in this area. Since Reid (Chapter 5) details much of this recent work, we are content here simply to record our belief in the potential importance of developments in this area.

BEHAVIORAL ASSESSMENT: OVER-ALL EVALUATION

Alcoholism involves a single "target behavior"—immoderate drinking—whose parameters can be traced with precision. In part for this reason, and in part because of the importance of doing so, efforts to develop behavioral assessment procedures to describe drinking by alcoholics have accelerated in recent years.

Assessment methods that actually involve alcohol consumption —laboratory assessment procedures—have notable strengths. They are reliable, rigorously quantifiable and salient to the problem of alcohol misuse. As a result, the operant, ad libitum and taste-test drinking assessment methods have become of great value to investigators studying environmental, psychological and interpersonal variables that influence drinking. On the other hand, these procedures share two important shortcomings. First, there are equivocal data to support the widespread assumption that drinking behavior observed in laboratory settings is in fact representative of drinking in natural environments. Thus results of one study which attempted to validate a laboratory assessment procedure (163) suggested that analogue drinking is like in vivo drinking only to the extent to which both settings share the antecedents and consequences that control an individual's drinking behavior. A second study (28) yielded comparable data: Barroom patrons consumed their drinks in significantly less time and with fewer sips than subjects observed in a laboratory.

Further, none of the assessment procedures which involve alcohol consumption can be used to assess abstinent alcoholics because all require alcohol consumption. As a consequence, they cannot be used for abstinence-oriented therapy outcome research. It is for these reasons that we view so hopefully such developments in assessment as the Sobells' Drinking Disposition follow-up format and improvements in procedures for assessing behavior in the natural environment. Such approaches to evaluation promise a usefulness much broader than methods developed for use only in the behavioral laboratory.

4

Behavioral Assessment of Social Drinking and Alcoholism

G. Alan Marlatt

Ninety-nine bottles of beer on the wall,
Ninety-nine bottles of beer;
Take one down and pass it around,
Ninety-eight bottles of beer on the wall.

ALTHOUGH WE DID NOT know it at the time, as we sang this endless ditty in the summer camps of our youth, we were paying lip service to the underlying assumption of the behavioral approach to drinking behavior. It did not occur to us then to wonder if the consumption of so much beer constituted a pathognomonic symptom of an underlying disease. We just continued to chant the lyrics, counting off bottles of beer to pass the time on a hike until our counselors told us to be quiet.

Today there is considerable controversy surrounding the measurement of drinking behavior and its correlates. It all depends on the nature of the questions being asked. For those who accept the notion of the disease concept of alcoholism (138), the questions take the following form: What is alcoholism? How do we know when someone is an alcoholic? Is he (or she) or is he not an alcoholic? The assumptions which prompt these questions also serve as the basis for the type of checklist or questionnaire frequently seen in popular publications under the heading, "Are You An Alcoholic?" ("If you answered Yes to seven or more of the above items, the chances are high that you have an alcoholism problem.") In this approach, the emphasis is on the diagnosis of alcoholism as a disease entity. As with most diseases, a person either "has it" or does not, although sometimes a further attempt is made to diagnose the particular "stage" of alcoholism the individual is in.

The traditional diagnostic procedures assume that alcoholism is a dichotomous variable, and the primary aim is to identify the presence or absence of the disease in any given individual. This dichotomy also is reflected in the outcome measures selected to evaluate response to treatment: A "cure" for alcoholism is reflected by the simple absence of drinking behavior, and a "relapse" is designated by any resumption of drinking. Although there may be agreement concerning the definition of successful treatment outcome among adherents of the disease approach to alcoholism, there is little agreement on the definition of alcoholism itself—not that there has not been a great deal of effort expended in the attempt to establish defining criteria. In a review of traditional diagnostic procedures, Miller (215) concluded that there is little consensus about the definitive criteria for the diagnosis of alcoholism.

The search for diagnostic criteria covers a wide range, including the investigation of underlying personality factors, physiological factors such as tolerance to alcohol and withdrawal symptoms, pathognomonic drinking symptoms (e.g., morning drinking, loss of control, blackouts), and the physical, psychological and social effects of drinking. Miller (215) provides an excellent review of this literature, with particular emphasis on the many paper-and-pencil tests that have been used in attempts to detect or select alcoholics from the general population. These tests range from "indirect" personality inventories derived from the MMPI (173) to "direct" screening devices such as the Michigan Alcoholism Screening Test (MAST) (259). The indirect tests attempt to diagnose alcoholism by comparing the responses of alcoholics in treatment with those of various nonalcoholic groups on a variety of test items associated with particular personality traits. Direct tests, on the other hand, are constructed by selecting items that pertain to drinking behavior itself. Common to both approaches is the assumption that these tests can be used to identify a pattern of symptoms or personality profiles associated with alcoholism. Attempts to establish the validity of these instruments encounter the same problem the tests were designed to answer: the lack of established diagnostic procedures for selection of the criterion group of alcoholics.

Behavioral assessment procedures avoid this problem of diagnostic circularity altogether. They do this by asking a different set of questions in the first place. Instead of asking "What is alcoholism?" the questions take the following form: How can we describe the pattern of this individual's drinking behavior? What are the antecedents and consequences of his drinking? Under what conditions was this behavior acquired, and how is it maintained? What factors can be manipulated to produce a change in this person's drinking? Here the assumption is that drinking is a learned behavior and that individuals vary in the amount of alcohol they consume under different environmental conditions. Drinking is thus viewed as a continuous variable, and the approach to assessment is a differential one—in contrast to the dichotomous or binary approach of traditional diagnostic procedures. Individuals are compared on the basis of their drinking behavior and associated effects, with no attempt to assign them to categories such as alcoholic, prealcoholic or nonalcoholic.

Rather than focusing on symptom clusters or personality types, the behavioral approach concentrates on the environmental or situational determinants of drinking and its reinforcing consequences. In the broader context of behavioral theory, this approach to assessment has been variously defined as functional analysis (27), behavioral diagnosis (142), behavioral personality assessment (109) or psychosituational assessment (25).[1]

Methods of behavioral assessment serve three main purposes: (1) They provide descriptions of drinking practices in various populations, as a form of behavioral epidemiology. (2) They predict and evaluate the effectiveness of treatment interventions with problem drinkers and alcoholics. (3) They assess the effects of potential environmental and situational determinants of drinking behavior, including investigations of the reinforcing properties of alcohol. This chapter reviews the following methods of assessment: (1) self-report measures of drinking behavior, including self-monitoring procedures; (2) direct observational measures of drinking behavior, consisting of operant and ad libitum procedures employed in research settings, observation of drinking behavior in the natural environment, and measures of BAC; and (3) an unobtrusive measure of alcohol consumption, the taste-rating task. The recent reviews by Briddell and Nathan (36), Miller (200, 202) and Nathan and Briddell (223) further describe these measures.

SELF-REPORT MEASURES

It has become fashionable of late to state that self-reports of drinking behavior are "notoriously unreliable" and of questionable validity. The evidence in support of these assertions is rather meager, however. The available data suggest only that retrospective accounts of pretreatment drinking histories given by alcoholics are often unreliable. In one frequently cited study, for example, Sum-

[1] For a general discussion of the behavioral assessment approach with a variety of clinical problems, see the above publications and a number of recent books on this topic (60, 185, 218).

mers (284) reported that alcoholics in treatment tended to give varying accounts of their pretreatment drinking histories in the course of two interviews over a 2-week interval. Despite the fact that this study examined only the inter-interview reliability of the reports, the report was entitled: "Validity of Alcoholics' Self-Reported Drinking History." There is good reason to mistrust both the reliability and validity of these retrospective accounts given by alcoholics, however, because of the combined effects of factors such as memory lapses (especially blackouts), bias and response to the demand characteristics of the treatment setting. Because of these factors, it is frequently recommended that collateral sources of information, including public records and the reports of "significant others," be consulted to substantiate the alcoholic's self-reports. It should be noted, however, that the reports given by significant others, including the family and friends of the patient, may also be of questionable validity. Guze and his associates (119, 120) found that the reports of the drinking behavior of alcoholics given by relatives were often more distorted than the patients' self-reports.

Should it be concluded that self-report data have no place in the assessment of drinking behavior? By discarding this source of information, we may lose our only access to reports of drinking that occurs in the absence of others. It makes more sense to conceive of self-reports as one of several response measures open to investigation. A comprehensive assessment strategy would include multiple measures of drinking behavior, including direct observation of alcohol consumption, physiological concomitants of drinking, and measures of cognitive attitudes and beliefs, as well as verbal self-reports. Only through this multifaceted approach can we develop an understanding of how these measures interrelate and whether the various indices are independent or interdependent (162). In addition, information should be gathered concerning the determinants of the reliability and validity of self-report data. Factors such as the subject's motivational state (e.g., orientation toward abstinence, desire to please the therapist or experimenter), the presence or absence of experimenter bias or expectancies for particular results, and the social desirability of the behavior being recorded should be systematically manipulated to determine their effects on the accuracy of self-reports.

A recent study provides an excellent example of this experimental approach to self-report data. Sobell and Sobell (268) interviewed a group of outpatient alcoholics about their social and drinking histories. The subjects were interviewed on two occasions 3 weeks apart, with identical critical items included among filler items in both sessions. At the end of the second interview, subjects were given the opportunity to go back and change any of their answers. To determine the influence of motivational factors, the subjects were given one of three instructional sets prior to changing their responses to the test items. For example, in one group the instructions were: "I have actually obtained copies of your hospital and arrest records to check the accuracy of the answers you have given in the interviews, so before we end this interview I'll give you an opportunity to change your answers to certain questions if you want" (268, p. 36). In this particular study, few subjects chose to change their answers as a function of the experimental manipulations, but the design illustrates one way in which potential determinants of self-report data can be investigated. The authors checked the validity of the subjects' reports by comparing them with official records and documents. Reliability was assessed by comparing the subject's responses to the same items in each of the two interviews. It was found that 91.98% of the responses were reliable and 85.98% were valid. Only 4.87% of the answers were underestimates and 9.23% overestimates when compared with an objective criterion. The authors concluded that the obtained self-report data concerning the correlates of drinking behavior in these subjects "were found to be sufficiently valid to support their use as a primary source of life history data when compared with official records" (268, p. 40).

Self-Monitoring Procedures

Most of the criticisms concerning the reliability and validity of self-reports are directed at retrospective accounts of drinking behavior, e.g., pretreatment drinking histories given by alcoholics. In many instances, however, it is necessary to obtain accounts of ongoing drinking behavior. These reports may be used to assess drinking behavior that occurs either before treatment begins (baseline assessment) or after completion of a treatment program (follow-up assessment). Continued monitoring of drinking behavior is particularly important in programs that have controlled drinking as a treatment goal. For these purposes the best method is to have the patients record their drinking behavior on a day-to-day basis. Special forms can be developed which require the patient to report the exact amounts of alcohol consumed each day, the time period for each drinking occasion, the social and situational setting in which drinking occurs, and the antecedents and consequences of each drinking act. The Sobells have described an instrument of this type, called the Alcohol Intake Sheet (267).

Self-monitoring procedures are frequently used to record a variety of behaviors in the behavior modification field (145). There are a number of factors that can influence the accuracy of this form of ongoing self-report. The therapist can train clients in the details of the recording procedure before beginning the self-monitoring period, thus avoiding some of the pitfalls associated with retrospective accounts. Difficulties that might develop in the recording procedure can be worked out in regular weekly meetings with the patient. The therapist can reward the patient for turning in carefully prepared reports. Social reinforcement should be contingent on the accuracy and care that goes into the reports, rather than on the amount of drinking reported, so as to avoid the influence of experimenter bias and expectancy effects. To increase the patient's motivation to cooperate in the self-monitoring program, the therapist might request that the patient pay a monetary deposit in advance, which would be earned back in weekly amounts contingent on the return of carefully prepared reports.

Much research is needed to evaluate the effectiveness of self-monitoring procedures in the assessment of drinking behavior. The reactivity of these measures has yet to be fully determined. As the individual becomes more aware of the extent of his or her drinking behavior as self-monitoring continues, it is likely that this awareness may lead to a reduction in subsequent drinking for a short time. The validity of the data obtained must be checked by referring to collateral sources of information on a regular basis. Despite these problems, the use of self-monitoring to assess ongoing drinking behavior has much to recommend it.

Self-reports of drinking behavior are frequently used to evaluate the effectiveness of treatment programs with alcoholics. These reports can provide valuable information about the comparative effectiveness of various treatment methods if the investigators choose to go beyond a simple dichotomous assessment of abstinence versus relapse as the primary measure of treatment outcome. For relapsed patients, it is of considerable interest to know how much they are drinking, how frequently and how it affects their general life status. Self-monitoring data may be combined with other assessment procedures to provide a detailed picture of each patient's drinking behavior following treatment. An excellent example of such a detailed follow-up assessment procedure based on self-report data is provided by the Sobells' evaluation of an individualized behavior therapy program for alcoholics (272, 273, 278). Following completion of the treatment program, patients were contacted at intervals of 3–4 weeks for a period of 2 years. Many collateral sources were checked in an attempt to verify the accuracy of these reports. Included among their many outcome measures is a description of the patient's drinking behavior, termed the Daily Drinking Disposition. For this measure, alcohol consumption on each day was assigned to one of four independent categories: (1) drunk days, equivalent to the consumption of more than 6 oz of 86-proof distilled spirits (43% alcohol); (2) controlled drinking days, with consumption of 6 oz or less of 86-proof distilled spirits or the equivalent; (3) abstinent days, on which no drinking occurred; and (4) incarcerated days, in which the patient was either in jail or in a hospital setting. In addition to reporting the general results for each of the treatment conditions under evaluation, the report of the 2-year follow-up gives individual drinking profiles, which show the number of controlled drinking and drunk days for each patient in the study. (See Chapter 10 for further description of this project.)

Questionnaires and Survey Methods

Drinking behavior has also been assessed by the use of standardized questionnaires and interview surveys. The emphasis in these instruments is on establishing relatively objective, quantifiable indices of drinking rates and patterns. Cahalan and his colleagues at the University of California made extensive use of structured interviewing techniques in their epidemiological studies of American drinking practices, described in Chapter 2. In their study of American social drinking patterns, Cahalan and associates (43) asked the subjects to describe the quantity of alcohol (beer, wine and distilled spirits) they typically consumed on an average drinking occasion and to estimate how many drinking occasions occurred during specified time intervals. On this basis, a single Quantity-Frequency-Variability (Q-F-V) index was obtained to describe the subject's drinking habits. Population norms were then established to permit assignment of individuals to one of several drinking categories. In the national survey described by Cahalan and his co-workers (43), the sample population ($N = 2746$) was grouped into five drinking categories: (1) abstainers (32% of the population studied); (2) infrequent drinkers, who drink at least once a year but less than once a month (15%); (3) light drinkers, who drink at least once a month but limit their drinking to one or two drinks per occasion (28%); (4) moderate drinkers, who drink at least once a month, typically several times, but who usually drink no more than three to four drinks per occasion (13%); and (5) heavy drinkers, who drink nearly every day (with five or more drinks per occasion at least once in a while) or who drink about once a week with five or more drinks per occasion (12%). The authors (43) also describe a related drinking measure, the Volume–Variability (V-V) index, which offers several advantages over the earlier Q-F-V index. A recent report by Bowman and colleagues (35) introduces yet another index, the Volume-Pattern index (V-P), which the authors describe as superior to the Q-F-V and V-V indices. In our studies with social drinkers, we developed a multiple-choice questionnaire containing the interview items developed by Cahalan et al. (43), which we use to screen subjects for prior drinking experience. We also developed a computer program to score this questionnaire and to provide the Q-F-V and V-V indices for each subject.

In behavioral treatment programs for alcoholic patients, there is a need for a structured, standardized assessment procedure that focuses on the patient's drinking rates and patterns. This information can then be used to plan a treatment strategy tailored to the individual's unique drinking behavior. Instruments of this type are particularly valuable when it is impossible to obtain a direct sampling of the patient's drinking behavior, as is typically the case in many treatment settings. The Drinking Profile (181) is an instrument originally developed by Marlatt for use with inpatient alcoholics who participated in an aversion therapy treatment program.[2] In its present form it may be used with problem drinkers or alcoholics in either an inpatient or outpatient setting.

The Drinking Profile is a structured questionnaire best administered on an individual basis by a trained interviewer. In addition to a number of detailed demographic items, the Profile contains a variety of questions pertaining to drinking patterns and behavior, including the initial development of the drinking problem, typical drinking patterns (for both steady and periodic drinkers), physical symptoms and behavioral problems associated with drinking, periods of abstinence and drinking settings. Other items are designed to provide information about beverage preferences and drinking rates, and to estimate pretreatment drinking levels. A final section contains items in which the patient is asked to specify his own rea-

---

[2] MARLATT, G. A. A comparison of aversive conditioning procedures in the treatment of alcoholism. Presented at the annual meeting of the Western Psychological Association, Anaheim, California, April 1973.

sons for drinking (antecedent and consequent events) and to respond to questions relating to motivation for past and present treatment and expectations of treatment outcome. Many of the items in the Profile are quantitatively specific and can easily be coded for purposes of computer analysis. A scoring manual has also been developed to code and categorize the open-ended questions.

DIRECT OBSERVATIONAL MEASURES

During the past decade many behavioral research studies with alcoholics and social drinkers have employed direct observational measures of alcohol consumption. Unlike the self-report measures reviewed above, these observational procedures permit an objective and reliable assessment of actual drinking behavior in controlled laboratory settings and the naturalistic environment. In contrast to the indirect or unobtrusive behavior measures reviewed in the final section of this chapter, direct measures include those procedures in which the subjects are usually aware of the fact that their drinking behavior is being observed and recorded (except when the subject's drinking is covertly observed in the naturalistic setting). It is possible, therefore, that the subject's awareness of the purpose of the direct assessment procedure may affect his or her drinking behavior. This issue is discussed below in the section on unobtrusive measures.

Operant Measures

Over a decade ago, a report appeared which challenged the then existing prohibition against administering alcohol to alcoholics. Mello and Mendelson (194) proposed a radical idea: behavioral assessment of alcoholism which involved actual observation of the drinking behavior of alcoholics. In their study, and many subsequent ones prompted by this pioneering effort, alcoholics were admitted to a research ward where their drinking could be directly observed under controlled laboratory conditions. The basis of the operant assessment strategy is that alcohol is dispensed to the subject as reinforcement for a specified behavioral response. The subject is required to "work" for his alcohol by performing a series of behaviors ranging from simple motor responses (lever-pressing or passing fingers over a photoelectric beam) to more complicated personal or social behaviors. The amount of work performed by the subject can then be taken as a measure of motivation for alcohol or can be used to evaluate the relative effectiveness of alcohol as compared with other sources of reinforcement, e.g., money or socialization. The use of operant procedures in the laboratory setting provides a parallel to the natural environment, where the alcoholic must "work" to obtain funds to support his drinking habit.

Since research employing operant and other direct measures of drinking behavior has been extensively reviewed by others (36, 203, 222, 223), only an overview of assessment procedures is presented here. Operant measures have been employed for a number of experimental purposes. The initial use of this procedure was to provide a descriptive topology of the drinking behavior of alcoholics housed in a research ward for periods ranging from several days to several weeks (195). Important data concerning the rates and patterns of alcohol consumption and related physiological and emotional effects were obtained from these studies, summarized by Mello (189). Operant measures have also been employed to provide a comparative description of the drinking behavior of men alcoholics and social drinkers (224) and women alcoholics (289).

A second use of operant measures is to compare the reinforcing effect of alcohol with other reinforcers. Will an alcoholic work more for alcohol or for the opportunity to be released from a period of social isolation? Several studies (e.g., 224, 289) required subjects to earn points on an operant manipulandum which they could then "spend" for either the purchase of alcohol or time out from an imposed period of isolation.

Operant measures have also been used as dependent measures in studies that tested the effects of manipulated variables thought to influence drinking behavior. Miller and his colleagues manipulated such factors as social stress (212) and the presence or absence of visual cues (bottles and pictures of various alcoholic beverages) associated with drinking (211) to determine their effects on subjects' willingness to work for alcohol. Finally, it was demonstrated in a recent study (209) that operant responding for alcohol by alcoholics in an inpatient treatment program is related to treatment outcome. The patients who were rated during follow-up as more successful were found to show fewer pretreatment operant responses for alcohol than patients rated as treatment failures. The use of operant assessment procedures as potential predictors and measures of treatment outcome remains to be fully explored.

Ad Libitum Consumption Measures

Ad libitum measures of alcohol consumption differ from operant measures in that the "work" requirement to obtain alcohol is eliminated; alcoholic beverages are freely available to the subjects during specified time intervals. One of the first attempts to incorporate this assessment procedure was instituted by investigators at Patton State Hospital in California. The drinking behaviors of alcoholics and social drinkers were compared in a simulated bar setting in the hospital. In the first study in this series (255), subjects attended a 3-hour drinking session in the bar and were allowed to order up to 6 oz of 86-proof distilled spirits (43% alcohol) or the equivalent. The drinking patterns of both groups of subjects were compared, and it was found that alcoholics ordered more straight (versus mixed) drinks and took larger sips per drink than the social drinker control subjects. These findings were replicated and extended in a subsequent study (271). (Chapter 10 provides a more detailed description of this research program.)

Ad libitum measures have also been used to predict and evaluate the response to various treatment interventions. In the course of their controlled drinking treatment program at Patton State Hospital, the Sobells (272) interposed three drinking "probe" sessions at selected time intervals during the treatment period. Subjects were free to drink during these probe periods without the aversive contingencies that were in effect during the ongoing treatment program. In an investigation of the effectiveness of electric shock as an aversive control procedure, Wilson and co-workers (312) monitored alcoholics' ad libitum drinking on a 24-hr basis, during which time alcohol was continuously available on request. In a recent study Skoloda and associates (265) found that ad libitum drinking by alcoholics during treatment may predict drinking behavior following discharge from the hospital. During the treatment phase of their Fixed-Interval Drinking-Decision (FIDD) program, patients could choose to consume up to 2 oz of 40% ethanol each hour of the day. Patients who did not choose to drink during these periods showed the greatest improvement during a 6-month follow-up, compared with those classified as moderate or heavy drinkers on the basis of their prior ad libitum consumption.

Naturalistic Observation of Drinking Behavior

Studies that show a relation between operant or ad libitum laboratory measures of consumption and the posttreatment drinking behavior of alcoholics assessed during follow-up speak directly to the question of the predictive validity of these measures. Unfortunately, many of the follow-up procedures used in these investigations rely on self-report data and other retrospective accounts of drinking behavior following treatment. To date, there have been no studies that directly compare the results of drinking in the laboratory analogue tasks described above with direct observations of drinking in the naturalistic environment. Such studies are necessary to establish the validity of laboratory-based measures of alcohol consumption.

Investigators have only recently begun to develop observational systems that can be applied in naturalistic settings such as bars or cocktail lounges. Ethical concerns typically preclude the possibility of observing subjects in these settings without their knowledge or prior consent. Despite these limitations, a few reports of naturalistic observation studies have appeared in the literature. Sommer (281) pioneered this area of research with his study of the drinking behavior in a Canadian beer parlor. A more recent observational study of drinking in a similar setting was reported by Cutler and Storm (73). Kessler and Gomberg (148) described the behavior and drinking patterns of men in New England bars, and in the present volume Reid describes a sophisticated observational system he applied to a study of drinking behavior in an Oregon bar (Chapter 5). The next few years should yield a wealth of information from such observational studies.

Measures of Blood Alcohol Concentration

Various instruments are available to estimate or measure the concentration of alcohol in the bloodstream. These devices can tell us whether an individual has been drinking and to what degree, but they provide no information about the nature of that drinking (rate, patterns or even the type of alcohol consumed). Nevertheless, blood alcohol tests do provide a reliable and objective index of alcohol consumption and are of considerable value to the behavioral investigator.

The most widely used instrument of this type is the Breathalyzer (Stephenson Co., Red Bank, NJ), which provides a chemical analysis of the alcohol content of alveolar air. The subject exhales into a breath intake tube to begin the test operation, and the final results are calibrated on a linear scale to yield the percentage of alcohol in the blood. A number of alternative instruments operate on the principles of chemical analysis, osmometric methods, gas chromatography, and infrared absorption. Cravey and Jain (71, 137) recently reviewed and compared the major instruments available. Many of these instruments are too bulky and complicated to use in most field settings. As an alternative method, the Sobells used an inexpensive portable test called the "Mobat" (276). Because it is not as accurate as the more expensive instruments, however, the Mobat should be used only for gross screening procedures. Instruments to measure blood alcohol concentration (BAC) have been put to a variety of uses in behavioral studies. Many treatment programs use the Breathalyzer to train alcoholics and social drinkers to monitor and estimate their own BACs based on a variety of external and internal cues, using feedback from the Breathalyzer as the criterion measure (e.g., 171). Caddy reviews the literature on blood alcohol discrimination training in Chapter 8. BACs were also used as a measure of treatment outcome in several studies. In one study breath tests were administered on a random basis, and with little advance warning, to an alcoholic treated on an outpatient basis (213). BACs have also been obtained as a pre- and posttreatment measure of treatment outcome (85).

THE TASTE-RATING TASK: AN UNOBTRUSIVE MEASURE

In direct observational measures of drinking the subject is usually aware of the experimental purpose of the assessment procedures. As in any such procedure, the degree to which the respondent is aware of the purposes of the test or task may influence the validity of the findings. The question then arises: Is the subject's alcohol consumption as indicated by the laboratory or research ward analogue measures representative of his drinking behavior in the naturalistic environment? If the subject is aware that his drinking is being investigated in these relatively artificial situations, does the presence of observers or other recording instruments significantly alter the nature of the behavior? Alcohol consumption, particularly for the problem drinker or alcoholic, is frequently viewed as a socially undesirable behavior. Does the subject deliberately reduce his alcohol intake in the laboratory to conform to these implicit social desirability demands?

Experimental demand characteristics (229) may also have the opposite effect, leading to an artificial increase in drinking behavior. Subjects who participate in many of the research ward studies reviewed in the preceding section are typically Skid Row alcoholics who elected to take part in an experiment in lieu of a jail sentence, or who volunteered because they needed the money paid for their participation. It is possible that these participants may develop the belief that a "good subject" in this kind of experiment should drink heavily during the course of the study—after all, they are being paid to drink. Some subjects may believe that if they do not drink they will be released from the study, thus losing their pay and access to a relatively comfortable living environment (with free room and "booze"). While the instructions given to subjects in the research ward studies may partly alter some of these expectations, the nagging question of validity remains.

These problems increase substantially when subjects are brought into the laboratory for a single drinking session. For example, suppose an investigator wishes to assess the effects of fear or anxiety on alcohol consumption in social drinkers. He then selects a group of subjects, perhaps college students, and asks them to report to the laboratory for a study of drinking practices. How is the experimenter going to measure their drinking behavior in this setting? It is unlikely that use of operant or ad libitum measures of consumption yields valid results when the subject realizes the purpose of the study: to find out how much he or she drinks under the experimental conditions. The presence of the experimenter, consent forms, one-way mirrors, and other assorted recording and observation devices increases the salience of demand characteristics and may render the obtained findings invalid.

Many of these issues apply to the assessment of any behavior in a contrived or artificial setting. For example, recent studies demonstrated the influence of demand characteristics in the objective assessment of avoidance behaviors, particularly the "behavior avoidance test" used as a pre- and posttreatment measure with snake phobic subjects (24).

In the personality assessment field, projective tests are often advocated because it is said that subjects are less likely to "fake" or distort their replies than they would with objective tests having higher face validity. In an attempt to overcome these problems, investigators have sought to develop unobtrusive assessment procedures (301). The aim of these procedures is to make the subject less aware of the true (i.e., the experimental) purpose of the measure, or less aware that a particular behavior or response is the focus of observation. Frequently a "cover story" is given which directs the subject's awareness away from the target behavior by providing him or her with an ostensible purpose or explanation that is actually unrelated to the true purpose. Although this approach may involve some initial deception on the part of the investigator, the subject is typically told the true purpose of the measure at the end of the experiment. The intent of this strategy is to obtain "clean" data, relatively free from the influence of demand characteristics and other sources of bias. The taste-rating task has been developed as an unobtrusive measure of alcohol consumption that can be employed in the laboratory setting.

Development and Description of the Taste-Rating Task

Visitors to the Napa Valley wineries in California unknowingly served as an impetus to the development of the taste-rating task. While serving as clinical psychology intern at Napa State Hospital, I participated in a number of weekend tours of the local wineries. After roaming for an hour or so through rooms filled with crushing machines and oaken casks, the visitor is treated to a sojourn in the "tasting room," usually considered the high point of the tour. The bartender or winemaster serves an array of wines and emphasizes the correct way to sample each wine's taste and bouquet. Although the majority of visitors play the role of connoisseur, carefully sniffing and sipping the wines presented, other visitors take full advantage of the ad libitum atmosphere by ordering one or more glasses of all available wines, quaffing them down in rapid succession. Under the ostensible guise of wine tasting, these visitors manage to do substantial free drinking. Local residents have learned to stay off the Napa Valley highways on busy weekends.

A second impetus for the development of the wine-tasting task came from the work of Schachter. In one study Schachter and his colleagues (253) attempted to show how the manipulation of anxiety (fear of receiving a painful electric shock) affected the eating behavior of obese and normal subjects. Faced with the need to develop an unobtrusive measure of eating, these investigators made use of a task in which subjects were asked to make comparative taste ratings of various brands of crackers. Subjects were presented with an ad libitum supply of the crackers and were asked to rate them according to various dimensions of taste, e.g., salty, dry. After the task was completed, the experimenters noted the actual number of crackers eaten to determine whether the prior anxiety manipulation was associated with increased consumption. Thus, although the subjects were led to believe that the purpose of the task was to make comparative taste ratings of crackers, the true purpose was to provide a measure of food consumption.

We decided to try the same approach to develop an unobtrusive measure of alcohol consumption. Although the specific details of the taste-rating task vary from study to study, the following description is typical of the procedure. The subject is told that the purpose of the experiment is to investigate various determinants of the ability to make fine taste discriminations among several wines. In one study, for example (51, *p. 408*), the subjects were read the following instructions:

> The overall purpose of this experiment is to investigate various determinants of the ability to make fine taste discriminations with alcoholic beverages. As you probably know, people differ in their ability to make fine discriminations in tastes. While some individuals, the real connoisseurs, are capable of making exceedingly fine discriminations in taste, others seem to be unable to make even gross discriminations. One possible factor which may affect one's ability to make taste discriminations is the degree of experience one has had in tasting and drinking alcoholic beverages, such as different wines. In order to test out this possible relationship, we have selected subjects with varying experience along this particular dimension based on your responses to the Drinking Habits Questionnaire you filled out in class.

For the task itself, the subject is seated at a table and presented with the alcoholic beverages to be rated (three decanters of wine, for example), empty glasses and a number of rating forms. A memory drum is also placed on the table, containing a list of the taste characteristics to be rated (the advantage of the memory drum is that the subject does not know the total number of adjectives on the list and is thereby prevented from pacing his performance during the task). Our list contains over 60 adjectives, more than any subject could complete in the time allotted. The subject is not told how long the task will last (again to prevent self-pacing) but is told to continue making ratings until the experimenter returns. In most of our studies the actual time period ranges from 15 to 30 minutes.

An ample supply of alcoholic beverages is presented to the subject (typically 72 fluid oz, divided equally among three decanters) to encourage ad libitum consumption. Any beverages may be compared, depending on the subject's preferences and other factors. In most of our studies with college students we used wine because of the cultural emphasis on subtle taste differences between wines, as compared with other alcoholic beverages. Other beverages (e.g., distilled spirits or beer) may be used, however. In the sample instructions which follow, the subjects are asked to compare three varieties of wine: burgundy, rosé, and chablis (each containing 12% alcohol):

The taste-rating task involves filling out these taste-rating forms. If you look at this memory drum, you can see that there is a slot that lets you read the words on the paper inside. There are a number of words on the paper roll, and you can always turn to the next word in line by turning this knob on the side of the machine, like this [experimenter demonstrates]. Now you try it just to make sure you know how it operates. Okay. You will notice on these rating forms that there are three columns: one column is labeled burgundy, one rosé and the other chablis. In other words, there is one column for each type of wine on the table.

All of the words in the memory drum are adjectives that describe how a wine might taste, such as "strong," "sweet," "bitter" and so forth. By sampling the drinks, I want you to determine which wine the word *best* describes and also the one the adjective applies to *least*. For example, the adjective in the slot right now is "strong." If we were to start now, your job would be to taste the three wines and then decide which of the wines is the most strong and which is the least. Once you decide, take the taste-rating form and write "most strong" in the column designating the wine you feel was the strongest, and write "least strong" in the column for the wine you feel was the least strong. Once you do that, turn to the next word in the memory drum and do the same thing for that adjective. It may not seem to you that all of the adjectives are applicable but try to come to a decision on those words anyway. Feel free to sample as much of each wine as you need in order to make up your mind. Just pour the wine from the decanters into these glasses as you go along. Once we start, you can go at your own pace. The important thing is that you make your judgments as accurately as possible. There is also some water here in case you feel like rinsing your mouth out or taking a drink.

The subject is then left alone in the tasting room to make the ratings. During this period, we covertly observe the subject through a disguised one-way mirror to record the number of sips taken (a "sip" is defined as a discrete touch of the glass to the subject's lips). Frequency of sips is tallied on a 5-min basis to provide a measure of sip rate at various time periods. After the subject completes the task, the experimenter determines the amount of beverage consumed by subtracting the amount of beverage left from the original amount presented. To estimate the consumption changes over the course of the task period, we calculate the amount consumed per sip by dividing the total consumption by the total frequency of sips taken by each subject. Finally, the subject is administered a Breathalyzer test 30 min after completion of the task to determine the final BAC.

Another version of the taste-rating task was developed independently by Miller and Hersen (206). In their version, the subject is presented with a number of glasses placed on a table. Each glass contains exactly 100 cc of either an alcoholic or nonalcoholic beverage. The glasses are opaque to disguise the fact that each contains the same amount of beverage. The subject is asked to rate the taste of each drink on a number of dimensions (e.g., "sweet" or "sour"). After the task is completed, the amount of each beverage consumed is determined. Miller and Hersen first used the taste-rating task as a measure of the effectiveness of electrical aversion therapy with alcoholic patients.

Illustrative Applications of the Taste-Rating Task

In our laboratory the taste-rating task was first applied in an analogue study designed to investigate the role of cognitive factors in the determination of loss-of-control drinking (183). This study is described in some detail to illustrate how the task may be used to assess the effects of various determinants thought to influence drinking behavior.

Loss-of-control drinking, usually defined as an alcoholic's inability to control his intake after having consumed at least one drink (138), is an important symptom in the disease model of alcoholism. Involuntary drinking of this type has been described as the primary symptom of gamma alcoholism, denoting the existence of "helpless dependence or addiction, the essence of the disease" (146). From this perspective it is assumed that loss-of-control drinking is mediated by underlying physiological processes activated by the physical presence of alcohol in the bloodstream. Another possible explanation is that loss-of-control drinking is a learned behavior based on the alcoholic's expectations of the reinforcing effects of alcohol. In an attempt to gain these expected effects, an alcoholic must consume a greater number of drinks than a normal drinker because of greater tolerance to alcohol.

Our first experiment (183) was an attempt to determine whether it was the actual presence of alcohol or the subject's expectancy of the alcoholic content of the drinks that led to increased drinking rates. In a 2 × 2 factorial design subjects were assigned to conditions in which they were led to expect that the beverage they would be drinking was either alcoholic or nonalcoholic. The actual presence or absence of alcohol in the drinks was also varied as an independent factor. To do this, we needed a beverage in which the presence of alcohol could not be reliably detected for use in the two placebo control groups. After considerable experimentation, we settled on a mix of vodka and tonic for this purpose. Pilot work showed us that with a mix of one part vodka to five parts tonic the presence of vodka could not be detected by subjects on a better-than-chance basis. We could then assign half our subjects to a condition in which they were led to believe that they would be drinking vodka and tonic and half to a group believing they would be drinking only tonic. Unknown to the subjects, each of these two groups was again divided in terms of whether vodka was actually added to the drinks.

Subjects in our study were thus told they would be making comparative taste ratings for either three kinds of vodka mixed with tonic or three varieties of tonic, depending on the expectancy condition. Both nonabstinent men alcoholics and matched social drinker control subjects who volunteered to participate were selected as subjects. After receiving a one-drink primer, each subject was taken individually to the tasting room, where they received the task instructions. Each subject was presented with three unmarked decanters, each with a capacity of 24 fluid oz, and three empty glasses. For the groups expecting alcohol, the experimenter filled each decanter with a mix of vodka and tonic (1 : 5), pouring the three brands of vodka (Smirnoff, Petrushka and "Brand X") into the respective decanters. For subjects in the no-alcohol deception group, the vodka bottles had been prefilled with colorless decarbonated tonic water. Similarly, for subjects expecting no alcohol the decanters were filled with three brands of tonic (Canada Dry, Schweppes and "Brand X"), while those in the deception subgroup received a vodka and tonic mix prefilled in the tonic bottles. While the subject covered his eyes, the decanters were shuffled around and labeled A, B and C for purposes of rating. The instructions for the taste-rating task were then read to the subject. These instructions were similar to those described above, except that subjects were told they would be comparing the tastes of three different vodkas (or tonics) instead of wines.

The results, in brief, showed that cognitive factors play an important role in determining drinking behavior. In terms of the beverage factor, the only significant determinant of consumption was the subject's expectation of whether the drink contained vodka (a mean of 9.12 oz for subjects expecting only tonic compared with 17.77 oz for subjects expecting alcohol). Neither the actual beverage administered nor the interaction of expectancy set and beverage was a significant factor in the analysis. A significant main effect was also obtained for the subject population factor, alcoholics consuming more beverage (mean 16.80 oz) than the social drinkers (11.08 oz), averaged over all conditions.

We used the taste-rating task as an analogue measure of drinking behavior in a number of subsequent studies. Our over-all strategy in this research program was to investigate potential determinants of alcohol consumption suggested in theoretical writings or selected on the basis of prior research. Nonabstinent alcoholics and heavy social drinkers served as subjects in these studies.

From a behavioral perspective, one important direction for research is the investigation of parameters of reinforcement assumed to govern excessive drinking. Considerable attention has been paid to the tension-reducing properties of alcohol as a possible source of reinforcement (182). It has been pointed out by several investigators (50) that although it may be found that alcohol reduces tension or anxiety, this finding does not necessarily imply that increased tension causes increased drinking. Nevertheless, full examination of the relationship between induced tension states and subsequent drinking would be of considerable interest. We examined the role of three potential sources of tension or arousal as determinants of drinking: fear of pain, threat of interpersonal evaluation and anger.

In the first of these studies, Higgins and Marlatt (130) assigned alcoholics and social drinkers to either a high- or low-threat condition prior to their participation in the taste-rating task. Subjects in the high-threat group were led to believe that they would receive a painful electric shock midway through the tasting task, whereas control subjects expected to receive a very mild level of electrical stimulation which would be barely noticeable and completely painless. Drinking rates during the taste-rating task, however, failed to show a significant difference between either the alcoholic or nonalcoholic subjects as a function of this fear manipulation. Although alcoholics consumed significantly more alcohol than social drinkers during the task, the fear arousal failed to alter consumption by more than half an ounce in either group of subjects. Many workers in the alcoholism field would suggest that it is not fear of pain itself that is related to increased drinking (although anxiety is defined operationally as fear of pain in many psychological studies), but that drinking may increase in situations in which the individual is threatened by interpersonal sources of anxiety, such as fear of criticism or evaluation by others.

In our second study, Higgins and Marlatt (131) attempted to instill a sense of impending social evaluation in subjects participating in the taste-rating task. The subjects in this study were men classified as heavy social drinkers. In the high-threat condition subjects were asked to participate in a second study immediately following the taste-rating task in which they would be interacting with a group of women peers who would be rating the subject along selected dimensions of personal attractiveness. Control subjects also expected that they would take part in a group experiment following the taste task but did not anticipate being evaluated and judged by the other subjects. All subjects then took part in a taste-rating task in which they were asked to make comparisons among three wines. Unlike the fear-of-pain manipulation described in the first study, the fear of interpersonal evaluation had a significant impact on drinking rates. Subjects who expected to be evaluated drank almost twice as much wine as subjects in the low-threat control group.

In an investigation of the determinants of relapse in alcoholics who had been treated in an inpatient program,[2] I found that almost a third of all relapses occurred when the patient became involved in a situation in which he became frustrated and angry. Instead of openly expressing these angry feelings or dealing with them in a constructive manner, the patients began drinking again. Consequent to these findings, an analogue study was designed to assess the effects of induced anger on drinking behavior in the taste-rating task. Marlatt and colleagues assigned heavy social drinkers to one of three experimental conditions (184). In two of the conditions subjects were deliberately criticized and angered by a confederate prior to participation in the tasting task. A third group served as nonprovoked controls. The subjects in one of the angered groups were allowed the opportunity to express their anger by retaliating against the confederate who had insulted them. It was hypothesized that angered subjects who expressed their anger by retaliating against the person who had initially provoked them would drink less than angered subjects who were deprived of this opportunity. The results supported our hypothesis. Angered subjects in the no-retaliation condition consumed the most wine in the taste-rating task. Subjects who were allowed to express their anger against the confederate drank significantly less than the no-retaliation group. The consumption level of the nonangered control subjects fell between the other two groups. This study was the first in the taste-rating series to show a drop in alcohol consumption as a function of our experimental manipulations.

The taste-rating task was also used to investigate the role of social modeling influences in the determination of drinking behavior.

Caudill and Marlatt (51) asked heavy social drinkers to participate in the taste-rating task in the presence of a partner. The subjects, both men, were instructed to work on the task independently, with a minimum of communication. Unknown to the real subject, the other "subject," acting as a drinking model, was a confederate of the experimenter. The model played the role of a "heavy" or a "light" drinker; the third condition was a no-model control group. Subjects were asked to rate three burgundy wines in the tasting task. In the heavy-drinker modeling condition, the model consumed 700 ml of wine (equivalent to a full bottle) during the 15-min task, compared with the light-drinker model, who consumed only 100 ml. The results showed that modeling influences can exert a powerful effect on drinking in this setting: Subjects who observed the heavy-drinking model drank twice as much wine as subjects in the no-model control condition (an average of 364 vs 181 ml); those who observed the light-drinking model drank 22% less than those in the control condition (down to 142 ml). Although these differences were obtained in a contrived laboratory task, the results have been replicated and extended in the naturalistic setting by Reid (Chapter 5).

Reliability and Validity of the Taste-Rating Task

Replication of the laboratory study of modeling influences by Reid's research in the naturalistic setting provides some support for the external validity of the taste-rating task. In addition, there is some accumulating evidence pertaining to the discriminative and predictive validity of the task. Two studies described in this chapter showed that nonabstinent alcoholics consume significantly more alcohol than nonalcoholics in the tasting task (130, 183). Heavy social drinkers consumed more alcohol than moderate or light social drinkers when asked to rate alcoholic and nonalcoholic beverages.[3] Consumption scores on Miller et al.'s version of the taste-rating task given to alcoholics at the beginning of an inpatient treatment program predicted the response to treatment as determined during follow-up assessment (209). Responses to the task also predicted the drinking behavior (assessed by operant responses for alcohol) in a group of women alcoholics observed in Tracey and Nathan's re-

---

[3] MARLATT, G. A. and KOSTURN, C. F. The taste-rating task; an unobtrusive measure of alcohol consumption. [Unpublished research, University of Washington, 1975.]

search ward setting (289). Some evidence of the task's reliability was also established. In a group of 12 male heavy social drinkers who were administered the taste-rating task on 2 occasions 6 weeks apart, the test–retest reliability for the consumption scores was .72.[4]

Future Directions

Although these data provide encouraging support for the validity and reliability of the taste-rating task, much more research is needed. We have yet to determine the correlation between performance on the tasting task and other measures of consumption, including self-report measures, self-monitoring of consumption in the natural environment and performance in other laboratory consumption tasks. These questions must also be asked of the other laboratory analogue tasks described in this chapter, including the operant and ad libitum measures.

Future research must examine the relationship between the various behavioral assessment procedures; physiological correlates of alcohol consumption should be included. We do not yet know the pattern of relationships between self-report, behavioral and physiological measures of alcohol consumption. Although much remains to be done, a great deal has already been accomplished. We have learned more about the parameters of drinking behavior during the past 10 years than ever before. Many myths about the nature of social drinking and alcoholism have been exploded as investigators increasingly turned their attention to the direct observation of drinking behavior.

[4] MARLATT, G. A., PAGANO, R. R., ROSE, M. M. and MARQUES, J. A comparison of relaxation procedures as they affect drinking behavior in male social drinkers. [Unpublished research, University of Washington, 1975.]

5

Study of Drinking in Natural Settings

John B. Reid

WHILE RETURNING from a trip to Seattle, I was unable to book my usual flight to Eugene, Oregon (a flight that stops only briefly in Portland). Instead, I boarded a DC-9 which made three stops between Seattle and Eugene. As we prepared to take off, the stewardess announced that because of the short air time between stops the drink cart would not be used for the sale of cocktails. Instead, anyone desiring a drink could place an order directly with the stewardess.

Since I have long been interested in the effect of situational cues on behavior, I made a bet with myself that few drinks would be sold on this flight because a powerful set of stimuli for airplane drinking (i.e., the drink cart and an attractive woman asking each person if he wishes to order) was missing. Sure enough, only 4 of the 103 passengers ordered a drink on the first leg of the journey (flight time was 28 minutes). On the next hop (flight time 18 minutes), only 1 of the 86 passengers ordered a cocktail. The last leg of the journey had a flight time of 35 minutes, and the stewardess decided to use the drink cart; 42 of the 97 passengers ordered at least 1 cocktail. Given that at least 10% of these travelers were problem drinkers (perhaps even delta- or gamma-type alcoholics), I was struck by the notion that drinkers who ordinarily show an inability to abstain from liquor when it is available do in fact abstain if familiar characteristics of the drinking situation are changed.[1] As I saw

---

[1] It is also fascinating to watch drinkers and waitresses in cocktail lounges of large airports. The pace of drinking and serving of cocktails is often quite hectic. Not only is the traveler desirous of getting served quickly, but the waitresses are speedy and check drinks frequently, often offering to bring a patron a second drink when his first glass is still half full. It could be difficult for a problem drinker to live up to his vow of "only one drink" in such a setting. It would be exciting to make systematic observations of drinking and serving behavior in airport bars.

these people ordering drinks, I had visions of bribing stewardesses to randomly use and not use the drink cart on a series of flights, counting both the number of passengers over 21 years of age and the number of drinks sold. As my mind wandered further into the specifics of the study (e.g., ethical considerations, assessment of observer reliability, control over time of day, day of week, etc.), the cart passed my seat and I automatically ordered a drink.

The purpose of this chapter is to urge investigators to place greater emphasis on observational methodology to create an additional data base from which to evaluate and even generate theoretical hypotheses about alcoholism. An attempt is made here to show that a historical disinterest in the collection of systematic observation data by theorists in the area of alcoholism may have led to a serious underestimation of the degree to which problem drinkers vary across time and situations in their consumption of alcohol. An attempt is made also to show that recent laboratory and clinical studies provide an empirical basis for the assumption that situational, cognitive and motivational variables are potent determinants of drinking patterns. Finally, the strengths and weaknesses of an observational approach to the study of drinking (in terms of validating laboratory findings and generating testable hypotheses) are discussed in the context of a modest study of drinking in a barroom setting.

How Do Alcoholics Drink? Do They Drink Differently From Those Who Study Them?

In 1960 Jellinek (138) attempted to review and organize what is known about the behavior of alcoholics. Although Jellinek stated repeatedly that his ideas represented a conception of alcoholism rather than a formal theory (and went on to support that assertion by weighing medical, legal, religious and scientific opinions), his notions about the nature of alcoholics have been interpreted by scientists in the field as though they were based on systematic observation. Specifically, his ideas about loss of control as the central behavioral characteristic of gamma alcoholics have been treated by some laboratory scientists as though they were documented by controlled observational studies. Even some contributors to the present volume have designed studies to test whether loss of control in alcoholics could be temporarily altered as a function of situational or expectancy variables (e.g., 183) or permanently altered as a function of specific treatment (e.g., 274). The implicit assumption underlying these and similar investigations is that Jellinek's notions about loss of control as discriminating between alcoholics and social drinkers in vivo were accurate. Even though loss-of-control behavior has not been observed to differentiate alcoholics from nonalcoholics in laboratory studies, or even to hold for alcoholics across various situations or cognitive set manipulations, the idea of loss of control as an important variable which separates alcoholics from social drinkers has remained intact.

It is not my purpose to challenge the validity of loss of control or the inability to abstain as useful constructs for the understanding of self-destructive drinking. In my judgment, however, there is no evidence which meets even minimal standards of scientific objectivity in support of the ecological validity of these constructs. In examining the literature, I was unable to find a single observational study to show that loss of control is less prevalent among social drinkers than among diagnosed alcoholics.

There are many assumptions in addition to loss of control which together form the basis for the disease theories of alcoholism, just as there is a wealth of armchair speculation and expert opinion about how alcoholics differ from social drinkers in the way they drink alcohol; there are few solid data about either matter.

In fact, the most informative first-hand descriptions of how alcoholics drink outside institutions, jails and laboratories have been published by novelists such as Weiner (302) and a few ethnographers and sociologists such as Cavan (56) and Le Masters (165). A basic problem is the fact that numerous investigations conducted in laboratory settings were based in part on ideas about how alcoholics drink in their day-to-day life—ideas that were never properly tested.[2] The result may well be that 20 years from now we will have abundant data about how alcoholics can behave under various

[2] Although there is a wealth of clinical information (e.g., verbal reports of alcoholics and their relatives in doctors' offices, clinical observations in institutions and jails, discussions with Alcoholics Anonymous members), it is of unknown validity or reliability. Such information should obviously serve to generate hypotheses to be tested by questionnaires with known psychometric characteristics or direct observational procedures with controls. Unsystematic clinical observations, however, should never take the place of hard data for the support of hypotheses or for rationales for laboratory experimentation. A popular example of how unsystematic observations by theory-minded practitioners can lead to totally wrong conclusions is described by Chase (58). By looking at pellagra patients around the turn of the century, eugenics-oriented doctors concluded definitely that pellagra was a genetic disorder, endemic to areas populated by "chronic pauper stock." Because of this strong conviction by clinical authorities, data to show that the disease was caused by environmental variables that could be altered (i.e., dietary deficiencies) were ignored for many years.

conditions—which may be irrelevant to how they actually behave in the natural environment.

IS A COMPLETE EXPLANATION OF ALCOHOLISM FOUND THROUGH EXCLUSIVE STUDY OF THE NATURE OF ALCOHOLICS?

One of the ultimate criteria for the validity of theories and experimental data in the area of alcoholism is the degree to which they account for drinking patterns in everyday life. Until several years ago it was almost universally believed that once a person had developed a self-destructive drinking pattern he could never change that pattern, and that his behavior vis-à-vis alcohol was unvarying across situation and time, over cognitive sets and emotional states. Thus it was reasonable to assume that research in the natural environment would be a futile exercise. During the last decade, however, many studies have demonstrated that alcoholic drinking patterns vary across time and place, and can vary as a function of emotional state, cognitive set and reinforcement patterns.

Since a host of well-controlled investigations to support this assertion are described in other chapters in this volume, only a few studies are presented here to illustrate the wide variety of factors that must be thoroughly investigated before an adequate theory of alcoholism can be formulated.

It is certainly the case that many if not most bona fide alcoholics never learn to master the art of controlled drinking. Well-documented case histories, however, have shown that an indeterminate proportion of such individuals do in fact make controlled drinking adjustments, sometimes without the aid of therapeutic intervention (78, 147, 217, 243, 260). Although the phrase "once an alcoholic, always an alcoholic" has a nice ring as a battle cry for total abstinence, it is probably an oversimplification.

The "one drink, drunk" doctrine that has become common in discussions of the invariability of loss of control among alcoholics may have to be changed to "one drink, drunk—maybe." The operant analyses conducted by Nathan and his associates (225) and by Cohen and her associates (65) show that drinking by alcoholics is under the reinforcement control of environmental contingencies. The classic study by Sobell and Sobell (274) shows beyond a doubt not only that alcoholics may be taught to drink in a normal manner via operant treatment procedures but that this newly taught skill may generalize across time and situation.

Finally, Marlatt and associates provided data that may force us to elaborate on the "one drink, drunk" rule. Marlatt showed in laboratory analogue studies that: (1) alcoholics show loss-of-control drinking patterns when they think they are drinking alcohol, regardless of whether their drinks actually contain alcohol (183); (2) certain emotionally charged interpersonal situations may cause anyone to drink with abandon (155); and (3) a heavy drinking confederate can effectively influence normal subjects to drink at rates similar to those of alcoholics (51).

The rapid accumulation of studies such as those cited above force us to reconsider the natural environment as an additional data base for generating information about problem drinking behavior. Specifically, two sorts of questions can be answered only by systematic studies of alcohol consumption in situ. First, how do the drinking behaviors of alcoholics and social drinkers differ? Behavioral norms for social drinking must be developed so we do not fall into the trap of attributing as unique to alcoholism those behaviors which are actually shared by problem and social drinkers. Further, a thorough understanding of the actual manner in which nonalcoholics drink will help to decide which specific behaviors of alcoholics should be changed through programs such as those pioneered by the Sobells (274). With actual comparative data describing the similarities and differences in the drinking patterns of alcoholics and social drinkers, we can develop extremely precise behavioral goals for alcoholism treatment programs. At the same time, we may be able to develop a continuous, rather than a dichotomous, classification scheme for problem drinking that facilitates diagnosis for the purpose of early identification and specific intervention.

The second question to be answered by systematic research in natural settings is concerned with the ecological validity, or generalizability, of laboratory findings. As pointed out earlier, a spectrum of variables affects drinking patterns of social and problem drinkers in laboratory and institutional settings. A crucial and heretofore missing step in such research is to discover the extent to which such variables carry weight in vivo. Caudill and Marlatt (51), for example, showed that heavy drinking models can reliably elicit heavy drinking in normal subjects in a highly controlled laboratory environment. Is it true that such systematic modeling effects can be observed in a complicated barroom setting? The validity of such laboratory data will be determined to a significant extent by their replication in natural settings.

DEVELOPMENT OF NORMS FOR DRINKING BEHAVIOR IN NATURAL SETTINGS

The first attempt to collect systematic observational data on drinking behavior in vivo was made in 1965 by Sommer (281). The purpose of his investigation was to gather data on the consumption patterns of isolated versus group drinkers in 32 taverns in a Canadian city. In an initial study he found that 142 group drinkers consumed about twice as much beer as 142 isolated drinkers during observational periods lasting 1 hr each. He also found, however, that the group drinkers stayed about twice as long in the pubs as did their isolated counterparts. His conclusion, then, was that group drinkers drink more than isolates simply because they stay longer in the tavern. In a second study Sommer observed 110 isolates and 156 group drinkers throughout their stay in the same 32 bars. Replicating the first study, he showed that group drinkers drank more than isolates because they tended to stay longer. Actual rates of drinking (about 3.5 14-oz glasses of beer per hour) did not differ between the two groups. In other words, Sommer demonstrated that in a tavern situation the total amount of alcohol consumed might be better predicted by time in the bar than by the rate of drinking.[3] Sommer also provided initial information on the normal or average rate at which people drink in taverns. Unfortunately, no standard deviations were provided to allow empirical derivation of "abnormal" drinking rates.[4] Moreover, in this early study no information was provided concerning observer reliability in recording number of drinks consumed or time of stay in the taverns.

Another such observational study was reported almost a decade later by Kessler and Gomberg (148). Six behaviors having to do with the process of drinking (number and type of drinks ordered, sips per drink, time to consume drink, time in bar and alone versus with others) and four demographic variables (type of clothing, height, weight and age estimates) were recorded over 1 hr for each of 53 subjects in 15 cocktail lounges. Interobserver reliability assessments of their paper-and-pencil recording procedure were also carried out; with the exception of height estimation ($r = +.58$), which could probably have been increased by more intensive ob-

---

[3] It may be that one important skill we must teach nonabstinent alcoholics is the art of scheduling their time, looking at clocks and gracefully leaving taverns.

[4] It might also have been interesting if comparable tavern data had been analyzed to determine whether different establishments produce different drinking patterns.

server training, all variables attained high levels of reliability given the complexity of the observational situation.

The results reported by Kessler and Gomberg (148) closely matched those of Sommer (281): The adjusted average drink rate was approximately 3 per hour—providing support for the ecological validity of the laboratory analogue study by Sobell and colleagues (271) in which social drinkers averaged 28 min per drink; there were no differences in rate between solitary and group drinkers and, unlike Sommer's findings, no differences in time spent in the bar. Although no mean rate was presented, most drinkers took 4–12 sips per drink. This finding also provides some validity for findings in laboratory analogues of drinking behavior. Marlatt and associates (183), for example, reported an average of about 9 sips per 6-oz mixed drink for social drinkers.

Kessler and Gomberg's study was a landmark in that it demonstrated for the first time that important variables could be recorded reliably in the natural environment. Furthermore, their data essentially replicated those of Sommer (281), showing that observational data have a reasonable amount of validity (generalizability) across situations.

Cutler and Storm (73) carried out an extensive study in which 877 subjects were observed drinking in four Canadian beer parlors. Observations were carried out by three-person teams composed of two observers and a coder. Data on number of drinks, time per drink, and time in bar were recorded, as was the size of the group with whom the subject drank, several demographic variables, and estimates of blood alcohol concentration (BAC). The study essentially replicated the work of Sommer (281) and Kessler and Gomberg (148) in showing that (1) the average drink rate was close to 3 per hr, and (2) the total amount consumed was highly related to time spent in the bar ($r = .81$). Their conclusion that group size was moderately correlated with number of drinks ordered ($r = .34$) was in accord with the finding by Sommer (281) that group drinkers consumed more than isolates. This study marked the first time that BAC of drinkers in taverns was estimated; 13% of the sample left taverns with estimated BACs of over 0.08%. It might have been interesting if Cutler and Storm had compared the drinking patterns of intoxicated subjects with those of their entire sample.

There are two potential problems with this study. First, each observer had responsibility for coding the behavior of patrons at two tables. This sometimes meant that an observer had to observe 24 subjects simultaneously. It seems doubtful that this sort of procedure can yield fine-grain data on drinking behavior; and, not surprisingly, Cutler and Storm provided no data on interrater reliability. Second, observers passed their messages to a recorder, who then coded the information, sometimes on 48 subjects simultaneously. This procedure adds an extra link in the data transformation chain which may not have been necessary and must certainly have contributed error to the data collected.

All three investigations provided similar results, indicating that data collected in barrooms show a high level of generalizability across settings. The normal rate of drinking is about 3 drinks per hour in beer halls (73, 281) and a bit over 2.5 drinks per hour in establishments that serve distilled spirits (148). (In a pilot study described in the next section, we also found a rate of 2.5 drinks per hour for patrons in a cocktail lounge.) Rate of drinking appears to be consistent across time: There is no systematic trend for normal drinkers to speed up or slow down as a function of time in the bar. This finding, coupled with the fact that group drinkers tend to stay in bars longer than isolates and thus to drink more, leads to a tentative hypothesis that situational and social interactional variables may act to homogenize the consumption rates of barroom drinkers.

A step that should be taken next in normative observational research is to identify nonabstinent, previously diagnosed alcoholics and record their drinking rates in situ. It would be enlightening to discover whether alcoholics drink at twice the rate of normals in bars, as predicted from the laboratory study by Sobell et al. (271), or whether they simply stay in the bar twice as long, as implied by the observational studies.

The studies by Sommer (281), Kessler and Gomberg (148) and Cutler and Storm (73) represent an important first step in creating an accurate definition of normal drinking patterns in vivo which serve as a measure against which to compare analogous patterns in alcoholics. Such normative data can also serve as a standard against which to assess some aspects of the validity of analogue drinking situations. It is also true, however, that the methodology of such observation studies must be improved if we are to gather fine-grain data on such drinking patterns. Reliable data on such factors as sip rate or on specific aspects of social interaction or mood states in such settings require that more efficient coding methods be developed and that we take more care in measuring observer reliability (it is the assessment of reliability that gives observational research the edge over the personal experience of experts). For reasonably intensive descriptions of methodological alternatives and their relative merits, see Barker (17), Johnson and Bolstad (139), Jones and co-workers (141) and Wright (317.)

ASSESSMENT OF GENERALIZABILITY OF LABORATORY MANIPULATIONS TO NATURAL SETTINGS

Although it is certainly true that normative observational studies can be carried out in natural settings and that such studies provide important information for the definition of problem drinking and the interpretation of laboratory studies, it would be extremely useful if such research tactics could be used to test the generalizability of data gathered in laboratory manipulation studies to natural settings. To determine the feasibility of naturalistic observation for such validity checks, my colleagues and I attempted to replicate one laboratory manipulation study in a bar setting.[5] Although our work to date is pilot in nature, some reasonably firm conclusions can be drawn about the possibility of such studies. The study described below was an attempt to replicate the recent laboratory experiment reported by Caudill and Marlatt (51) in a natural bar setting.

Bandura (12) reviewed a large number of studies which document the fact that models can systematically influence the actions of others over a wide spectrum of social behaviors. There are also numerous studies which suggest that interpersonally warm models produce stronger effects than cold models (129). Using an analogue drinking situation (a wine-tasting task), Caudill and Marlatt exposed social drinkers to either warm or cold models who modeled either high or low drinking rates. There was also a no-model control condition. The time allowed for drinking was 15 min. The dependent measures used were amount consumed, sip rate, BAC and a measure of task-oriented behavior.

Caudill and Marlatt found that (1) subjects exposed to the high-drinking models drank significantly more wine, took more sips and consumed more per sip than subjects in either the control or low-model conditions; (2) there was a statistically insignificant trend for subjects in the low-model conditions to drink less, take fewer sips and consume less per sip than subjects in the no-model control condition; (3) no significant amount of variance on any measure was accounted for by the personal behavior (i.e., warm versus cold) of the model. Because the results of this study were quite clear, it seemed the sort of experimental design that might lend itself to replication in a bar setting.

[5] REID, J. B. and HEMPEL, U. Modeling effects in a bar setting. [Unpublished ms., Oregon Research Institute, 1975.]

To do this we devised an observational system that allowed us unobtrusively to record the number of drinks consumed, number of sips per drink and time spent in the bar. We also wished to devise a methodology that would provide a means to collect data on a wide array of variables in future studies (e.g., latency between sips; various types of social interaction; initiations made by waitresses, bartenders and other patrons).

After experimenting with the pencil-and-paper coding strategies used by Sommer (281) and Kessler and Gomberg (148), we rejected them because (1) they were conspicuous and awkward, especially in a dark cocktail lounge; (2) it was difficult to record time continuously during an observation; and (3) it was impossible to record rapid social interaction or several process variables simultaneously. The methodology used by Cutler and Storm (73) was rejected on similar grounds; however, we did adopt their use of an audio cassette recorder as a starting point.

The data-collection system we developed is as follows: A small, high-quality cassette audio recorder is carried in the purse of a woman observer. The microphone is positioned below the observer's throat, concealed by her clothing. The female observer is accompanied by a male "chaperone," who behaves as though he is personally involved with her. This is done for three reasons. First, we found that cocktail waitresses approached single men or single women at a much higher rate than they did our affectionate couples (an average of every 12, 21, and 34 min, respectively).[6] Second, we found that attempts were made by patrons to engage single men and women in conversation (especially the single women), but our couples were seldom bothered by customers. Third, the man could also carry a concealed cassette recorder. Both members of the pair could make simultaneous but independent observations of the same subjects, a procedure that allows for on-site reliability assessment of the data collected.

Our observers came into the bar, selected adjoining seats that provided a view of all bar stools, ordered glasses of wine, and then engaged in a "private" conversation. The woman observer actually whispered coded information into her microphone. The code itself is simple. The tape recorder is switched to the record position and

[6] This methodological finding is worth following up. If indeed cocktail waitresses treat patrons differently as a function of their assumed status, different classes of people may be under different social control in the same bar setting (e.g., known controlled drinkers versus known alcoholics).

the observer simply enters an identification number for the subject and says "start" as she begins a recording session. The total time spent by a subject in the tavern or the time between drinks and sips can be retrieved simply by measuring the temporal distance between any two entries on the tape (such temporal data are accurate, on a good machine, to within about 0.4%). The existence of this time line during all observations makes the calculation of rate scores straightforward. Coding of drinking and sipping behaviors was done in a simple narrative fashion: It was possible during the pilot work to record reliably (1) number and rate of drinks consumed (100% agreement); (2) number and rate of sips (mean, 97% agreement); (3) time spent in bar (mean discrepancy, 3 sec during half-hour periods); (4) number of initiations made to the subject by waitresses, bartenders and other patrons (100% agreement); and (5) number of initiations made by the subject to others (100% agreement). Although we are now starting to collect data on the content of conversations, no reliability data are yet available.

We tested the validity of this coding system: 93 subjects were observed at a cocktail lounge in order to compare the data collected with those reported in other observational studies. All observations were carried out between the hours of 5 and 6 PM on weekdays. The result of this validity check was that the mean adjusted drink rate for the 93 subjects was 2.46 ($\pm$0.41 SD) per hr, slightly lower than but nonetheless comparable to findings by Sommer (281), Kessler and Gomberg (148) and Cutler and Storm (73).

The first study employing this coding system was designed to approximate closely the experimental design employed by Caudill and Marlatt (51), i.e., subjects were exposed to either warm or cold models who drank at high or low rates. Twenty-five men patrons of a cocktail lounge were observed. Subjects were included in this study if they had been seated at the bar for at least 20 min between 5 and 6 PM and if they were alone so that our models could sit next to them. Subjects were not aware they were being observed.[7]

Five men graduate students (average age 29.8 years) were trained as models. They were selected on three criteria: (1) appearance similar to that of regular patrons in the bar (i.e., relatively short hair

---

[7] Extreme care was used to ensure that no information was recorded that might identify the subjects. Moreover, it was decided to terminate a "trial" if the subject ordered more than three 1-oz drinks (or equivalents) during his entire stay at the bar. No subject, however, consumed more than three drinks during a total stay at the bar.

and somewhat conservative clothing); (2) self-reported high tolerance for alcohol; and (3) ability to initiate and maintain conversation with a patron. For the "warm" conditions, models were taught to initiate topics of general interest (i.e., weather, sports, current events, family, job, etc.), to establish and maintain eye contact, and to turn their bodies toward the patron to indicate interest in the ongoing conversation. In the "cold" condition they were taught to sit next to the patron but not to talk to him. In case the patron initiated talk in this condition, the model answered only briefly, indicating no interest in conversation.

Five women observers were involved in the study; they used the observation system described above. All observers were well known in the bar as "regulars." They consumed one or two drinks during the 1-hr session, which was conducted in a small, middle-class bar in a medium-sized town.

Entering the bar at 5 PM, a model sat beside a single patron, avoiding "observer" seats. Optimal observer positions were at the end of the bar because these allowed the best view of the model and patron. If those seats were occupied when the observers entered, they sat in seats in the lounge that afforded an unobstructed view of model and patron.

In the warm condition the model opened the conversation as soon as there was a patron beside him. The opening remark was always: "Hi, how are you today?" The model then continued with a remark about the weather. At this point the conversation could cover almost any topic. Only two topics were explicitly avoided: drinking and sex. The first was avoided because this topic could be seen as an additional drinking cue; the latter was omitted because it might distract the patron's attention from the model in the direction of the barmaid or other women patrons. The topics actually covered were sports, politics, family and job.

In the cold condition the model just sat beside a single patron, not initiating conversation with him. If the patron initiated conversation with the model, he answered very briefly with yes or no, indicating that he did not want to be disturbed. The cold models stared straight ahead or into their glasses.

The modeling conditions consisted of a high-consumption, a low-consumption, and a no-model control condition. Since the pilot study had shown that the average rate of drinking was 2.46 drinks per hr in this bar, the high-consumption models consumed 5 drinks per hr (whisky with ice or water) in order to be considerably above the average drink rate. The low-consumption models drank 1 per hr.

In the no-model control condition, single patrons were randomly selected for observation.

The dependent measures were number of drinks ordered, sips per drink and time in bar. Five subjects were randomly assigned to each of the following conditions: high, warm model; high, cold model; low, warm model; low, cold model; and no-model control.

As in our pilot work, interobserver reliability was high. Observer agreement was perfect on number of drinks consumed and time of stay. Agreement on number of sips per drink was 97%. The reliability of transcription of the audiotapes was 100% on number of drinks and time of stay, and 96% on sips per drink. Reliability of calculation of adjusted rates per hour for number of drinks consumed was also perfect.

TABLE 1.—*Mean (± SD) Number of Drinks per Hour, Sips per Drink, and Time of Stay at the Bar by Subjects in Each Experimental Condition*[a]

	WARM MODEL		COLD MODEL		NO-MODEL CONTROL
	High Consumption	*Low Consumption*	*High Consumption*	*Low Consumption*	
Drinks per hour†	5.56 ± 1.29	1.74 ± 0.57	3.06 ± 0.87	2.64 ± 0.53	2.76 ± 0.81
Sips per drink†	6.70 ± 1.43	11.30 ± 2.80	9.76 ± 2.25	9.20 ± 1.64	7.90 ± 0.74
Time of stay (min)*	26.60 ± 7.60	46.60 ± 18.38	31.60 ± 7.40	22.40 ± 2.61	38.20 ± 10.90

[a] $N = 5$ per cell.
* Over-all F significant at $p < .05$.   † $P < .01$.

Means and standard deviations of each of the dependent variables are presented in Table 1. The data on number of drinks per hour clearly replicate the findings of Caudill and Marlatt (51): The modeling conditions did in fact produce significantly different drinking rates. Planned comparisons between treatment means revealed the following significant differences in consumption rates: (1) warm, high model > warm, low model ($p < .01$); (2) warm, high model > control ($p < .01$); and (3) warm, low model < control ($p < .10$). The cold model groups did not differ significantly from each other or from the control group.[8] Two differences between our results

[8] The four model conditions were also compared using a 2×2 ANOVA design. High-model conditions produced more drinking than low-model conditions ($p < .01$). Warm models produced more drinking than cold models ($p < .10$). The interaction between high–low and warm–cold model conditions was significant ($p < .01$), indicating the high–low effect to be strongest for warm models.

and those of Caudill and Marlatt were also identified: First, warm models produced greater effects than cold models; and second, warm, low models effected a marginally significant reduction in drinking rate compared with the control condition.

The data on sips per drink were also similar to those reported by Caudill and Marlatt in that a significant difference was found between model conditions. Planned comparisons revealed the following significant differences between groups in sips per drink: (1) warm, high model < warm, low model ($p < .01$); (2) warm, low model > control ($p < .05$). Again, no reliable differences were found in the cold-model conditions. However, the finding that subjects in the warm, high-model condition took fewer sips per drink than did subjects in the warm, low-model condition is comparable to the findings of Caudill and Marlatt.[9]

Although the data on time of stay do not compare with any measure in the Caudill and Marlatt study, they merit some discussion. As can be seen in Table 1, time of stay differed significantly across conditions ($p < .05$). Since no predictions were made about the order of group means, a posteriori (Scheffé) contrasts were carried out. Each contrast was significant at the $p < .01$ level. Thus subjects in the cold, low-model condition left the bar significantly more quickly than did subjects in other conditions, suggesting the importance of social interaction in barroom behavior. Since the closest person to them had neither drunk at a high rate nor talked to them, there was no reason for them to remain in the bar. Without exception, subjects in the cold, low-model condition finished 1 drink and left the bar. By contrast, the subjects who stayed longest in the bar were those in the warm, low-consumption modeling condition, suggesting that warm social interaction is a powerful reinforcer for remaining in the bar setting. Finally, the subjects in the warm, high-model condition left the bar significantly more quickly than control subjects. All subjects except one (who had only 1 drink) consumed 3 drinks in this condition. The short average time of stay for subjects in this condition probably indicates that although they drank quickly they left when they had reached their

[9] The four model conditions were also compared using a 2 × 2 ANOVA design. High-model conditions produced significantly fewer sips per drink (i.e., more gulping) than low-model conditions ($p < .05$); the differences produced by warm and cold models were not significant. There was a significant interaction between the warm–cold and the high–low model conditions ($p < .025$), indicating again that warm models produced the largest effects.

subjective limits. Thus the modeling effects observed in this study must be viewed with caution.

Although modeling effects were potent, they did not lead to drunkenness in any subject. The highest BAC reached by our subjects, estimated by observers as they left the bar, was 0.08%. A possible constraint in this regard was the fact that the study was carried out between 5 and 6 PM, a time when most people feel pressure to leave a bar in time for dinner.

Although the sample in this study was admittedly small ($N = 5$ per cell), it nonetheless served to demonstrate the possibility of conducting manipulation studies in bar settings. As pointed out before, such studies can provide validity checks on laboratory studies and point the way to extensions of laboratory experiments. In this example there is reason to suggest that the Caudill and Marlatt study be replicated, using longer drinking periods and a more complicated social situation which might add salience to the warm–cold model manipulation.

On the negative side, this study brings up a host of ethical problems (the reason we collected data on only five subjects per cell). Although no subject had more than three 1-oz drinks during the study, and no subject was legally intoxicated when leaving the bar, the question of subjecting uninformed and nonconsenting individuals to manipulations is serious. It would certainly be possible to argue that informed consent is not necessary so long as subjects are not exposed to unusual risk. In the present study it could be argued that most bar patrons are commonly exposed to high-drinking models, and consumption of as many as three drinks is not abnormal in that setting. However, there are a number of alternate research strategies possible which avoid the issue of informed consent. Two such strategies are briefly described.

First, we were able in subsequent pilot studies to recruit regular bar customers as observational subjects. They were paid for their participation and informed that they would be asked to observe other customers and to provide subjective impressions about the interpersonal transactions occurring in the bar. They were also informed that participation in the study might influence them to drink more or less than usual. The customers they were asked to observe were of course our models. Additional trained observers were also present and unobtrusively recorded number of drinks ordered and sips per drink for the "observer-subjects" in the usual manner. The subjects were then asked to provide the observer with their perceptions of the bar as they were driven home. If the data collected in this way replicate our initial observation study, it might more easily be concluded that manipulations in natural settings present a viable and ethical research strategy.

A second possible strategy, which we have not yet evaluated, is a quasi-experimental approach that requires manipulation of data based on time series analysis rather than on manipulation of subjects. We start with the hypothesis investigated in our observation study, i.e., that a person's rate of bar drinking increases if he is exposed to a sociable, heavy-drinking model. Instead of using confederates as models, observers would be sent into a bar to record the drinking rates of 30 patrons. Only those patrons who are alone at the beginning of an observational period would be included. Drink rate and sips per drink would be recorded for each subject. If another patron takes a seat next to the subject, his drink and sip rates, as well as his interactions with the subject, would also be recorded. After the observation has been made, the second drinker could be empirically classified as a warm or cold, high- or low-rate model. Data on the initial subject would be on a time line, and his or her rates of sips and drinks before and after the entrance of the "natural" model could be compared. The data on each subject would be treated as an $N = 1$ study.[10, 11] Collecting such data on about 30 subjects should provide at least 2 or 3 replications for each condition (i.e., warm–cold, high–low models; no-model control).

Given that these and other ethical problems can be solved, observational studies in the natural environment can and should serve as an important data base for understanding drinking behavior in our culture.

A FINAL REMARK

An attempt has been made to show that observational studies in bars can provide important normative data on social and alcoholic drinking, and can provide validity checks on laboratory studies. There is no reason why we cannot collect similar data in the home

[10] JONES, R. R., VAUGHT, R. S. and REID, J. B. Time series analysis as a substitute for single subject analysis of variance designs. Presented at the American Psychological Association meetings, Montreal, 1973.

[11] JONES, R. R., VAUGHT, R. S. and WEINROTT, M. Time series analysis in operant research. [Unpublished ms., Oregon Research Institute, 1975.]

setting,[12] in the parks and alleys of Skid Row areas, at executive cocktail parties or on airplanes. An examination of drinking patterns across a variety of settings may well provide critical information on situational and social determinants of drinking behavior.

[12] During the last decade our group collected a large amount of data on a wide variety of behaviors in the home setting (141, 231, 242).

BEHAVIORAL TREATMENT OF ALCOHOLICS

This section is the largest of the book—and rightly so because behavioral efforts to treat alcoholics have a very long history, virtually the longest of any behavioral treatment effort. It is also the largest because more researchers and clinicians have been involved in efforts to develop behavioral treatments for alcoholics than in more basic areas, e.g., assessment of drinking behavior and research on the etiology of alcoholism. The development of consistently successful behavioral treatment methods for use with alcoholics would be an immense boon to mankind, and for that reason this topic is clearly the most important in this book.

The section begins with a chapter by Nathan, who first considers the controversial question of goals of alcoholism treatment —specifically, abstinence versus controlled drinking. Nathan then considers several methods for dealing with an alcoholic's associated behavioral deficits and excesses, as well as procedures for modifying those elements in his environment which support his alcoholism.

Wilson (Chapter 7) considers in depth the extensive literature on aversive treatment of alcoholics, including electrical, chemical and covert aversion methods. He emphasizes new methodological developments which now permit a more accurate assessment of the assets and liabilities of the aversive procedures. From this analysis emerges the conclusion that electrical aversion appears to have little value in alcoholism treatment whereas chemical aversion may well be of some value.

Caddy (Chapter 8) details his group's program of research into techniques for blood alcohol concentration (BAC) discrimination training, which they have been pursuing since 1970. In that context, Caddy also describes research by others with much the same goals, as well as the uses to which BAC discrimination training can be —and has been—put for therapeutic purposes.

Miller (Chapter 9) reviews the impressive array of studies on broad-spectrum behavior therapy for alcoholics that he and his group at the Jackson (Mississippi) Veterans Administration Hospital completed during the past few years. Undertaken with in-patients and outpatients, serving individual patients as well as their families, using analogue as well as long-term follow-up assessment procedures, this body of research is unique in the behavioral literature on alcoholism for its diversity and innovativeness in the pursuit of effective behavioral treatment methods for diverse groups of alcoholics.

As unique in its own way is the program of behavioral research M. Sobell and his colleagues began at Patton (California) State Hospital during the late 1960s, which he reports in Chapter 10. Studying inpatient alcoholics from a consistently behavioral point of view, their research program yielded a variety of useful basic research findings (e.g., on the topography of "micro" drinking by alcoholics) before culminating in the first large-scale comparative study of behavioral treatment programs. These programs aimed, respectively, at abstinence and controlled drinking.

In a discussion of alternative approaches to follow-up of treatment for alcoholism, L. Sobell (Chapter 11) draws on her own experiences with the study, in which she was responsible for much of the follow-up, as well as on her experiences in three other alcoholism treatment programs (in a state hospital, a county alcoholism clinic and an alcoholism program in an urban community mental health center). Her emphasis is not exclusively on the technical issues that follow-up of research programs must confront, however; she also stresses the importance of routine follow-up of any alcoholic treated by any treatment, emphasizing the "hows" of follow-up along with the "whys."

6

Overview of Behavioral Treatment Approaches[1]

Peter E. Nathan

UNTIL RECENTLY the only acceptable goal of alcoholism treatment was total abstinence. Choice of this unitary treatment aim stemmed from the widely held belief that alcoholism is a progressive, irreversible physical disease characterized by loss of control over drinking during periods of drinking and profound craving for alcohol during periods of abstinence (138, 172, 305). Moreover, the conviction that as little as a single drink by an abstinent alcoholic inevitably precipitates loss of control over drinking has been reinforced through the years by Alcoholics Anonymous, which considers total abstinence to be the only treatment option.

Researchers have recently questioned this unitary orientation to the goals of alcoholism treatment by demonstrating in the laboratory that one drink, or several, does not always produce irresistible craving and loss of control over drinking (74, 176, 183, 196, 308). To the same end, Bigelow (26) and Cohen (67) and their co-workers report that volunteer alcoholic subjects chose to drink moderately, despite the availability of large quantities of alcohol, in order to live in an enriched rather than an impoverished ward environment (67) and to spend time with other alcoholics rather than be alone (26). Researchers conclude from these and similar studies that alcoholics can moderate their drinking voluntarily even after they have begun to drink again. As a consequence, these investigations suggest that controlled drinking may be an appropriate treatment goal for some alcoholics. In fact, other investigators (233, 235) have reported on some alcoholics who voluntarily returned to moderate levels of drinking in the absence of specific therapeutic intervention.

[1] Preparation of this chapter was facilitated by U.S. National Institute on Alcohol Abuse and Alcoholism grant No. AA00259 to the author.

Impelled by these findings, clinical researchers launched several experimental treatment programs that have controlled drinking as a primary treatment goal. Several of these studies are reviewed in the chapters which follow. What I wish to note here is that on the basis of the admittedly preliminary outcome data reviewed below, as well as the suggestive evidence cited above, controlled drinking may well be an appropriate treatment objective for some alcoholics—just as it is almost certainly an inappropriate goal for others. What we do not know, but need very much to know, is the nature of reliable pretreatment predictors of differential responses to abstinence-oriented and controlled-drinking-oriented treatment programs. In other words, the data we have available suggest that we move from questions concerning the legitimacy of more than one treatment goal for alcoholism—because maintaining more than one appears to have proved legitimate—to the matter of how to identify those individuals who should aim for abstinence and those who should strive for a goal of controlled drinking.

For this purpose I believe that a thorough behavioral assessment must precede any attempt at intervention and any choice of treatment goal for an individual alcoholic. Furthermore, given the preliminary nature of controlled-drinking research, I believe that extreme caution should be exercised before encouraging a problem drinker to attempt to "control his drinking" rather than to stop it altogether. Specifically, it is unwise to agree on controlled drinking as a treatment goal for a patient unless that individual has repeatedly tried and failed to achieve abstinence in abstinence-oriented programs. I also believe, even more emphatically, that no currently abstinent patient should experiment—with or without a therapist's help—with controlled drinking as an alternative to abstinence.

Among the factors that should be weighed in deciding on the best treatment goal for an alcoholic patient are the following: (1) Does the patient use alcohol to lubricate social situations or to reduce tensions? Would moderate amounts serve the same salutary purposes? (2) How supportive would the patient's social support systems be of his decision to continue to drink moderately? Is anyone in the environment so strongly opposed to the concept of controlled drinking that he would sabotage such treatment efforts? (3) Does the patient's job require that he remain abstinent, or is the job such that it could be performed adequately (or better) at modest levels of alcohol in the blood? (4) What prior treatment experiences has the patient had? Has he failed repeatedly to achieve abstinence in traditional treatment programs? How does he feel about controlled drinking treatment? Is he realistic about its hazards and its limits?

MODIFYING MALADAPTIVE DRINKING BEHAVIOR: AVERSIVE CONDITIONING

Wilson reviews the current status of electrical, chemical and covert aversion conditioning for alcoholics in Chapter 7, so I do not review the many studies in this area here.

MODIFYING MALADAPTIVE DRINKING BEHAVIOR: OPERANT CONDITIONING PROCEDURES

In contrast to the aversive conditioning procedures—which aim to modify or eliminate alcoholic drinking by pairing it with an aversive event in such a way that it acquires aversive properties—the operant treatment approaches modify the drinking response by punishing its appearance, thereby reducing its frequency. Despite their recent origin, the few operant treatment programs designed to modify excessive drinking by alcoholics show considerable promise.

Cohen and her colleagues (67) and Bigelow and his co-workers[2] undertook such a series of pilot investigations at the Alcoholism Behavior Research Unit, Baltimore City Hospitals. Cohen et al. reported that five of five alcoholic subjects in the research unit voluntarily moderated their drinking when (1) moderate drinking—no more than 5 oz of beverage alcohol a day—was associated with an enriched living environment, and (2) not doing so—drinking 6–24 oz—was associated with an impoverished environment. The enriched environment allowed subjects to work in the hospital laundry 4 hr a day for a dollar an hour, have use of a private telephone, have access to a fully equipped recreation room, participate in daily group therapy, eat a regular hospital diet, possess a bedside chair and receive visitors. The impoverished environment permitted none of these "extras."

Bigelow and co-workers[2] explored the effects on drinking of a brief period of isolation that was contingent on drinking. Isolation—a period during which 10 min of confinement to a small booth followed every drink of an ounce of 95-proof (47.5% alcohol) distilled spirits (up to 12 oz a day)—preceded and followed baseline drinking periods of indeterminate length. The 10 alcoholic subjects consumed

[2] BIGELOW, G. E., LIEBSON, I. A. and GRIFFITHS, R. R. Experimental analysis of alcoholic drinking. Presented at the annual meeting of the American Psychological Association, Montreal, August 1973.

95% and 92% of the alcohol available to them during the pre- and postisolation periods, respectively, but only 52% during the contingent isolation phase. This result suggests that isolation was so aversive to these subjects they avoided it even at the expense of alcohol consumption.

Alcoholics who possess robust social reinforcers outside the hospital were examined in a second study described by Bigelow et al.[2] The chance to earn permission to attend a family gathering or to visit a girlfriend was made available to the two subjects contingent on their consumption of 5 oz of alcohol or less a day. One subject drank more than 5 oz a day (on only 1 of the study's 16 days), and the other drank none at all. Together these studies show that alcoholics may in fact drink in moderation when the contingencies for doing so are tied directly to the availability of potent reinforcers.

Bigelow and his colleagues tested the power of alcohol itself as a reinforcing consequence for moderate drinking by alcoholics in the final experiment detailed in their 1973 report. Not one of five alcoholics drank excessively (more than 8 oz a day) when contingent alcohol was available if subjects did not exceed predetermined moderation criteria. By contrast, when no contingencies were attached to drinking, all five subjects drank as much alcohol as was available to them.

Miller and his colleagues (208) recently designed an unusual single-subject operant treatment study that also evaluated the effectiveness of contingent reinforcement for reduced blood alcohol concentrations (BACs). A single outpatient alcoholic was the subject of the study. The patient's BAC was assessed in his home or his place of employment by a research assistant dispatched twice weekly at unpredictable times to collect breath samples for later analysis by gas chromatography. Contingent reinforcement—$3 in the form of hospital commissary coupons—was given for each zero BAC reading after an initial baseline (nonreinforcement) period during which breath samples were also collected. Once the 3-week contingent reinforcement period began, the research assistant returned to the patient's home or job after each chromatographic analysis either to deliver the reinforcement coupons or to inform the patient that he had failed to meet the requirement criterion. After 3 weeks of this schedule a 3-week noncontingent reinforcement phase was introduced, during which the patient received commissary coupons following each breath test regardless of his BAC. The contingent reinforcement phase was then reinstated for the final 3 weeks of the study.

The two contingent reinforcement periods were much more effective than either noncontingent reinforcement or no reinforcement in reducing the patient's drinking. Although the practicality of the treatment method must be questioned on the basis of cost effectiveness—the high cost in paraprofessional time spent locating the patient, taking breath samples from him, analyzing them, and then delivering the reinforcement or announcing its absence—some elements of the procedure may have value in the context of an intermittent follow-up procedure designed to assess BAC in the natural environment.

Wilson and co-workers (312) recently reported that drinking by alcoholics can be effectively suppressed by strong contingent electrical shock. Thus when a painful experimenter-administered shock routinely followed consumption of a 1-oz drink of beverage alcohol, a substantial decrease in drinking from the baseline, nonshock levels was observed; when contingent shock was subsequently withdrawn, subjects returned to much higher consumption levels. During a second phase of the same study shock was self- rather than experimenter-administered. The results of this punishment procedure showed that drinking by one subject was completely suppressed during and after the contingent self-shock sequence, and another maintained a controlled pattern of consumption during the same period. Although these findings are admittedly preliminary, they do suggest that self-punishment, like the other modes of contingent control reviewed here, may effectively modify drinking by some alcoholics. We believe, accordingly, that the self-punishment model of aversive control warrants intensive study.

MODIFYING MALADAPTIVE DRINKING BEHAVIOR: BAC DISCRIMINATION TRAINING

In 1970 Lovibond and Caddy (171) described the first research program designed specifically to investigate the therapeutic potential of BAC discrimination training. With that study these two clinical researchers opened a new field of inquiry into previously unexplored determinants of alcohol consumption and its modulation. In Chapter 8 Caddy details that study, as well as additional studies in that area.

MODIFYING BEHAVIORAL EXCESSES AND DEFICITS: SYSTEMATIC DESENSITIZATION

Although many or most behavioral therapists consider systematic desensitization to be the treatment of choice for the neuroses, the procedure, a cornerstone of behavior therapy, has only rarely been utilized as the sole component of a behavioral prescription for alcoholism. In fact, only Kraft and Al-Issa (156, 157) reported using systematic desensitization alone with alcoholic patients. These two clinical studies report the successful use of systematic desensitization to reduce the anxiety that interfered with the social functioning of eight young alcoholics. The anxiety was so severe it was believed to have played an important causal role in the development of each person's alcoholism. Each of these eight subjects who underwent systematic desensitization were thought to have improved their social functioning and reduced their drinking by the end of treatment. Unfortunately, extensive follow-up data on these patients were not reported.

MODIFYING MALADAPTIVE DRINKING BEHAVIOR: BROAD-SPECTRUM AND MULTIFACETED BEHAVIORAL THERAPIES

Somewhat over a decade ago Lazarus, then as now a major figure in the field of behavioral therapy, proposed a "broad-spectrum" behavioral approach to alcoholism that combined systematic desensitization with a variety of other behavioral techniques. This treatment package was designed to modify an alcoholic's excessive drinking and his associated behavioral excesses and deficits (164). The elements of Lazarus's broad-spectrum behavioral therapy package for alcoholism included (1) medical treatment of alcohol-related physical problems; (2) aversion conditioning to attempt direct modification of the patient's drinking behavior; (3) tests and interviews to identify "specific stimulus antecedents of anxiety" in order to construct anxiety hierarchies for systematic desensitization; (4) assertiveness training, behavioral rehearsal, and hypnosis to "countercondition anxiety-response habits"; and (5) development of a relationship with the patient's spouse, to help him or her identify and then alter his or her role in the patient's alcoholism. This early commitment to a multifaceted behavioral approach to an alcoholic's associated behavioral problems foreshadowed subsequent developments generally, as well as Lazarus's own innovative approach to behavior therapy. The extent of Lazarus's vision in this regard is suggested by the fact that most current efforts to treat alcoholism are multifaceted; most endeavor to confront as many as possible of the patient's problems associated with his excessive drinking.

Wilson and Rosen (313) chose this treatment strategy when they planned a behavioral treatment program for a 30-year-old male alcoholic. Deciding early in treatment that the most appropriate goal for this patient was controlled drinking, they proceeded to employ BAC discrimination training, aversion conditioning, behavioral rehearsal, assertiveness training, self-monitoring of alcohol consumption and contingency contracting to modify the patient's drinking as well as to improve his ability to deal with stress in familial and social settings. A 6-month follow-up revealed that the patient had maintained a stable pattern of controlled drinking.

In later chapters Miller (Chapter 9) and M. Sobell (Chapter 10) report their efforts to implement large-scale broad-spectrum behavioral treatment programs for in- and outpatient alcoholics. I therefore complete this review of multifaceted behavioral treatment by making brief reference to clinical researchers other than Miller and Sobell who reported this kind of work.

Pomerleau and Brady (239), for example, described a multifaceted treatment package for use with a particular subset of outpatient alcoholics—those with sufficient motivation to change their drinking habits and who are willing and able to invest $300 in their own treatment. A small portion of this sum is returned each treatment session, contingent on the patient's cooperation with a multifaceted treatment package that includes self-monitoring of alcohol intake, contingency management techniques, explicit efforts to shape more adaptive drinking behavior, and practice in social behaviors incompatible with uncontrolled drinking (e.g., playing bridge or chess). Of seven patients treated in a pilot test of this treatment approach, six quickly reduced their drinking; a lengthy follow-up of substantially more patients has not yet been reported, so this multifaceted treatment package must be considered experimental.

Whereas Pomerleau and Brady's study was designed to maximize the chances of successful treatment by simultaneously providing patients with an array of behavioral change methods, Hedberg and Campbell (126) compared the therapeutic efficacy of four specific therapeutic procedures. After randomly assigning 49 alcoholics to 1 of 4 outpatient treatment groups (behavioral family counseling, electrical aversion, covert sensitization, and systematic desensitization) and treating them for a year, Hedberg and Campbell concluded the following: Behavioral family counseling was most effective in modifying alcohol consumption; systematic desensitization, although useful, was less effective than behavioral counseling; covert sensitization and electrical aversion were, respectively, relatively and completely ineffective in this regard. Although the design of this study did not permit assessment of the interactive effects of a multifaceted alcoholism treatment program (i.e., the combined effects of family counseling and desensitization), it nonetheless represents a step in this important direction.

A more recent study with conceptual similarities to that of Hedberg and Campbell was reported by Vogler and associates (294), who compared the efficacy of 2 broad-spectrum behavioral therapy packages that differed markedly in their composition. A total of 42 alcoholics completed the inpatient portion of the study and its subsequent 1-year follow-up. The 23 patients in group 1 received comprehensive behavioral treatment while they were inpatients. This included videotaped recording and replay of intoxicated behavior, alcohol education, BAC discrimination training, aversion training for overconsumption (drinking so the BAC was above 50 mg per 100 ml) and for "alcoholic drinking" (gulping instead of sipping, drinking straight alcohol instead of mixed drinks, etc.), and behavioral counseling. Group 2 patients received only alcohol education and behavioral counseling as well as the standard hospital milieu "treatment" both groups received. Regular booster treatment sessions were then given to members of both groups over the succeeding 1-year follow-up period.

At the 1-year follow-up, the two treatment groups did not differ in rates of abstinence or controlled drinking: 62% were either abstinent or drinking in a controlled fashion at that time. Similarly, the groups did not differ in their patterns of positive change in four of five specific drinking and drinking-related behaviors after treatment (preferred beverage consumed, drinking companions chosen, drinking environment and number of days per month lost from work because of drinking). The one behavior that did differentiate the two groups was alcohol intake: Group 1 decreased from 17.2 to 3.5 gallons of absolute alcohol a year; group 2 decreased from 11.8 to 6.9 gallons (the national average is 2.6 gallons per adult per year). This difference in rates of decrease in consumption was significant beyond the .01 level.

This study merits discussion here for several reasons: (1) Some of the subjects in both groups maintained a pattern of controlled drinking throughout the entire follow-up year; (2) subjects in both groups did better than expected during the year on a variety of alcohol-related behaviors; and (3) only one index of treatment outcome (amount of alcohol consumed) differentiated the two treatment groups. These results suggest, first, that continued research on behavioral treatment designed to teach controlled drinking should be supported. They also reaffirm the importance of booster treatment sessions to a successful outcome; in fact, it is possible that both treatment groups did well during follow-up largely because booster sessions were regularly programmed for both. The Sobells reach similar conclusions about the therapeutic value of their intensive follow-up programs (Chapters 10 and 11). Finally, the results of this study reemphasize that the manner in which outcome data are cast in alcoholism treatment studies profoundly affects the conclusions that can be drawn from them. If one believes that the rate of abstinence or of controlled drinking is the best index of behavioral gain, it would have to be concluded that the added behavioral treatment given group 1 in this study had no beneficial impact on their drinking. However, if, like the authors of the study, one examines several other less obvious indices of change, the additional treatment group 1 received could be justified. The central problem that remains is how to choose among these indices of improvement: Since they do not cohere, on which ought one to rely?

MODIFYING THE NATURAL ENVIRONMENT: COMMUNITY-REINFORCEMENT COUNSELING AND CONTINGENCY MANAGEMENT

Like most people, alcoholics live in the midst of persons who are important to them. These persons may include, at any given time, spouses, parents, children, employers and friends. The alcoholic influences—and is influenced by—this matrix of relationships. Thus, behavioral researchers have begun to study the impact of these reciprocal influences on the development and maintenance of alcohol misuse.

Goldman and associates (111), for example, studied the drinking rates of four alcoholics and the effects of group versus individual decision-making on whether to drink. Hersen and colleagues (128) studied relationships between the verbal and nonverbal interactions of an alcoholic and his wife; and in a related project Miller and Hersen (207) found that a therapeutic change in the troubled relationship of an alcoholic and his wife had a beneficial impact on his drinking.

Behavioral researchers and therapists have begun to place increasing emphasis on helping alcoholics develop more adaptive responses to stressful interpersonal situations. This doubtless reflects their growing realization that there is an intimate relationship between interpersonal competence and alcohol misuse. The Sobells and Miller and his colleagues deserve credit for pioneering this new effort.

One direct effect includes the attempts recently reported to extend behavioral intervention to "alcohol abuse in the natural environment" as opposed to more traditional treatment within laboratory, clinic or hospital settings.

The community-reinforcement approach to alcoholism proposed by Hunt and Azrin (136) represents one of the first efforts at comprehensive intervention in the natural environment. To launch the study, 16 hospitalized alcoholics were placed in 2 matched groups on the basis of marital status, age, education, vocational status and number of previous hospitalizations. The control group of 8 patients received standard hospital milieu therapy as well as counseling on the health hazards and interpersonal problems associated with continued drinking and detailed information about local A.A. groups. The 8 patients in the experimental group received community-reinforcement counseling along with the standard hospital treatment.

Community-reinforcement counseling provided for direct modification of the patients' interpersonal and environmental support systems. An experienced behavioral clinician helped each patient find employment, improve family and marital relations, enhance social skills and find new nonalcohol-related social activities. Precisely how the clinician undertook these rehabilitative efforts is not detailed in Hunt and Azrin's report. His labors must have been arduous indeed, however, in view of the very limited personal and vocational skills these patients were able to bring to the treatment situation.

Because alcoholics with effective social, family and vocational ties have better prognoses for successful rehabilitation than those without such environmental supports, the community-reinforcement counseling portion of the Hunt and Azrin study must have heightened prospects for successful treatment outcome. The study went further, however, by providing continued access to the newly developed "natural reinforcers" (e.g., good job, wife's sustained attention, effective social relationships) contingent on continued abstinence. This contingency arrangement was coordinated during weekly visits by a counselor for the first month following hospital discharge; visits were less frequent during the remainder of a 6-month follow-up period.

At the 6-month follow-up the community-reinforcement group had spent significantly less time drinking, unemployed, away from home or institutionalized than the control group. These data support the view that direct environmental manipulation, especially when combined with contingent access to important environmental reinforcers, is almost certainly of value in treating alcoholics. Despite the promising nature of these data, however, two cautions should be observed. The first concerns the obvious high costs of this program: Few communities could afford the expense of the intensive individual supervision and counseling this program provided on a community-wide basis. What could be done for 16 men would be impossible to do for 5000 or 50,000. Second, the direct therapeutic efficacy of the unique "active ingredient" employed in this study —contingent access to familial, vocational and social reinforcers —cannot be distinguished from the benefits patients derived from help in finding a job, improving social skills, and increasing marital communication. Since control patients received neither this help nor contingent access to the same range of reinforcers, the two groups cannot be compared. On the other hand, the study does reaffirm the importance of any and all help therapists can give patients in improving social, vocational and personal skills.

For several years Bigelow, Liebson and Griffiths and their coworkers at the Baltimore City Hospitals have focused most of their efforts on ways to extend contingent control of drinking behavior achieved in the laboratory setting to equivalent control in the natural environment, where continuous monitoring of behavior and systematic delivery of reinforcers for moderate drinking or abstinence are impossible. These efforts received initial impetus from therapeutic success with a heroin addict who simultaneously had a high intake of alcohol (168). This patient was treated by making his maintenance on methadone (a potent reinforcer) contingent on simultaneous ingestion of disulfiram. Regular ingestion of disulfiram, in turn, prevented the patient from drinking since he knew that alcohol–disulfiram reactions are extremely aversive. Encouraged by this initial success, the researchers then went on to treat nine more multiply addicted men in precisely the same way (169). Treatment continued to be successful. The patients drank alcohol on only 1.4% of the days methadone maintenance was contingent on abstinence, but on 19.2% of days it was not.

Four hospital employees were referred for treatment because they were in danger of being fired for "work decrements related to excessive drinking" and underwent a variant of this treatment.[3]

---

[3] BIGELOW, G. E., LIEBSON, I. A. and LAWRENCE, C. Prevention of alcohol abuse by reinforcement of incompatible behavior. Presented at the meeting of the Association for the Advancement of Behavior Therapy, Miami, December 1973.

They were given the opportunity to continue their employment contingent on regular disulfiram ingestion. Each was required to report to the hospital's alcoholism clinic for disulfiram each day before work. Failure to report resulted in no work and no pay that day. At the time the 1973 report was written, the four had accumulated over 1000 treatment days: "None of the patients has ever failed to satisfy the contingency" during follow-up periods of varying lengths.

The same investigators describe another outpatient contingency program in the same report, this one requiring seven alcoholics to make cash security deposits with a therapist to ensure their continued attendance at an alcoholism clinic where they received disulfiram. The security deposit could be earned back by regular clinic attendance; failure to report to the clinic resulted in immediate loss of a small portion of the deposit to charity. At the time of the report, the seven patients in the program had accumulated 835 days under contract, six had achieved the initial contracts, four patients agreed to contract for additional periods of abstinence despite the "heavy response requirements involved in participation in this kind of program" and the sizable financial commitment involved in the initial security deposit.

Miller and his colleagues have also begun to explore the utility of contingency contracting in both analogue and actual "natural environment." The first of two reports on this work contrasted the effects on analogue drinking by inpatient alcoholics of four kinds of behavioral contract (208). The second (201) involved a comparative study of the efficacy of a multifaceted behavioral intervention program providing Skid Row outpatients access to a variety of goods and services in return for moderation in their drinking. Miller gives further details about these studies later in this book (Chapter 9).

BEHAVIORAL TREATMENT: A BRIEF PERSPECTIVE

This review of the research, together with my familiarity with the research described elsewhere in this section, leads me to attempt this very selective summary of the current state of knowledge in a very broad treatment area.

(1) No data yet exist which indicate that any of the aversion conditioning methods (including electrical, chemical or covert aversion) has the capacity alone to effect change in excessive drinking on even a short-term basis. In fact, data exist which suggest that electrical and covert aversion probably do not even add to the capacity of multifaceted behavioral treatment programs to effect such

changes in drinking behavior. Although still tentative, findings relating to the efficacy of chemical aversion indicate that this behavioral treatment approach may well show promise.

(2) Despite their success in controlled laboratory studies, behavioral treatment approaches such as operant conditioning and BAC discrimination have not yet withstood the test of broad-scale application in the natural environment. That clinical researchers have begun such tests, however, is reassuring as to future developments in the field.

(3) What has been done "in the real world," together with results from laboratory studies, strongly supports the following conclusion: There are multifaceted therapeutic programs which simultaneously attack several areas of maladaptive functioning in a given individual (e.g., deficits in assertiveness, social skills and vocational competence). These programs are more effective—they change more areas of behavior—than procedures that deal with only a single "target behavior" (e.g., excessive drinking).

(4) On the basis of admittedly limited data, the most persuasive evidence seems to indicate that controlled drinking is a viable goal for some alcoholics. The identity of these alcoholics and the criteria that should be employed to select them for such a treatment goal remain to be determined. Until that time, extreme care must be employed in selecting alcoholics for any treatment that does not have abstinence as its goal.

7

Alcoholism and Aversion Therapy: Issues, Ethics and Evidence[1]

G. Terence Wilson

A SURVEY of the attitudes of members of behavior therapy associations in the United States and Britain toward homosexuality showed that aversive procedures were clearly the preferred techniques in the treatment of homosexuals (80). Had a similar survey been conducted on behavioral therapists' practices with alcoholics, the same result almost certainly would have been found. Eysenck and Rachman, for example, noted that early behavioral approaches to the treatment of sexual disorders, which emphasized aversion conditioning almost exclusively, were "inspired by the earlier attempts to cure alcoholism in this manner" (92, *p. 163*). Similarly, Franks (99) remarked on the conceptual and procedural parallels between the behavioral treatment of alcoholics and sexual deviants. As a result, behavior therapy with alcoholic patients is still all too often equated with aversive control, a subject which has triggered public and professional controversy. Illustrating the controversial nature of this topic, a fairly recent article on aversion therapy in *The Wall Street Journal* (250) raised the possibility that aversion therapy is merely "old-fashioned torture." In contrast, the director of an alcoholism treatment center in Los Angeles was quoted as enthusiastically endorsing the utility of aversion conditioning: "We are using brainwashing—but for the good of people" (250). On the other hand, no less distinguished a figure than psychologist Perry London was reported as commenting that "Aversion therapy just doesn't work worth a damn" (250).

In order to analyze the sometimes heatedly debated nature of aversion therapy and alcoholism, it is necessary to distinguish between empirical, conceptual and ethical issues. Although there is

[1] The preparation of this chapter was supported by a grant from the National Institute on Alcohol Abuse and Alcoholism (AA 00259-06) to Peter E. Nathan.

overlap, with a broad range of literature pertinent to one or more sets of issues, the remainder of this chapter is organized along these lines in the interest of expositional convenience.

EMPIRICAL CONSIDERATIONS

Discussions of the aversive control of alcoholism are often flawed by the failure to differentiate between the several treatment techniques and theoretical rationales subsumed under the general rubric of aversion therapy. A major distinction among methods is whether the aversive stimulus is electrical, chemical or imaginal.

Electrical Aversive Stimulation

Kantorovich (143) reported the first systematic application of conditioning principles to the treatment of alcoholics, pairing electric shock with the sight, smell and taste of alcohol. There followed an almost 30-year hiatus until the advent of behavior therapy as an explicitly formulated, systematized approach to assessment and therapy. Since then electrical aversion conditioning has become the most widely used and intensively researched form of aversion therapy. Much of the literature has been critically appraised by Nathan (222), Nathan and Briddell (223) and O'Leary and Wilson (228). The present chapter summarizes previous critiques, covers additional findings and focuses on specific theoretical and methodological issues.

In a widely cited clinical outcome study, Blake (29, 30) described an escape-conditioning technique in which the patient terminated a painful shock by spitting out the alcohol he had been instructed to sip but not swallow. At a 1-year follow-up this procedure reportedly produced significant improvement in approximately 50% of the alcoholics treated. However, the absence of an appropriate control group and the concurrent use of other therapeutic procedures render any meaningful interpretation of the effects of aversive conditioning itself impossible. Vogler and colleagues (296) compared Blake's (29) escape-conditioning paradigm with pseudoconditioning (random shock), sham conditioning (no shock), and routine hospital care in the treatment of 51 alcoholics. There were no significant differences between the groups in terms of proportion of relapses at an 8-month follow-up; and although the authors claim that relapse took significantly longer in the aversion conditioning group, this difference was obtained by contrasting this group with all the others combined rather than by statistical comparisons between pairs of treatment groups. Moreover, a 1-year follow-up showed that the conditioning group did not differ from the pseudoconditioning group on any of the rehospitalization criteria used to gauge therapeutic efficacy (297). The results indicating statistically greater improvement in a booster conditioning follow-up group cannot be properly interpreted because patients were assigned to this group on a nonrandom, post hoc basis.

In a similarly designed study with alcoholics in Germany, Vogler and colleagues (295) compared four treatment groups: (1) a contingent shock group; (2) a random shock group; (3) a "mixed" treatment group including contingent and random shock; and (4) a control group which received standard hospital treatment such as detoxication, improved diet, exercise and group psychotherapy.

A 12-month follow-up of 32 of the 40 subjects in the first 3 experimental groups indicated that 21, 38 and 40%, respectively, were abstinent. An estimated 7% of the control group subjects were abstinent, legal problems preventing the collection of full follow-up data. Statistical comparisons showed no significant differences between the three groups that received shock, although when combined they were significantly superior to the control group. The failure of the contingent shock group to show greater suppression of drinking than the random shock group (indeed the latter was more effective) suggests that whatever the therapeutic value of these treatments it cannot be attributed to any aversion conditioning process.

Hallam and co-workers (123) found that their electrical aversion conditioning method was not only unsuccessful in promoting therapeutic change, it failed to produce the predicted conditioned cardiac or galvanic skin responses (GSR) to alcohol-related stimuli during treatment. Similar results were obtained in a controlled outcome study by Regester (241). Alcoholics treated with a respondent aversion conditioning procedure did not differ from control groups in terms of mean weekly consumption of alcohol at a 6-month follow-up. Of theoretical importance is the fact that there were no significant correlations between an objective, independent index of the level of aversive conditioning (a conditioned GSR criterion) recorded during the last treatment session and five behavioral measures of drinking at the 6-month follow-up.

In other treatment studies Lain and Schoenfeld (160) compared classic and avoidance conditioning paradigms (with electric shock as the unconditioned stimulus) to two control groups in attempting to modify alcoholics' preconsummatory responses of looking at alcohol-related stimuli. The aversion conditioning failed to signifi-

cantly alter visual attention to the alcoholic stimuli. Claeson and
Malm (62) compared two groups of alcoholics receiving electrical
aversion therapy. The groups differed only in terms of the range of
alcohol-related stimuli that were systematically paired with the
shock. Forty per cent of both groups were abstinent at a 6-month
follow-up and 24% at 12 months. In a control group of "somewhat
less heavy drinkers" (raising questions about satisfactory match-
ing—and with control treatment unspecified), 18.2% were abstinent
at the 6-month follow-up. The definition of abstinence in this study
provides an instructive example of the problems involved in outcome measures in the alcoholism treatment literature. Relapse was
defined as readmission to an institution for alcoholics. The rationale
for this criterion was that "all the patients were such addicts that if
they once began to drink again, it would surely lead to . . . readmission to hospital" (62, p. 664). There is no guarantee that those
alcoholics who were not rehospitalized were abstinent, however,
making this a poor index of treatment efficacy. The assumption that
their patients would be readmitted to the hospital if they resumed
drinking is a classic example of the uncritical acceptance of the "dry
or drunk," or loss-of-control notion implicit in the disease theory of
alcoholism, which has been severely criticized (41, 228, 308).

A well-controlled treatment outcome study by Marlatt[2] compared
electrical escape conditioning, avoidance conditioning and punishment paradigms with pseudoconditioning, as well as no-treatment
control groups, with a population of hospitalized alcoholics similar
to those treated by Vogler et al. (296). Carefully conducted follow-
up studies at 3 and 15 months after therapy showed no differences
among groups in terms of total abstinence. However, the punishment group differed significantly from control groups at the 3-
month follow-up in terms of mean weekly consumption of alcohol. These data are difficult to interpret as demonstrating the role
of aversion conditioning principles because of the failure of either
the escape or avoidance conditioning groups to show any significant
improvement over the control groups. Moreover, the punishment
group was no longer significantly different from the other treatment
groups at the 15-month follow-up.

The anticipatory avoidance conditioning technique, which purport-
edly has been shown to be successful with homosexual patients (96),

[2] A comparison of aversive conditioning procedures in the treatment of alcoholism. Presented at the annual meeting of the Western Psychological Association,
Anaheim, California, April 1973.

has also been used with alcoholics. Adapting this method, Hedberg and Campbell (126) administered electric shock contingent on the presentation of alcohol-related visual stimuli chosen for their relevance to the individual's drinking pattern. It is clinically noteworthy that of the 12 alcoholics assigned to this treatment condition only 4 remained in the treatment program beyond the third session; and of those 4, only 1 showed any improvement at a 6-month follow-up. MacCulloch and colleagues (175) reported similarly negative results with this technique in the treatment of alcoholic patients.

Evaluation of all the above studies is complicated by the fact that assessment of outcome has been based on subjective judgments of whether the patient is abstinent at various follow-up periods of many months' duration. Within the context of social learning theory, Bandura (12) pointed out that outcome evaluation of treatment must distinguish between the initial induction of behavioral change, its generalization beyond the treatment center, and the maintenance of treatment-produced gains over time. The absence of treatment effects several months after discontinuation of therapy does not necessarily mean that aversion conditioning techniques are ineffective. There may have been initial therapeutic gains, but they may not have been maintained.

Since the use of aversion therapy is predicated on the assumption that it suppresses drinking by endowing the alcohol with conditioned aversive properties, it seems desirable to demonstrate such aversions in a laboratory setting before testing their efficacy in a complex clinical outcome study. This initial laboratory-centered approach would also permit the rigorous, objective measurement necessary to specify the processes responsible for behavioral change. Evaluation procedures that rely on self-reports, even in those instances where attempts are made to corroborate the reports by interviewing others who are significant in the patient's environment, or by checking arrest or rehospitalization records, are of questionable reliability and validity.

Miller and co-workers (210) obtained an objective measure of alcohol consumption when the electrical escape conditioning method was applied to alcoholics and compared the results with those in two control groups which used (1) a conditioning procedure using barely perceptible shock intensity, and (2) a confrontation therapy condition for the treatment of hospitalized alcoholics. Under the guise of an analogue taste test, subjects were asked to rate the tastes of alcoholic and nonalcoholic beverages. They were instructed to sample as much of the beverage as they needed to make accurate judgments. The amount of alcohol consumed during the taste test served as the pre–post measure of treatment success, and the ratings provided an index of subjects' attitudes toward alcohol. No significant differences in alcohol intake or in attitudes toward alcohol were found between the three groups, all of which showed similar decreases in drinking of about 30% on the posttest. Miller et al. (210) endorsed the conclusion of Hallam et al. (123) that the effects of respondent electrical aversion conditioning with alcoholics may be related more to general treatment factors (e.g., therapeutic instructions) and placebo effects than to any specific conditioning process.

As useful as the taste test is as an objective analogue outcome measure of alcohol consumption, and despite the fact that it appears to discriminate reliably between alcoholics and heavy social drinkers (183), it is possible that its time-limited and relatively artificial nature renders it insufficiently sensitive to therapeutic effects (223). Accordingly, Wilson and colleagues (312) assessed the effects of the electrical escape conditioning procedure on free-operant drinking baselines in a naturalistic situation that allowed prolonged drinking.

In a series of 3 studies at the Rutgers Alcohol Behavior Research Laboratory, an inpatient treatment facility, 8 alcoholics were variously allowed unrestricted alcohol intake—up to a maximum of 30 oz per 24-hr period—in order to establish an objective measure of realistic drinking patterns. Following an initial 3-day baseline phase, subjects were administered 30 trials of either aversion conditioning or a control treatment procedure (in which the electric shock preceded the alcohol stimulus) on each of the succeeding 3 or 4 days (depending on the experiment). No alcohol was available to subjects during treatment days. The shock parameters and procedure were modeled after those of Blake (30) and Vogler et al. (296). After a second posttreatment ad libitum drinking period the treatment procedures were reversed in a crossover design for a second 3- or 4-day treatment phase. A third baseline drinking period was programmed to evaluate the impact of the treatment reversal phase. Neither method had any discernible effects on alcohol consumption except in the case of one subject, who displayed a substantial reduction in drinking following the escape conditioning treatment. This subject, however, returned to excessive drinking within a week of being released from the laboratory and was rehospitalized. Subjects' attitudinal responses as measured by a semantic differential test indicated similar transient placebo effects for both treatments.

It is possible, of course, that the number of aversion conditioning trials administered was insufficient to produce conditioned aversions strong enough to suppress drinking. However, the data show no evidence of any trend suggesting that an increased number of trials would reduce subsequent drinking. Miller et al. (210) obtained similarly negative results despite the administration of 500 aversion conditioning trials. Furthermore, the shock intensities employed were comparable to those reportedly used to produce the apparent clinical successes.

There are important clinical limitations on the extent to which aversion treatment procedures can be employed. All eight subjects reported the procedures to be distinctly unpleasant. The dramatic attrition rate in Hedberg and Campbell's (126) electrical aversion conditioning treatment underscores this point, as does the fact that when frequencies and intensities of shock similar to those in the Wilson et al. (312) study were used, two subjects voluntarily withdrew from the treatment program at the Rutgers Laboratory (314). Consistent with the findings of Miller et al. (210), the data yield no evidence that the escape conditioning procedure resulted in any permanent conditioned aversion response to the properties of alcohol.

The foregoing review of the evidence on electrical aversion conditioning strongly disputes Eysenck and Beech's (91) conclusion that it represents the "optimal" behavioral treatment method for alcoholism. Equally misleading is Davidson's (77) statement, in a review of the literature on aversion conditioning for alcoholics up to and including the year 1972, that "electrical aversion strategies have shown consistently positive results" (*p.* 576). In addition to the negative findings of the Miller et al. (210) and Wilson et al. (312) studies, which appeared subsequent to his review, inadequacies in some of the studies Davidson uncritically accepted as evidence also tend to invalidate the claim to efficacy.

Aside from Blake's (30) report, Davidson cites the results obtained by Mills et al. (217) and Lovibond and Caddy (171). In the former study, 13 hospitalized alcoholics were trained to drink like social drinkers by restricting the quantity of the alcohol they drank and the manner in which it was consumed. In view of earlier findings which indicated that social drinkers mix drinks which they sip, whereas alcoholics tend to gulp their drinks straight, Mills et al. made electric shock contingent on the alcoholics' failure to sip and mix their drinks in a simulated bar setting. A 1-year follow-up indicated that a larger proportion of these 13 patients were functioning adequately compared with an untreated control group (254). In the absence of appropriate controls for attention-placebo influences, however, nothing can be said about avoidance conditioning. Furthermore, a close look at the data shows that 4 patients who sipped and mixed their drinks from the outset of the treatment program, and hence received virtually no avoidance training to drink in a moderate fashion, did not differ subsequently from those who had experienced shock. This finding suggests the obvious—that factors other than avoidance conditioning accounted for the results.

In the Lovibond and Caddy (171) study, alcoholics were trained to discriminate accurately differences in their blood alcohol concentrations (BAC), following which they were shocked contingent on their drinking in excess of a predetermined BAC but not when they drank below this criterion level. Patients in the control condition received identical treatment except that shock was administered on a noncontingent basis. The authors reported that 65% of the patients in the experimental group were completely successful in maintaining moderate drinking habits after treatment based on a 16- to 60-week follow-up, whereas the control patients showed little improvement. These data must be interpreted with considerable caution, however, since many of the control patients dropped out of the study after a single session. This attrition rate means that treatment factors are confounded with self-selected patient characteristics.

Finally, the avoidance conditioning procedure used by Mills et al. (217) formed part of Sobell and Sobell's (274) multifaceted treatment program. Although it is impossible to ferret out the critically effective agents in their treatment package, it is highly unlikely that the avoidance conditioning method was as significant a factor as Katz and Zlutnick (144) suggest. Throughout therapy the number of inappropriate drinking behaviors emitted during probe (no shock) days was significantly greater than during treatment sessions in which the avoidance contingency was in effect. This simple discrimination learning by alcoholics attests still further to the fact that electrical aversion conditioning of this kind does not produce generalized suppression of drinking in the absence of external contingencies, a finding elaborated on below (312).

In sum, evidence on the efficacy of electrical aversion conditioning of the kind described above is overwhelmingly negative. Its use as a treatment modality with alcoholics should be discontinued.

Chemical Aversion Conditioning

Typically, nausea-producing drugs (e.g., emetine and apomorphine) have been employed as agents of chemical aversive stimulation. The pioneering treatment studies initiated by Lemere and Voegtlin (166) at the Shadel Sanitarium in Seattle, Washington, during the 1930s remain the most comprehensive and impressive application of this method to date. The details of their therapeutic procedures, the early attempts to replicate them at other treatment facilities, the nature of their results and the implications for treatment of alcoholics have been carefully described and discussed in several other sources (12, 98, 228, 240). The present chapter addresses only more recent developments in this area.

Wiens and colleagues (303) reported detailed statistical analyses of patients treated at the Raleigh Hills Hospital in Portland, Oregon, a private facility devoted exclusively to the treatment of voluntarily admitted alcoholics; pharmacological aversion conditioning (emetine) modeled after Lemere and Voegtlin's original procedures is used there. The mean age of the patients was 48.5 years and the mean educational level 13.8 years (a relatively well-educated sample); only 7.7% reported being unemployed. Slightly over 37% depended on personal financial resources, the remainder on some form of insurance or employer reimbursement.

A 12-month follow-up of patients treated during one randomly chosen year (1970) showed the impressive abstinence rate of 63% (the correspondence with Lemere and Voegtlin's 60% success rate is striking). This figure represents data from 92% of the 261 patients treated that year; patients who could not be contacted were counted as failures.

Obtaining long-term follow-up data on most of their original patients constituted an impressive accomplishment. Sobell and Sobell (275) noted that most follow-up studies are typically unable to locate a sizable proportion (20%–50%) of alcoholics treated. The importance of reporting complete follow-up data is, as Franks and Wilson (101) point out, due to the fact that patients who are not included in follow-up studies are usually functioning poorly. Exclusion of these treatment failures from the findings artificially inflates apparent success rates. Additionally, the maintenance of close contact with patients throughout the follow-up period increases the probability that the self-reports obtained were valid (268).

A significant finding of Voegtlin and co-workers (293) was that posttreatment abstinence rates were positively related to the number of reconditioning or booster sessions in which their patients participated. As discussed by Bandura (12), the over-all results of the Voegtlin et al. study showed that an alcoholic favorably disposed to posttreatment booster sessions had an 86% probability of maintaining abstinence for at least 1 year. Among the patients of Wiens et al. (303) who remained abstinent for 1 year, 67% completed an average of six sessions of booster treatments. These results indicate the utility of systematically scheduling booster sessions to promote maintenance of treatment-produced improvement. The suggestive nature of these clinical observations is strengthened by the fact that the efficacy of booster sessions has been demonstrated by well-controlled research on other addictive behavior.[3]

As with the Lemere and Voegtlin (166) data, it is impossible to assess unequivocally the role of emetine conditioning in the therapy program investigated by Wiens et al. (303). Several confounding factors that could influence outcome are inherent in the treatment. For example, patients received informal therapy sessions from counselors—recovered alcoholics who themselves had been successfully treated with chemical aversion conditioning and whose optimism about the program generated a favorable therapeutic climate. Furthermore, these patients were relatively better motivated and of higher educational and socioeconomic levels than alcoholics treated in most other behavioral programs, factors known to indicate a favorable prognosis (223).

Yet despite the methodological limitations of these findings, their suggestive value is strong. Bandura's (12) point with respect to the presence of "contaminating" sources of social support and influence in a program of this type is particularly pertinent here: "by the time alcoholics appear for aversion therapy they have been recipients of considerable wise counsel, impassioned appeals by significant people in their lives, repeated admonitions, rewards, and a variety of remedies to no avail. Treatment outcomes are frequently attributed to common social influences as though these were encountered for the first time in the treatment situation" (12, *p. 541*). Controlled outcome studies designed to test the efficacy of this promising form of aversion conditioning are overdue.

This treatment method has generated little relevant research.

---

[3] KINGSLEY, R. G. and WILSON, G. T. Behavior therapy for obesity; a comparative investigation of long-term efficacy. [Unpublished ms., Rutgers University, 1975.]

However, Burt (37) examined the circumstances of relapse in 34 alcoholics who had been treated with nausea-inducing chemical aversion conditioning. Specifically, the physical location, social environment and type of beverage consumed during the first drinking episode following treatment were compared with each patient's most frequent habits prior to therapy. Although the arbitrary manner in which this specific sample of patients was selected precludes much meaningful interpretation of the data, some interesting findings emerged. Length of abstinence ranged from 2 weeks to 93 months (mean 8.8 months). Only 5 patients reported nausea and 3 reported being frightened by the first posttreatment drink. Moreover, 75% relapsed with their previously preferred beverage. This raises the question whether an aversion to alcohol had been successfully conditioned during treatment or whether treatment effects were attenuated or "extinguished" during follow-up.

Ironically, one of the major reasons behind behavior therapists' neglect of Lemere and Voegtlin's encouraging clinical findings was the belief that electric shock is clearly preferred to nausea-inducing drugs as the unconditioned stimulus (UCS) in conditioning paradigms. Yet as Wilson and Davison (309) later pointed out, the relevant experimental literature suggests that shock is not the optimal stimulus; rather, successful conditioned aversion to the taste and smell of alcohol may require a more "biologically appropriate" aversive stimulus such as nausea-inducing drugs like emetine.

Since this proposition has not yet been directly tested with human subjects, the clinical prescription about favoring nausea-inducing drugs over electric shock was derived from animal conditioning results (258).

One of the problems in extrapolating from this data base has been that in rats preconditioned familiarity with the substance to be aversively conditioned or with the noxious agent itself greatly decreases the development of any conditioned aversion. As alcoholics are more than a little familiar with alcohol and nausea, there is reason to expect aversion therapy to fail. However, Elkins (87) recently showed that these studies involved only one pairing of the target substance (CS) with the aversive UCS. Using multiple conditioning trials and discrimination training (the standard clinical treatment procedure with aversion therapy), Elkins (87) successfully conditioned an aversion in rats to a substance as familiar as tap water. These findings suggest that preconditioning exposure to the CS and UCS need not impair classically conditioned aversion reactions.

Elkins (88) also found marked individual differences in the strength of aversion reactions this procedure produced in rats. He likens this finding to Voegtlin's (291) often overlooked report that a few patients with normal nausea responses to emetine (evidenced physiologically and behaviorally) failed to develop an alcohol aversion, even after numerous conditioning trials. Whatever the basis for these individual differences, it may well be that not all alcoholics are candidates for aversion therapy. Predictive patient selection criteria, unfortunately so lacking in all areas of behavior therapy, might greatly improve the success of aversion therapy for alcoholism.

Suggestive support for Wilson and Davison's (309) thesis that nausea-inducing drugs are "biologically appropriate" aversive stimuli for alcoholism treatment can be gleaned from the unusually effective treatment of cigarette smoking with the rapid smoking technique (154, 167). As Danaher and Lichtenstein (75) observed, the strong nausea-producing effects of rapid smoking provide a plausible explanation of treatment success.

Finally, if the repeated association of physiological malaise (nausea) with alcohol is crucial in developing a conditioned aversion reaction, ways of inducing this unconditioned response other than by injection, ingestion, or both, of harsh substances like emetine should be explored. One alternative is the use of symbolically generated nausea, as discussed below. Another possibility under investigation at the Rutgers Alcohol Behavior Research Laboratory is the use of varying degrees of motion sickness, which may be safely produced by mechanical rather than chemical means.

Nausea-inducing drugs are not the only form of chemical aversion treatment applied to alcoholics. Sanderson and colleagues (249) paired the sight, smell and taste of alcohol with the terrifying experience of being paralyzed for upward of a minute by the intravenous administration of succinylcholine, which induces paralysis and respiratory arrest. Despite initial claims for therapeutic success, however, subsequent better controlled studies not only showed that there is negligible treatment efficacy but also that the so-called classic aversion conditioning procedure failed to produce any differential effects from appropriate pseudoconditioning control procedures (94, 133). Given the absence of compelling theoretical reasons for using the latter method, its lack of empirical support, and the lack of ethics its use entails, it is important that the various types of chemical aversion treatment not be confused (77) and a potentially effective and acceptable technique prematurely dismissed.

Symbolic Aversive Stimulation

In an early study Miller (198) had patients smell and taste alcoholic beverages while being instructed to imagine typical hangover
feelings of severe headache, nausea and vomiting under hypnosis.
He reported that 20 of 24 patients treated with this procedure were
abstinent at a 9-month follow-up. Cautela (52) later described
essentially the same strategy, which he labeled covert sensitization. In his method imaginal representations of undesirable behaviors are repeatedly paired with aversive imagery concerning
nausea and general malaise after the patient is trained in deep muscular relaxation.

The therapeutic use of symbolic aversion is recommended on
several counts. Wilson and Davison (309) suggested that feelings of
physical malaise might be a more biologically appropriate stimulus
for developing a conditioned aversion than electric shock. Moreover, as a self-directed behavioral change technique it is ethically
more appealing than therapist-administered aversive stimuli and
might facilitate the generalization of therapeutic gains to the
patient's natural environment (287). Enthusiastic as clinical reports
of the efficacy of covert sensitization have been (54), evidence from
objective, experimental studies is lacking.

Anant (4) treated hospitalized alcoholics with five sessions of
covert sensitization. Reportedly, 96% of these alcoholics were abstinent at follow-up periods of 8–15 months, although only 3 patients remained abstinent beyond this period (5). These follow-up
data are totally inadequate given the failure to specify details such
as the number of alcoholics abstinent at different follow-up contacts
and the validity of the follow-up procedures. Since there was also
no control group, these findings are anecdotal at best. Using hospitalized alcoholics, Ashem and Donner (7) found that 9 sessions of
covert sensitization therapy produced abstinence in 6 of 15 patients
at a 6-month follow-up, compared to none of 8 alcoholics in a no-
treatment control condition. Failure to include an appropriate
attention–placebo control group precludes unequivocal interpretation of these data.

Hedberg and Campbell (126) included a covert sensitization
treatment condition in their comparative outcome study. Fifteen alcoholics received 20 hr of covert sensitization over a 6-month
period. Each session included 10 imaginal scenes; homework assignments were encouraged but not required. Of the 15 subjects, 6
(40%) had attained their goal of abstinence (or, in one case, con-

trolled drinking) while another 4 (27%) were rated as "much improved." The behavioral family counseling and systematic desensitization treatments each produced success rates of 87%.
The authors liken their results to those of Ashem and Donner (7). As with the latter study, however, the absence of appropriate control groups makes it impossible to conclude anything about the effects of covert sensitization therapy per se (let alone the aversion conditioning principles on which it is supposedly based) other than to note that it appears less effective than the other two behavioral treatments employed in this study.
Using single-subject methodology, Wilson and Tracey (314) investigated the effects of aversive imagery on free operant alcohol consumption in a controlled laboratory setting. Subjects were instructed to imagine strong feelings of nausea associated with the symbolic representation of various components of the entire complex pattern of internal and external stimuli that governed their alcohol consumption. Half of the scenes were punishment trials in which subjects imagined themselves feeling sick and vomiting uncontrollably; the other half were avoidance trials in which subjects obtained immediate relief from feelings of nausea without vomiting by ceasing inappropriate behavior. The rewarding nature of resisting the desire to drink was heavily emphasized. Subjects were closely questioned after each presentation to ensure that they were following instructions and to ascertain the clarity of their imagery.
In the first experiment in this series, 4 alcoholics were allowed alcohol ad libitum over a 2-day baseline drinking period. Thereafter 2 subjects received twice daily sessions of 10 trials each of an aversive imagery procedure while the other 2 were scheduled to receive an equal number of electrical escape conditioning trials. However, the latter subjects withdrew from the treatment program, stating that they found the electrical aversion conditioning too anxiety-producing. Following a second baseline drinking phase, the electrical aversion conditioning procedure was administered to the 2 remaining subjects. A final posttreatment baseline period completed the experiment. The 2 subjects showed decreases in alcohol intake of approximately 49% and 71%, respectively, following aversive imagery treatment. One subject indicated a slight increase in drinking after the treatment reversal, whereas the other ceased drinking entirely.
The loss of two subjects and the failure of the amount of drinking to return to the initial baseline level makes it impossible to interpret these data meaningfully. A second experiment replicated

these procedures with three additional alcoholics. One of these subjects reported an inability to generate aversive imagery despite the therapist's cues during the first treatment session and was excluded from the study. Of those remaining, subject 1 showed a significant reduction in drinking following electrical aversion conditioning and then ceased altogether. However, it is difficult to attribute this result to the aversion conditioning process. Close inspection of his drinking pattern reveals that he consumed 10 oz on the first post-treatment day and thereafter stopped drinking completely. This pattern is inconsistent with the tenets of conditioning theory, which would predict maximum suppression of alcohol intake immediately following treatment trials, with possibly a gradual recovery of the drinking habit as extinction effects set in. The consumption of 10 oz on the day after therapy not only suggests that aversion conditioning effects had at best produced only partial suppression but also would surely have served to facilitate the extinction process. A more plausible explanation of this behavioral pattern is suggested by anecdotal observations which revealed that subject 1 was extraordinarily highly motivated to stop drinking, and that during subsequent baseline drinking days he closeted himself in his room and avoided sitting around the living area or bar, where alcohol was available and subject 2 was drinking. Two weeks after being released, subject 1 was reported to have been rehospitalized for excessive drinking.

Neither the aversive imagery nor the electrical escape conditioning treatment produced a reduction in the alcohol consumption of subject 2. Failure of the aversive imagery procedure in his case is particularly noteworthy because of its very real effects on this subject during treatment sessions. He constantly stated how nauseated the aversive scenes made him feel and on two occasions actually vomited at the end of the session.

The results of a second replication of these procedures are shown in Figure 1. The first treatment phase produced similar decrements (41 and 36%, respectively) in the alcohol consumption of subjects in the electrical escape conditioning and aversive imagery treatment regimens. This decrease cannot be unambiguously ascribed to the effects of the specific treatments administered. Although similar studies in the same laboratory have shown that placebo influences have little effect when specifically controlled for, the crossover design used does not permit the role of a placebo effect to be discounted. The subjective drinking-urge data failed to

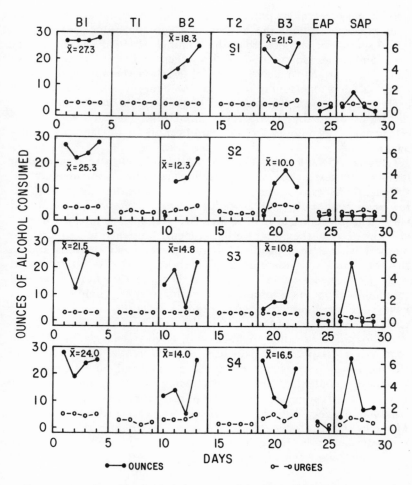

FIGURE 1.—*Amount of Alcohol Consumed by Each Subject During Various Experimental Phases*. B: baseline. T: electrical escape conditioning and aversive imagery treatments. EAP: experimenter-administered punishment. SAP: self-administered punishment.

reflect any differences and do not appear to be a suitable measure for assessing these subjects.

Over-all, the results of these experiments indicate no significant differences between the electrical escape conditioning and the aver-

sive imagery treatment procedures. An important clinical consideration, however, is that the aversive imagery procedure was clearly
less stressful for subjects than the administration of electric shock.
Two otherwise highly motivated subjects withdrew from experiment 1 rather than receive electrical aversion therapy, and several
other subjects anecdotally reported that being shocked was the less
preferred procedure. Callahan and Leitenberg (48) made similar observations when they compared symbolically generated and electrical aversion techniques in the modification of deviant sexual behaviors.

Cautela (55) and Wisocki (315) noted several factors that might
limit the success of covert sensitization, including poor imagery, insufficiently aversive scenes, incomplete homework assignments, too
few treatment trials, and procedural errors. Yet subjects reported
very clear imagery and intense affective response to noxious scenes,
and stated that they followed therapeutic instructions to use the
method whenever appropriate between treatment sessions and in
the free drinking situation. It could be argued that 80 treatment
trials are insufficient. Although it is possible that more extended
treatment might have produced superior results, clinical successes
have been attributed to covert sensitization after only 5 treatment
trials (52) or sessions (4).

Although the results obtained with covert sensitization thus far
have been disappointing, further research is warranted. As with
chemical aversion, there seem to be marked individual differences
in nausea induction in patients using aversive imagery (88).
Bandura's (12) suggestion that an optimal aversion procedure might
combine imagery with emetic drugs deserves particular attention.
Maletzky (180), for example, reports potentiating the effects of
symbolic aversion by pairing it with a foul-smelling substance
—assisted covert sensitization in the apparently effective treatment
of exhibitionism.

Operant Conditioning and the Aversive Control of Alcoholism

Unlike classic conditioning procedures which attempt to suppress
drinking by reducing the positively valenced properties of alcohol
per se, the operant conditioning approach emphasizes the response-
contingent consequences of which alcohol consumption is a function. Using a modified A-B-A-B single-subject reversal design, Wilson et al. (312) consecutively introduced and withdrew a punishment
procedure (contingent shock delivered immediately after consumption of each 1-oz drink) while alcoholics' drinking was continuously

recorded. Shock was self- rather than experimenter-administered from day 9 onward (Figure 2). Self-punishment was encouraged but not required. A variable-ratio schedule was implemented on day 11 to determine the degree to which punishment could be phased out while drinking remained suppressed. The punishment procedure effectively reduced alcohol consumption below pretreatment baseline levels. Moreover, the self-administered method appeared to be almost as effective as experimenter-administered shock.

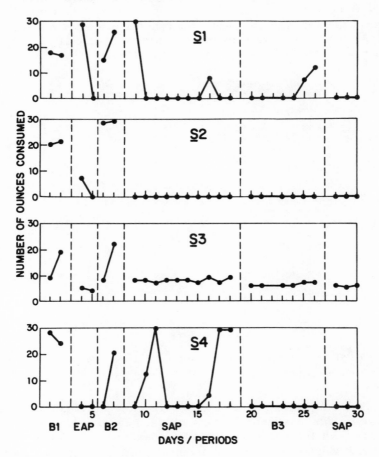

FIGURE 2.—*Amount of Alcohol Consumed by Each Subject During Baseline Drinking and Experimenter- and Self-administered Shock Conditions.* See Figure 1 for explanation of abbreviations.

The efficacy of response-contingent aversive stimulation is further documented in Figure 1. Whereas the electrical escape conditioning and aversive imagery treatments were largely unsuccessful, both experimenter- and self-administered punishment procedures (days 24–29) effectively reduced drinking.

A second experiment was conducted to show that this reduction in drinking was due to the punishment contingency itself rather than to more general placebo effects or demand characteristics. Figure 3 summarizes the results of the contingent versus noncontingent shock comparison. Clearly the contingent relationship between drinking and aversive consequences was both necessary and sufficient for effectively suppressing alcohol intake.

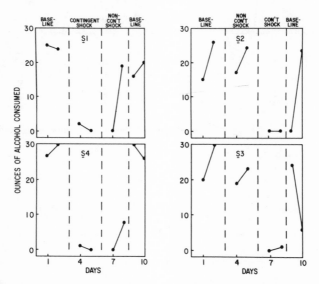

FIGURE 3.—*Amount of Alcohol Consumed by Each Subject During Baseline Drinking and Conditions of Contingent and Noncontingent Shock.*

The efficacy of these aversive control procedures contrasts sharply with the ineffectiveness of the escape conditioning technique with the same population of alcoholics in the same laboratory. It is unlikely that this difference in results is accounted for by the distinction between classic and operant conditioning techniques. Although the electrical escape conditioning and aversive imagery treatments are commonly regarded as respondent conditioning procedures, each involves a contingent relationship between response and aversive stimulus. The difference is probably due to the fact that in the punishment procedure shock was contingent on alcohol consumption during periods when alcohol was available. The electrical escape conditioning and aversive imagery treatments failed to endow alcohol with aversive qualities such that consumption was suppressed during the posttreatment assessment periods when subjects could drink with impunity. The efficacy of aversive control was maximal only when the punishment contingencies remained in effect.

Essentially the same findings were reported by Bigelow et al. (26). Ten alcoholics were allowed limited access to alcohol in an inpatient setting to establish a baseline of free operant drinking. The institution of a time-out procedure, in which 10 or 15 min of physical and social isolation were made contingent on the patient receiving a 1-oz drink of alcohol, reduced drinking by approximately 50% of baseline frequency in 9 of the 10 subjects. Drinking immediately returned to high levels when the time-out contingency was eliminated.

The major problem in applying this behavioral analysis of drinking to the therapeutic situation is to rearrange contingencies so as to facilitate long-term maintenance of abstinence or controlled drinking in the patient's natural environment. One strategy is to use contingency contracting (313).

Miller (199) had an alcoholic sign a mutually agreeable contract limiting him to a specified number of drinks per day. Any violation of this limit resulted in a $20 fine paid to his wife. She also withdrew her attention for a period; moderate drinking by her husband was rewarded with affection. Conversely, if the wife criticized the patient for appropriate drinking, she paid the $20 fine and temporarily lost his attention. After the patient had incurred several fines by exceeding his agreed on number of drinks, his drinking stabilized within acceptable limits. Using an alternative approach, Hunt and Azrin (136) developed a community-reinforcement program in which excessive drinking resulted in time out from vocational, social and familial reinforcers. Compared with a control group that underwent a conventional hospital program for alcoholics, patients in the reinforcement program showed considerable improvement. Throughout an independently conducted 6-month follow-up evaluation they spent significantly less time drinking, were more steadily employed, earned more money and left their families less often.

CONCEPTUAL ISSUES

Effective therapy for alcoholics requires flexible use of a multi-faceted social learning treatment approach (228). That aversion therapy in and of itself is not sufficient is reemphasized by Nathan and Miller in Chapters 6 and 9. As Wilson and Davison (310) pointed out in connection with the treatment of homosexuals, the almost standard application of aversion conditioning methods to alcoholics reflects a failure to evaluate the presenting problem adequately with behavioral assessments. Competent behavioral assessment involves two major facets: first, identification of all the variables that maintain such a complex disorder as alcoholism; and second, selection of the appropriate technique that will most effectively and efficiently result in the desired behavior change. Theoretically, the object of the exercise is to tailor specific treatment strategies to the individual's problems rather than to mold these problems to some preconceived therapeutic notions.

Behavior therapy is not a superficial approach in which a specific symptom (e.g., excessive drinking) is treated in isolation by a single, limited technique (e.g., aversion conditioning). Behavioral treatment is as concerned with modifying the "real causes" of alcoholism as more traditional therapies; the difference lies in what the respective approaches regard the causes to be. Psychodynamic theory favors hypothetical unconscious mechanisms; behavior therapy, in contrast, considers the causes to be the diverse antecedent, mediational and consequent variables that maintain the patient's difficulties. For example, automatically treating an alcoholic with aversion therapy because his excessive alcohol use is seen as a behavioral surplus that must be deconditioned or suppressed would be naive at best, irresponsible at worst. A full behavioral analysis of such a person might reveal that his intoxication is associated with depression, which in turn might be traced to recurring marital conflict. If therapy in a case like this does not address itself to the important antecedents—depression and marital strife—the probability is that the patient will resume drinking or adopt some other self-defeating behavioral pattern in trying to cope with an unhappy marriage. Clinical illustrations of the application of multifaceted behavioral programs (including aversion conditioning) to alcoholics are described by Lazarus (164), Sobell and Sobell (274) and Wilson and Rosen (313).

Within this framework, the major question is whether aversion therapy is a necessary ingredient of broad-spectrum treatment. Only future research can establish the efficacy of nausea-inducing methods, the most promising form of aversion conditioning. Furthermore, even if it is shown to be an effective treatment modality, it will remain to be demonstrated that this efficacy cannot be accomplished using alternative, nonaversive methods. It is clear that aversion therapy is not always necessary in rehabilitating an alcoholic; but it would be premature to rule out the possibility that, at least with some otherwise recalcitrant patients, it may yet be shown to be so.

ETHICAL CONCERNS

Several significant ethical issues bear on the practice of behavior therapy in general and aversion therapy in particular. Of paramount importance is the concept of informed consent. Obtaining the patient's informed consent is necessary regardless of the nature —aversive or otherwise—of the specific behavioral technique(s) used. As Friedman (102) observed, for consent to a therapy program to be valid it must be given voluntarily by a competent and knowledgeable patient. As a rule this poses no serious difficulties in applying aversion conditioning methods to detoxified, adult, outpatient alcoholics who seek treatment on a voluntary basis. For the patient to make an informed judgment about therapy, the full details of treatment procedures must be described. Moreover, in addition to the customary issues of treatment cost and duration, the therapist should provide the patient with information about probability of successful outcome and potential associated side effects, if any.

An unfortunate example of the violation of this basic principle of informed consent was reported by Sanderson et al. (249), who treated alcoholics with succinylcholine-induced paralysis. These patients were told only that the treatment would be "frightening but harmless." The patients were thus unprepared for the harrowing experience they subsequently suffered.

The availability of alternative forms of therapy should also be discussed. In most instances aversion therapy is administered only as a last resort, when more benign treatment methods have proved ineffective. Revocability of consent to therapy is another patient prerogative. Insofar as aversion therapy is often an extremely taxing experience, it is imperative that the patient be able to withdraw from treatment with impunity should he so desire. Hedberg and Campbell (126) and Wilson and Tracey (314) reported that patients in their respective electrical aversion conditioning programs decided to discontinue treatment on the grounds that the methods were too aversive.

If an alcoholic is institutionalized, the ethical concerns become more complex. The concept of informed consent is especially thorny in view of the questions raised about the voluntary nature of patients' decisions within institutional settings. At a minimum, however, in addition to freely given consent it is desirable that the patient have the option of participating in an alternative, nonaversive form of therapy. Goldiamond (110) provides an illuminating analysis of the issues involved and ethical safeguards that might be adopted in the treatment of institutionalized populations.

In the previous section it was concluded that preliminary clinical findings regarding the use of certain forms of aversion therapy are sufficiently encouraging to merit further investigation into their potential efficacy. There are some questions that need to be answered: Is chemical aversion conditioning effective? Even if it can be shown to work, is it necessary? Or are there more desirable alternatives that yield similar success? Assuming it is demonstrated to be superior to other modes of therapy, at least with certain alcoholics, the ethics of not administering such a treatment, provided appropriate ethical safeguards are observed, become questionable. It is not uncommon to have critics of aversion conditioning methods denounce the alleged indignities to which the patients are subjected. These objections sometimes overlook the fact that alternative forms of therapy might have failed to decrease the alcohol misuse. There is little dignity in an alcoholic's progressively tragic loss of job, family, health, and ultimately even life. The argument that discomfort or aversion per se renders a therapeutic intervention unethical is, as Begelman (21) has noted, a reductio ad absurdum.

Ethical evaluations of aversion therapy are sometimes distorted by confusion concerning the nature of behavioral treatment methods. Aversion therapy has been associated with the specter of brainwashing, the imminence of 1984, and the hypothetical horrors about mind control portrayed in the film *A Clockwork Orange*. There is growing public alarm that these are procedures that can control people without their knowledge and against their will. Yet the belief that humans can be automatically conditioned is largely a myth. As Bandura (14) points out, people do "learn through paired experiences, but only if they recognize that the events are correlated and summon up appropriate anticipatory reactions. So-called conditioned reactions are largely self-activated on the basis of learned expectations rather than automatically conditioned. The notion that one can create automatic internal inhibitors by imposed aversive conditioning, as graphically portrayed in A Clockwork Orange, may be captivating drama but it is faulty psychology" (14, p. 14).

Although this theme has been exploited by the media as well as by critics of behavior therapy, professional proponents of behavioral methods cannot be exculpated (14, 101). A technical argot which exclusively stresses external control inaccurately depicts man as a passive reactor to environmental forces (13) and unnecessarily elicits public displeasure.[4] Some behavioristic claims of the omnipotence of behavioral control simply compound arrogance with ignorance. In fact, a review of the available evidence indicates that conditioned aversion reactions cannot be developed all that easily (90) nor can they be firmly established without the patient's deliberate, conscious cooperation (79). It is difficult to conceive of a more terrifying assault on the senses than the misguided use of succinyl-choline-induced respiratory arrest and paralysis as an aversive stimulus. Yet this method failed to produce stable conditioned aversion responses.

Another informative example is the use of emetine conditioning (303), surely one of the most powerful and harsh behavioral change methods yet devised. The fact that even this treatment cannot be used to impose therapeutic goals and is optimally effective only when it assists an alcoholic in accomplishing his or her own purposes is described by a former patient in the Raleigh Hills program. Speaking of alcoholics, he suggests that aversion therapy helps restore will power. After treatment, "if he wants to, he can go to the nearest bar, gag down a few drinks and be off and running again." Indeed, Rachman and Teasdale (240) cite the case of a patient who extinguished treatment-produced aversion to alcohol by 4 hr of "dogged drinking" despite continuing emesis. For the more faint of heart who eschew this flooding procedure, systematically desensitizing themselves to the conditioned aversive stimulus of alcohol ingestion is said to require no more than a fortnight.

In short, considerations of ethics and efficacy demand that if aversion therapy is used the patient's informed consent to a trusted and respected therapist is a minimum necessity (311).

---

[4] WOOLFOLK, A., WOOLFOLK, R. and WILSON, G. T. A rose by any other name. . . . Labeling bias an attitude toward behavior modification. [Unpublished ms., Rutgers University, 1975.]

8

Blood Alcohol Concentration Discrimination Training: Development and Current Status

Glenn R. Caddy

THE DEVELOPMENT of the Breathalyzer (33), the Intoxilyzer (125) and a variety of gas chromatographs, all of which determine blood alcohol concentration (BAC) from alveolar gas analysis, now permits rapid monitoring of BAC as an accurate index of alcohol impairment. The almost universal implementation of prescribed maximum BACs for motor vehicle driving provides the most striking evidence of this fact.

This technological innovation was paralleled in the alcoholism treatment literature by an equally significant development: a series of reports describing a return to limited drinking by diagnosed alcoholics (32, 78, 232). These reports, in turn, generated research that began to test the assumptions underlying the prevailing abstinence dictum. Merry (196), for example, reported that abstinent alcoholics did not increase their craving for alcohol when they were surreptitiously given alcohol. In a similar vein, Mello (188) showed that alcoholics sometimes voluntarily stop drinking after several days of heavy drinking, and McNamee and colleagues (176) failed to find evidence of craving by alcoholics who had been drinking for several days.

It was within this general framework that a series of studies was begun in 1969 at the University of New South Wales, Australia, to assess the feasibility of training people to estimate their BACs accurately (38) and subsequently to employ this BAC discrimination training as a component in a program geared to reduce but not necessarily eliminate their use of alcohol (39, 171).

The assumptions underlying these studies were as follows:

(1) The estimation of one's own BAC is a very complex task. Although the BAC is primarily a function of the volume of alcohol

114

consumed, factors such as the type of beverage, the rate of ingestion, the nature and volume of the contents of the gastrointestinal
tract, together with the blood volume of the drinker, significantly
influence the rate and height of the BAC curve. If a drinker could
be trained to monitor his or her BAC accurately using the introceptive, proprioceptive and extroceptive cues that accompany changes
in the BAC, given the appropriate motivation, that drinker could use
this newly acquired skill to guard against intoxication just as a
driver may avoid exceeding the speed limit by closely monitoring
his speedometer.

(2) Within certain limits, increasing intoxication is paralleled by
recognizable and consistent changes in subjective states (86). These
subjective changes appear at BACs as low as 0.035% (118). Nevertheless, the relationship between BAC and intoxication varies considerably from one drinker to another. For example, it is common
knowledge that an alcoholic can appear sober yet have a BAC that
would cause the label "intoxicated" to be applied to the behavior of
a temperate user.

(3) Intoxication is under the control of the drinker and is an inevitable consequence of embarking on a drinking sequence that
either: (a) produces a rapidly rising BAC curve which is therefore
difficult to monitor and, given the initial ingestion, impossible to
modify; or (b) shows a slowly ascending BAC curve with attendant
subjective sensations which the drinker seeks to enhance or recap-
ture by continued drinking.

(4) In any research directed at reduced drinking by alcoholics,
drinking would be considered moderate only if a moderate BAC was
but rarely exceeded. Furthermore, if "loss of control" occurs at all
in alcoholics, it likely develops only after the drinker has achieved a
considerable level of intoxication (107).

In the first study in this research program (38), 51 male volunteer "moderate drinkers" were randomly allocated to either an experimental or a control group. These groups were further divided
into small testing groups ($N = 4$). Prior to the first drinking session, subjects were given general information detailing how various
hypothetical intake schedules might result in differing BAC curves as
well as a Behavioral Sensations Reference Scale (116), listing commonly experienced internal sensations that generally correspond to
various BACs.

All subjects were then given four drinks during each of three
2.5-hr drinking sessions. Each drink contained varying amounts of
absolute alcohol in a fruit juice base designed to camouflage the

concentration of the beverage. The volume of alcohol was varied across subjects and sessions in accordance with the intake schedule to which each subject was allocated, together with an adjustment made in consideration of the subject's body weight. The procedure of varying the intake schedules was introduced to reduce the possibility that estimates made in later sessions would be simply a reflection of actual BACs remembered from previous sessions.

In the experimental group, the procedures were identical during session 1 (pretraining) and session 3 (posttraining). The control group also received these procedures, although here all three sessions were identical. The procedure was as follows: administer drink, to be consumed in 5 min; wait 25 min; then obtain BAC estimates and analyze the breath sample. This sequence was repeated four times during each session.

During session 2 experimental group subjects received BAC discrimination training after each waiting period. During this training subjects were required to contemplate and verbalize the introceptive and proprioceptive cues indicating that they had been drinking and to relate these cues to those presented on the Behavioral Sensations Reference Scale. Based on these various sensations, a BAC estimate was then obtained, a breath sample was taken and analyzed, and the results were fed back to the subject. At this point subjects were required to consider the discrepancy between their estimated and actual BAC scores, and to review again the sensations they were experiencing in order to relate these sensations more precisely to a score in percentage BAC units. This procedure was repeated at least four times during each discrimination training session.

The data from this study indicated extremely high correspondence between the estimated and the actual BAC scores, with mean discrepancy scores below 0.01% across all cells of the experiment. Such accuracy produced a ceiling effect and hence an inability to show any significant differences between pre- and postfeedback training sessions in the experimental group.

To examine further the possible significance of BAC discrimination training, the discrepancy scores of 10 subjects from the experimental and control groups whose pretraining scores were lowest were compared across all sessions. An improvement in estimation accuracy was noted during and after training in both experimental and control subgroups; and though the scores from the experimental group were slightly lower in the posttraining session than those of the control group, this trend was not significant. The experimental subjects' mean pretraining accuracy score was 92.9% and their posttraining score 96.1% ($t = 3.55$, $p < .01$); in the control group the scores were 93.1 and 96.1%, respectively ($t = 3.67$, $p < .01$). Thus at least within the limits of intoxication sought during this study, both BAC discrimination training and structured practice with the aid of an external reference scale improved BAC estimation accuracy.

The finding that moderate drinkers could be trained to estimate their BACs with considerable accuracy led Lovibond and Caddy (171) to use BAC discrimination training as the basis for a discriminated aversive conditioning program with alcoholics. In this program 44 outpatient alcoholics who sought to reduce their drinking rather than abstain were trained to estimate their BACs accurately within the range of 0 to 0.08%. During this training subjects were permitted to drink with impunity up to 0.065%, but drinking beyond that level was punished with a series of highly aversive electric shocks. This procedure was incorporated within a more conventional therapeutic regimen, including an alcohol education phase, self-regulation training and individual and family psychotherapy. The results of this study are presented in Table 1.

Subsequently, Caddy and Lovibond (39), Maxwell and associates (186), Sobell and Sobell (267) and Vogler et al. (294) also reported significant success using BAC discrimination training in combination with a variety of other therapeutic components (e.g., videotaped self-confrontation of drunken comportment and assertiveness training) in aiding alcoholics to reduce their drinking.

Bois and Vogel-Sprott (31) employed a procedure and design similar to that used in Caddy's experimental group (38) to determine if nine male moderate drinkers could learn to assess their

TABLE 1.—*Treatment Outcome at 6-Month Intervals of 28 Patients Receiving Discriminated Aversive Conditioning*

	End of Treatment	6 Months	12 Months	18 Months	24 Months
Completely successful	22	21	16	10	5
Moderately improved	3	4	7	8	5
Slight/no improvement	3	3	3	7	5
No information	0	0	1	2	2
Total	28	28	27[a]	27	17[b]

[a] One patient died during the tenth month after treatment. The cause of death was unrelated to drinking.
[b] Ten subjects had not completed 24 posttreatment months at the time of follow-up.

BACs accurately under conditions of rising and falling BACs and to then self-titrate their alcohol intake to achieve a predetermined BAC within the range 0.04–0.06%. Three self-titration sessions were introduced after standard pretraining, training and posttraining sessions. Although no scale indicating commonly experienced sensations corresponding to various BACs was used and the volume of alcohol administered to each subject in each mixed drink during all sessions was not stated, the subjects were told that their BACs would not exceed 0.15% and that two martinis would produce a BAC within the range 0.05–0.08%.

This study found pretraining mean discrepancy scores of 0.22%, which were higher than those noted in the Caddy and Lovibond studies. With feedback, however, the mean discrepancy scores fell below 0.005%, with similar accuracy levels being maintained when feedback was removed.

The development of increased estimation accuracy noted during rising BAC curves was not found under conditions of falling BAC, where estimation errors (which were typically less than ±0.005%) resulted in a ceiling accuracy effect similar to that observed during rising BAC curves by Caddy (38). Bois and Vogel-Sprott did not vary the subjects' intake volume across days, and so confusion may exist in this study preventing assessment of the relative influence of perceived alcohol-related sensations and previous recall of the BACs achieved following each drink in the training session on BAC estimation accuracy. Nevertheless, during the self-titration sessions mean discrepancy scores continued to drop significantly without feedback, so by the third self-titration session the mean discrepancy score was less than 0.01%. Bois and Vogel-Sprott interpreted these findings as evidence to support the hypothesis that BAC discrimination is acquired on the basis of essentially internal, not environmental, cues.

In an effort to investigate further the determinants and extent of BAC discrimination training, Silverstein et al. (264) observed four male gamma alcoholics (138) over a 36-day period at the Rutgers Alcohol Behavior Research Laboratory. The study examined the alcoholics' baseline drinking behavior, the effect of BAC discrimination training on their BAC estimation accuracy and their ability to maintain control over their drinking with and without associated BAC feedback under various reinforcement contingencies.

The rather elaborate design of this study is presented in Table 2. The procedure employed during the BAC estimation training phase was similar to that used in the preceding studies. However, the fol-

TABLE 2.—*Design of Training Study*[a]

PHASE I: ESTIMATION TRAINING

	B1	T1	T2	T3	B2
			Training cycles		
	Estimation baseline	Continuous feedback, no reinforcement	Variable feedback, no reinforcement	Variable feedback, contingent var. reinforcement	Estimation baseline
	No feedback, no reinforcement				No feedback, no reinforcement
	Days 1–2	Days 3–4	Days 5–6	Days 7–8	Days 9–10

PHASE II: CONTROL TRAINING

	BC1	RS	C1	C2	C3	BC2	G
	Control baseline	Reinforcement sampling	Narrowing to acceptable range (0.07-0.09%)	Baseline with contingency	Contingency fadeout	Control baseline	Target generalization
	Ad libitum drinking	Programmed drinking	Partially programmed drinking		Ad libitum drinking		
	No feedback No reinforcement		Variable feedback		Fadeout	No feedback No reinforcement	
			Variable reinforcement				
			Target: 0.08%				Variable target
	Days 11–13	Days 14–15	Days 16–22	Days 23–25	Days 26–28	Days 29–34	Days 35–36

[a] Adapted from Silverstein et al. (264).

lowing procedural differences are noteworthy: (1) The subjects were not blind to the amount of alcohol they were ingesting. (2) With the exception of knowledge of dosage, subjects received minimal information on which to base their BAC estimates during non-feedback training sessions. They were told simply to convert their estimated level of intoxication into a number between zero and 40, where zero represented "cold sober" and 40 represented "extremely drunk, probably drunker than any of you has ever been." (3) The peak BACs achieved during this study were around 0.15%, approximately double the peak BACs sought by the previous studies. (4) Each pretraining and training session lasted up to 48 hr in contrast to the 2.5-hr sessons of the previous studies.

During the 26-day control training phase, subjects were introduced to various procedures designed to train them to use BAC estimates as discriminative stimuli for decisions about when and how much to drink. These procedures included a "self-titration" sequence during which subjects were required to maintain their BACs at 0.08% without feedback and a "reinforcement sampling" sequence during which reinforcement (in the form of convertible points) was provided for maintenance of a BAC below 0.08%.

Silverstein et al. (264) found that during the pretraining sessions their subjects were highly inaccurate at estimating their BACs, with discrepancy scores for the period averaging 0.112%. However, when BAC feedback was introduced an immediate increase in estimation accuracy was noted, with discrepancy scores after 1 day of feedback averaging 0.014%. Typically, no further gain in estimation accuracy was noted after this first day of discrimination training. On the first day feedback was withdrawn, each subject maintained approximately the same level of estimation accuracy he attained during training. On the next day, however, estimation accuracy deteriorated for all subjects, with discrepancy scores for three of the subjects averaging 0.030%. The fourth subject's estimates were reported as "essentially random." During the control training phase subjects maintained their BACs accurately at target level (0.08%) only while they received some BAC feedback. The addition of either a continuous or an intermittent reinforcement contingency during BAC discrimination training did not increase the accuracy achieved under nonreinforcement feedback training conditions.

The authors concluded that "the presence or absence of feedback, not its frequency or reinforcement accompanying it, powerfully affected the ability to estimate BAL [BAC] accurately. BAL feedback apparently served as an information anchor, in that its presence to even a minimal degree kept estimations accurate" (264, *p. 13*). They also noted that "our subjects said they learned to discriminate internal cue states associated with different BALs . . . nonetheless . . . the precise degree to which subjects actually relied on these internal cues [is] questionable" (264, *p. 13*).

Procedural and subject differences between the Silverstein et al. study and that of Bois and Vogel-Sprott (31) or Caddy (38) make any comparison of results difficult. It may be that the BAC estimation difficulties experienced in the absence of BAC feedback by the subjects of Silverstein et al. were related to a reduced interest in the task especially as the subjects' BACs approached 0.15%, or to the adaptation effects which, over a prolonged drinking sequence, may blur the "baseline anchor," or perhaps to a reduced ability on the part of highly tolerant alcoholic subjects to perceive small changes in BAC.

Lovibond and Caddy (171) reported considerable success in training their alcoholic subjects to discriminate various BACs accurately. This training, however, was restricted in BAC range and time, and had the advantage of a comprehensive alcohol-drinking education program designed to supplement the estimation of BACs based on the perception of essentially "internal" alcohol-related cues. Paredes and colleagues (230) also reported on BAC estimation training, in this case with one alcoholic. The high BAC estimation and self-titration accuracy scores noted in this study provide little additional information on the BAC discrimination accuracy of alcoholics because their subject received BAC feedback training on all sessions.

A yoked comparison assessing the BAC estimation accuracy of moderate drinkers and alcoholics appears worthy of consideration for future research. There is evidence indicating that, in comparison with moderate drinkers, alcoholics tend to (1) order "straight" drinks rather than mixed drinks, wine or beer; (2) take larger sips of their drinks; (3) finish their drinks more rapidly; and (4) have a longer inter-sip interval (255, 271). Studies such as these imply that the drinking behavior of alcoholics becomes patterned, and once the decision to drink has been made the actual drinking behavior involves no more thought than the drinking of a cool glass of water on a warm day. It is conceivable that as a drinker's tolerance increases, his ability to discriminate slight changes in intoxication decreases; and that with continued drinking, significant changes in BAC are required for increments in intoxication to be perceived. Certainly at a BAC of 0.08%, moderate drinkers see themselves as quite intoxicated, whereas alcoholics seem to perceive their drinking-relevant sensations yet evaluate them in relation to a completely different intoxication baseline. The only data available to date suggest that at high BACs alcoholics are either not capable or not motivated to maintain BAC estimation accuracy in the absence of feedback. There has been no research addressing the ability or motivation of moderate drinkers to estimate their BACs accurately at higher levels of intoxication, and so the influence of high BACs on this skill has yet to be ascertained.

To investigate further the extent to which BAC estimation accuracy is a function of the perception of internal or external cues, Caddy et al. (40) examined the influence of two levels of drinking-cue related information derived from two references scales, when all other external alcohol-relevant cues (e.g., drinking rate, dosage, timing of estimates) were minimized or held constant.

Twelve men volunteers who were moderate drinkers were randomly allocated to two equal groups; one group received the comprehensive Behavioral Sensations Reference Scale used by Caddy (38) while the other received an extremely limited reference scale showing only "0.00% completely sober" and "0.25% complete loss of coordination and increasing loss of consciousness." The design and procedure corresponded generally to that of Caddy's previous experimental group.

The means and ranges of the discrepancy scores derived for both reference scale conditions throughout this experiment are illustrated in Figure 1. No significant differences in discrepancy scores were found between the two reference scale conditions. This finding implies that extreme accuracy of estimation does not require the use of a detailed scale indicating the subjective sensations that typically correspond to various BAC ranges; it also lends further support to the hypothesis that, at least in the case of moderate drinkers, the BAC discrimination scaling task is based more on the subjects' internal alcohol-related sensations than on external supports. Despite the provision of differing intake schedules, BAC elevation typically occurred following the ingestion of each drink. Occasionally, especially during the training session, subjects reported a conflict between internal and external cues (e.g., "I can't be at 0.06%, but I sure feel it"). When a subject made an estimate that compromised the information from his internal cues, such an estimate often proved to be less accurate. This outcome, in turn, contributed to a trend toward increased confidence in BAC estimates based on internal cues. Observations similar to these were also made by Bois and Vogel-Sprott (31). This finding is at odds with the suggestion by

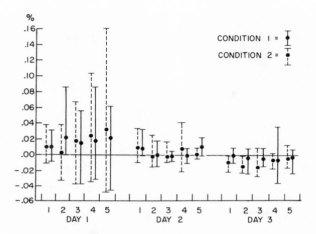

FIGURE 1.—*Means and Ranges of Errors of BAC Estimation Using the Detailed Scale (Condition 1) and the Limited Scale (Condition 2) during Trials 1–5 on Days 1, 2 and 3.*

Silverstein et al. (264) that BAC estimation accuracy may be more a function of the scale used to provide the frame of reference than a consequence of BAC discrimination training.

Unlike Caddy's (38) finding and in agreement with those of Bois and Vogel-Sprott (31), Silverstein et al. (264) found a significant difference in over-all discrepancy scores between the pre- and post-training sessions, with least accuracy appearing during pretraining when the estimated BACs were typically above the actual levels; this inaccuracy increased as the BAC curve rose. Feedback training not only lowered the estimated BAC scores in the direction of the actual scores, but also resulted in a reduction of the range of these estimates. Posttraining discrepancy scores reflected the continued maintenance of high estimation accuracy, this time with the estimates typically falling slightly below the actual BACs. By this third session it seemed likely that subjects had come to associate certain cues of intoxication with certain BACs; perhaps they were overcorrecting for the high estimates they had been told they had provided during the pretraining session.

With regard to within-session effects, when the data were collapsed across days and across reference scale conditions, an analysis indicated that discrepancy scores on trial 1 differed significantly from the scores on all other trials and in general showed the greatest accuracy. Similarly, discrepancy scores on trial 2 differed significantly from those on trials 4 and 5. This finding of decreasing estimation accuracy with increasing BACs was predominantly a function of the strength of the effect during the pretraining session. It seems that the first estimates necessarily would be reasonably accurate, for after one drink the zero baseline was not greatly modified. With increasing intoxication, however, this baseline reference point became blurred. Nevertheless, especially after feedback training, symptoms of intoxication became more salient with increasing trials and, with the information provided through feedback training, greater estimation accuracy became possible.

Again, these results indicate that moderate drinkers can come to estimate their BACs with considerable accuracy after only one BAC discrimination training session. During the pretraining session subjects reported employing strategies such as relating their degree of intoxication to their estimated ability to handle a motor vehicle, an essentially "internal and subjective" reference. It seemed that they attempted to use their own conceptualization of the legal driving limit (0.10% in California) to provide an anchor point in their scaling attempts. Such a strategy may have contributed to the tendency to overestimate during the pretraining phase, for during this first session 8 of the 12 subjects reported that it would be unsafe for them to drive a motor vehicle at that time, yet up to that point none of the subjects' BACs had exceeded 0.07%. Using similar peak BACs, Caddy (38) reported higher accuracy scores during the pretraining phase than were noted in the latter experiment. Interestingly, the Caddy study was conducted in Australia where the legal driving limit is generally 0.08%. At the completion of each of these studies, many of these moderate-drinking subjects commented that they now considered that the prescribed maximum BAC for drivers was more than fair.

It seems valuable to obtain a clearer understanding of the relative influence of internal and external cues in BAC discrimination than has been provided by any of the preceding studies. It may be, for example, that though the introceptively received cues of intoxication are potentially more sensitive, and therefore more important in BAC discrimination training, they are also especially subject to being compromised by environmental influences; this is because in the absence of evidence confirming the reliability of estimates based almost exclusively on internal sensations, we typically look outside ourselves for objectivity and reality. Additionally, an understanding of the extent to which a drinker can come to discriminate accurately and confidently his BAC using either internal cues, external cues or some combination of the two appears to be valuable in developing effective secondary and tertiary alcohol prevention programs incorporating BAC discrimination training. Such programs would be directed at those drinkers who seem not to know when to stop or to those who drive and therefore would benefit from an increased awareness of their safe driving limit (not necessarily the legal driving limit).

A recent study by Huber and co-workers (135) addressed the equivocal role of internal and external cues in BAC discrimination. In this experiment 36 moderate drinkers attended the three standard pretraining, training and posttraining sessions. During the training sequence subjects were taught to estimate their BAC from: (1) external cues based on the use of a programmed booklet explaining BAC–dose relationships (group E); (2) their perception of introceptive, proprioceptive cues or both, perhaps heightened by training in muscular relaxation designed to assist subjects to focus on these essentially internal sensations (group I); or (3) their perception of the combined influences of internal and external cues (group E + I). During a posttraining session half of the subjects in each of the three groups were tested under conditions where the amount of alcohol in each drink was known to them, and the other half tested with the amount unknown.

During the pretraining session mean discrepancy scores of 0.19% were obtained. During the training and posttraining sessions the scores dropped to 0.009% (identical for both sessions). This increase in estimation accuracy, however, did not reach significance when the data were analyzed across the three sessions. This study also found within-session estimation accuracy effects similar to those noted by Caddy et al. (40). During the pretraining session significantly lower discrepancy scores occurred on trial 1 than during subsequent trials; however, this difference in estimation accuracy across trials was not observed in either the training or the posttraining sessions.

Although no significant differences in over-all estimation accuracy were found between the three training groups, when groups I and E were compared during posttraining in the "unknown" condition there was a strong suggestion that the muscular relaxation training led group I to be especially sensitive to the internal cues corresponding to low BACs, whereas group E appeared to be relatively insensitive to the same cues. Thus Huber et al. concluded that nonalcoholics can learn to use internal cues to achieve considerable accuracy in BAC discrimination.

Of course neither this study nor any of those cited previously ensured separation of the various internal and external drinking-related cues. For example, in the Huber et al. study, although it may have been possible to minimize the external cues indicating alcohol consumption in the group stressing the internally perceived cues, in the group that stressed BAC discrimination based on external cues some internal cues inevitably would have been available.

This confounding could be examined in a study in which one group of subjects received alcohol in a drinking situation stressing external cues (e.g., noting the precise amounts and type of beverage chosen) while a comparison group was administered alcohol through intravenous infusion at a rate paralleling the BAC curve of subjects in the normal drinking condition. Such a technique would eliminate all the external drinking-related cues while still permitting complete control over the parameters of the BAC curve.

Although a drinker may be provided with a scale allowing the subjective cues that develop following alcohol consumption to be assigned a numerical value, BAC estimation accuracy may nevertheless reach some limiting value prior to some point of intoxication. After this "turning point," BAC discrimination accuracy may deteriorate. The Silverstein et al. (264) data provide some support for this hypothesis.

It may also be true that a high degree of BAC estimation accuracy can be achieved without discrimination training, or be maintained subsequent to such training, by providing a drinker with a specific profile representing the parameters of his own BAC changes derived from previous experience relating his BAC to specific external drinking cues. In fact, Vogler and colleagues (294) incorporated this approach into a treatment program by using the Alco-calculator (Rutgers Center of Alcohol Studies), a cardboard slide-rule from which a subject may calculate his BAC simply by knowing the quantity of alcohol in the beverage he has consumed.

With the exception of the study by Silverstein et al. (264), research in BAC discrimination training has not been used to investigate BACs above 0.08%. This restricted BAC ceiling was established in accordance with the assumption that moderate drinkers would rarely drink in excess of a BAC of 0.08%. Training procedures directed toward reduced drinking would be unlikely to investigate BACs above moderate levels. Of course such a limit also minimized the risk of aversive consequences such as nausea, which often follow overconsumption by moderate drinkers. It may be that the very nature of much drinking by alcoholics (e.g., ingesting "straight" drinks of high alcohol content during a short period at the beginning of a drinking session) necessarily results in a BAC increment of such magnitude that the subtle and changing cues noticed by moderate drinkers during a drinking occasion are lost to alcoholics. Thus with the inevitable delay between ingestion and the introduction of alcohol into the circulatory system, a state exists early in the drinking session wherein an alcoholic, even without further drinking, continues to experience an increasing BAC until the rate of absorption into the blood is matched by the rate of the elimination process. Under such conditions, having consumed alcohol the alcoholic may truly be said to be incapable of preventing a continued increase in his BAC. This may be an alcoholic's real "loss of control."

An intriguing finding by Schachter (251, 252) in a study of obesity may also be relevant to the operational dynamics of at least some alcoholics' drinking. Schachter reported a failure on the part of obese subjects to monitor the introceptive cues related to hunger. In his words, "eating by the obese seems unrelated to any internal visceral state but is determined by external food-relevant cues" (252, *p. 130*). In the case of alcohol use, evidence suggests that moderate drinkers experience a significant ongoing interaction between internal and external sensations related to their drinking, with emphasis on the internal ones. Alcoholics, perhaps like obese persons, may be influenced by external cues with little consideration of the internal state, and so they do not perceive many of the internal cues corresponding to low BACs. Another possibility is that when alcoholics are required to restrict the parameters of their drinking to match moderate drinker ingestion rates, they receive the internal alcohol-relevant sensations in much the same way as moderate drinkers. However, while the moderate drinker is labeling these cues indices of intoxication, the alcoholic is not debilitated by them, certainly does not consider himself intoxicated, and so deemphasizes them, for he does not view these particular cues as relevant to intoxication. Whatever the underlying mechanism, the alcoholic does not suppress his drinking behavior in response to the internal cues produced by rapid changes in BAC.

Interpretations such as these, addressing the operational components underlying at least some alcoholics' drinking, make no assumptions about the motivation of the drinker. There are no doubt some drinkers who set out to get drunk when they take the first drink. There are others who simply seek to have a "few drinks" but then overindulge. For those in the first category, abstinence and

moderation approaches fail. Without a thorough cognitive reap-
praisal and modification of the goals of alcohol use, such abusive
drinking will continue. For those in the second category, therapy
directed toward restricted drinking and incorporating BAC discrimination training offers a number of advantages (234).

A major premise underlying the so-called "controlled drinking"
programs (38, 39, 171, 186, 267, 294) is that the abusive drinker
has either never learned to drink in a regulated fashion or has
learned in a manner which causes problems. This pattern of drinking and its attendant difficulties are seen as multidimensional (134,
300); moreover, as Pattison (234) stresses, they require a multivariate treatment approach. Research by Caddy and Lovibond (39)
suggests the following requirements and stages of the process
operating during the changing of alcoholic drinking: (1) The drinker
must recognize the parameters of his drinking. That is, the pattern
of consumption must be analyzed in terms of intake volume, beverage alcohol content and time variables; and these must be shown to
be different from the drinking parameters obtained from moderate
drinkers. For most excessive drinkers this stage requires a detailed
alcohol-education program which illustrates the relationship between alcohol intake variables and the resulting BAC. (2) The
drinker must decide to change his stated drinking goals and establish an operational definition of the new drinking goal in terms of
BAC limits. (3) The drinker must then undergo training in restricted
drinking. During this phase BAC discrimination training could be
introduced. Discrimination training would serve to sensitize the
drinker to the internal cues which he would experience within the
BAC limits of his restricted drinking goal. It would also permit a
clearer perception by the drinker of the upper limits of his restricted drinking pattern.

For those drinkers who overindulge to the point of risking detec-
tion for driving with a BAC above the prescribed limit yet who do
not regard their drinking as a problem, a program geared toward
restricted drinking may not extend beyond this third training stage.
Those drinkers for whom alcohol has become a problem, however,
would require a treatment program that involved a modificaton of
much of their lifestyle. By the time alcohol is perceived as a problem, excessive drinking has generally become ingrained within the
total functioning of the individual. Behavior change under such circumstances requires far more potent intervention than that offered
by BAC discrimination training.

It is clear from this review that BAC discrimination training has not been widely used as a therapeutic component. Perhaps with the growing emphasis being placed on nonabstinence goals in alcoholism therapy and primary and secondary prevention approaches, BAC discrimination training will be more widely used.

9

Behavior Therapy in the Treatment of Alcoholism

Peter M. Miller

ALTHOUGH ONE MIGHT ASSUME that the application of behavioral approaches to the treatment of alcoholism is of relatively recent origin, references to the use of aversion conditioning with alcoholics date back to 1929 (143). Unfortunately, throughout this long history interpretations of behavioral strategies have been grossly oversimplified and misunderstood. For the most part, early etiological formulations were based on a simple conditioning model which postulated that repeated associations between alcohol consumption and the reduction of aversive emotional states (e.g., anxiety, tension, depression) increased the probability of alcohol misuse. Data to substantiate this explanation were based almost exclusively on animal analogue experimentation.

On the basis of this model, it was assumed that treatment should consist of a deconditioning procedure whereby the smell, sight and taste of alcohol would be repeatedly associated with unpleasant stimuli via aversive conditioning. These stimuli can be either electrical, chemical or verbal in nature. Electrical aversion therapy consists of administering, usually in a hospital setting, aversive electric shocks to the patient's arm, leg, hand or face contingent on his looking at, smelling or tasting a variety of alcoholic beverages. For example, Blake (29) used an escape conditioning paradigm in which shock was administered when the patient took alcohol into his mouth and terminated when alcohol was spit into a bowl. In chemical aversion therapy (166) the unpleasant stimulus is either nausea and vomiting induced by an emetic drug or brief respiratory paralysis induced by an apnea-inducing agent. A third form of this treatment, known as covert sensitization (52–54), uses verbal-cognitive aversive stimuli. Patients are exposed to repeated associations between thoughts of drinking and thoughts of unpleasant experiences (e.g., nausea and being injured in an automobile accident).

Patients are encouraged to practice these associations on their own and use the unpleasant thoughts to suppress strong urges to drink.

The widespread use of aversion conditioning by behavioral clinicians during the 1940s, 1950s and 1960s seems related to a number of factors. As with other treatment approaches, there was a strong desire to find a simple panacea for the treatment of alcoholism that would be economical in terms of time, money and personnel. The use was also reinforced by reports of clinical success, with abstinence rates ranging from 23 to 96% of patients treated (202). Unfortunately, these clinical reports were all confounded by relatively weak evaluation procedures together with the fact that conditioning factors per se (as opposed to other therapeutic influences such as advice given by the therapist or placebo factors) were never shown to be the potent ingredient in the treatment process. In addition, the widespread use of aversion conditioning that followed historically was based on two false assumptions: (1) Alcohol misuse can be explained primarily in terms of a simple conditioning model. (2) Since electrical and chemical aversion conditioning have been demonstrated to be effective in suppressing simple motor responses in animals and humans, they should also be equally effective in modifying drinking responses.

Unfortunately, the experimental data do not support a simple conditioning explanation of alcoholism. Rather, alcoholism appears to be a complex social-learning phenomenon related to various environmental, emotional, cognitive, social and physiological events. As yet, no one theory has been satisfactory in explaining the disorder.

In addition, the direct application of aversion therapy from animal laboratories to clinical situations appears to be a rather naive treatment strategy. "Automatic" suppression of alcohol consumption simply does not occur on the basis of such conditioning. Even experimental data lend support to this contention. For example, after conditioning cardiac rates in human subjects, numerous investigators (59, 227) found that such responses extinguished immediately when subjects were told they would receive no additional shocks. In addition, this phenomenon appears unrelated to either number of conditioning trials or intensity of the aversive stimulus.

Clinically, Hallam and colleagues (123), Miller and co-workers (210), and Wilson et al. (312) seriously questioned the efficacy of electrical aversion therapy with alcoholics, based on well-designed clinical–experimental investigations. Although a number of clinical outcome studies evaluating chemical and verbal aversion are available (4, 166), controlled experimentation has been inadequate. The few controlled studies available are characterized by numerous methodological weaknesses and often demonstrate simply that some treatment (only part of which involves aversion therapy) is better than no treatment at all (7).

This is not to say, however, that there have not been numerous clinical reports describing success with these techniques, although such success appears related to a wide variety of variables, e.g., patient expectancies, instructions and therapeutic demand characteristics. In fact many of the early clinical investigations of aversion therapies reported the use of extensive explanations and instructions to clients regarding the "expected" effects of treatment. Placebo factors were often enhanced unwittingly. For example, Miller (202) reports that, in the classic series of clinical investigations by Lemere and Voegtlin (166), "instructional set was an important aspect of treatment. Patients were told never to taste or experiment with liquor again. Instructions were geared to infer that conditioning effects were automatic and that alcohol would produce nausea and vomiting even after treatment had been discontinued." Although the influence of instructions and patient expectancies has been discussed in relation to behavior therapy in general (1), their importance in regard to reported success in aversion therapy has not been investigated comprehensively. Barlow and colleagues (18), however, demonstrated that in verbal aversion therapy contingent pairings are not always sufficient for behavioral change and that positive therapeutic instructions facilitate successful outcome.

Bandura (12) postulates that aversion therapy may be most effective when it allows the patient to revivify his negative experiences during conditioning sessions when confronted with alcohol stimuli. Thus aversion therapy does not seem to be "automatic" as was once assumed but functions as a self-management technique the patient can use to suppress his behavior temporarily.

The use of aversion therapy is currently being deemphasized and for the most part replaced by more sophisticated behavioral-change strategies. Current behavioral approaches emphasize teaching alternatives to alcohol misuse rather than simply attempting to suppress its occurrence. It is interesting that aversion therapy with alcoholics, which was first reported in the Soviet Union more than 45 years ago, still remains the major therapeutic modality in alcoholism treatment in that country (286).

The current status of aversion conditioning for alcoholic patients is extensively evaluated by Wilson in Chapter 7. His conclusions for the most part are in accord with those given here.

CURRENT TRENDS

Currently behavior therapists are taking a more comprehensive view of alcoholism and its treatment. Many contemporary behaviorists espouse an empirical rather than a theoretical orientation, which takes the form of a descriptive–explanatory model based on a functional analysis of drinking behavior. Excessive drinking is conceived as being related to a wide variety of specific antecedent and consequent events of a social, emotional, cognitive, environmental and physiological nature. Any one or a combination of these factors may precipitate alcohol misuse. Exact combinations of events related to drinking at any point in time may be highly complex. Much research has recently been devoted to examining the effects of these factors (e.g., social stress, visual alcohol cues, social pressure) on the drinking behavior of alcoholics and social drinkers. This literature has been reviewed at length elsewhere (36) and is described in other chapters in this book. The major point here is that a steady body of knowledge based on direct observations of alcohol misuse and events associated with it is being accumulated. This is a definite step toward establishing an effective set of treatment packages designed for various alcoholic populations (e.g., Skid Row, women).

GOALS OF TREATMENT

Based on functional behavioral analysis, the goals of behavioral treatment consist in modifying the antecedents and consequences of drinking and an alcoholic's responses to them. Thus goals might include (1) teaching an alcoholic alternative ways of coping with social–emotional antecedents of alcohol misuse; (2) teaching an alcoholic ways of altering antecedent conditions so that he is less likely to elicit excessive drinking; and (3) rearranging the social environment to make it more conducive to abstinence.

The ultimate purpose of these goals is to improve the patient's general psychological and physical functioning. Whereas past conditioning approaches focused mainly on reductions in drinking per se, the newer, more comprehensive behavioral treatment programs emphasize modifications in the patient's total life. In addition, abstinence is not necessarily the only or the best criterion of success. Controlled, social drinking is becoming a more acceptable treatment goal for some alcoholics.

There are three levels of intervention that become target areas in the treatment process:

(1) *Precipitating events.* Treatment is geared toward changing the individual's response to cues (e.g., via social skills training) or by modifying the cue itself (e.g., instructing an alcoholic to discontinue friendships with alcoholic friends).

(2) *Drinking behavior.* Treatment is geared toward teaching controlled, social drinking or toward abstinence via disulfiram treatment or community groups such as A.A.

(3) *Consequent events.* Treatment is aimed at manipulating the social environment via relatives, friends and employers or at teaching the patient to rearrange his environment via self-management skills (e.g., self-reinforcement for moderate drinking or abstinence).

MODIFICATION OF RESPONSES TO PRECIPITATING EVENTS

One of the major goals of alcoholism treatment consists in teaching patterns of behavior that are alternatives to or incompatible with excessive drinking. These new ways of responding allow the individual not only to avoid excessive drinking but also to obtain more satisfaction from abstinence by developing more efficient and adaptive coping skills. This therapeutic aim has the additional advantage of providing the patient with more control over his drinking and his general life functioning. Other behavioral strategies (e.g., aversion conditioning and operant approaches) rely heavily on external control so that others are "doing something" to the patient to change him. In many cases an alcoholic perceives such procedures as demeaning and often actively resists them. More importantly, since much of the problem behavior may occur without others present, long-term therapeutic success depends on the development of self-control skills. This is not to say, however, that external manipulation of an alcoholic's environment (in terms of allowing natural aversive consequences of excessive drinking to occur) are not extremely useful at times, particularly during the initial stages of treatment.

The types of skills in which alcoholics are deficient are varied. Most involve social–emotional behaviors and necessitate such procedures as relaxation training, assertion training, social skills training, marital counseling, and vocational and recreational training or retraining.

A number of clinical and experimental studies indicate that interpersonal situations requiring assertiveness (i.e., the appropriate expression of personal rights and feelings) are stressful for heavy drinkers and alcoholics and frequently create an occasion for excessive drinking (184, 212). In a recent study by Miller and Eisler[1] three issues related to this deficiency were evaluated: (1) the relationship between alcoholics' self-reports of their assertiveness compared with their actual assertive responses; (2) the relationship between alcoholics' assertiveness and their drinking behavior; and (3) the assertive behavior of alcoholic patients compared with that of patients receiving psychiatric treatment for other problems (i.e., nonalcoholics). Ten alcoholics and 10 nonalcoholics (matched for age and education) completed the Wolpe–Lazarus inventory (316), a measure of self-reported assertiveness, and 32 role-played videotaped interpersonal situations requiring assertive responses. Scenes included positive (e.g., expressing warm feelings or complimentary remarks) and negative (e.g., expressing feelings of irritation or disapproval) assertiveness. Videotaped responses were rated independently by two judges on a 5-point scale from 1 (very unassertive) to 5 (very assertive). In addition to measures of assertion, the drinking behavior of subjects in the alcoholic group was assessed via three 10-minute sessions on an operant drinking apparatus (209).

Table 1 illustrates the mean behavioral and self-report ratings of assertiveness based on responses to the role-played situations. The

TABLE 1.—*Mean Self-Report and Behavioral Assertiveness Ratings of Alcoholics and Nonalcoholics* [a]

	Alcoholics	Nonalcoholics	t
Self-reports (Wolpe-Lazarus)	20.30	14.30	3.17†
Positive assertion	2.98	2.44	2.50*
Negative assertion	2.55	2.31	1.13

[a] From MILLER, P. M. and EISLER, R. M. Assertive behavior of alcoholics: a descriptive analysis. [Unpublished ms., University of Mississippi Medical Center, 1975.]
* $P < .05.$ † $P < .01.$

alcoholics scored significantly higher on the self-report measure than did the nonalcoholics (maximum score 30). Thus the alcoholics perceived themselves to be more assertive than did the nonalcoholics. Behaviorally, however, the groups scored equally low in their ability to express negative feelings. The alcoholics were sig-

---

[1] MILLER, P. M. and EISLER, R. M. Assertive behavior of alcoholics; a descriptive analysis. [Unpublished ms., University of Mississippi Medical Center, 1975.]

nificantly better than the nonalcoholics at expressing positive feelings. In addition, a statistically significant negative correlation of −.63 was found between negative assertion and drinking on the operant task. Thus the less assertive an alcoholic was behaviorally, the more alcohol he was likely to consume.

Clinically, these results appear to have two implications. First, clinicians must be wary of exaggerated self-reports of assertiveness by alcoholics when establishing treatment goals. Assertive behavior should be assessed directly or via reports from others. Second, training alcoholics to express negative feelings may be more essential to therapeutic success than teaching positive assertiveness.

In addition to lack of assertiveness in peer, marital and employment areas, another behavioral deficit of alcoholics is difficulty in dealing with social pressure to take a drink. Foy et al. (97) recently developed a procedure to teach this ability. During each treatment session patients are exposed to a number of role-played situations (based on real-life encounters of each patient) in which two therapists attempt to coerce him into taking a drink. Arguments such as "One drink won't hurt you!" "What kind of a friend are you?" or "It'll make you feel better" are used. The role-played interaction is videotaped, and the patient's responses are rated on the following component behaviors: (1) Duration of looking; (2) Affect; (3) Changing the subject; (4) Offering an alternative ("Joe, why don't we have a cup of coffee together"); (5) Request for new behavior ("Joe, I've quit drinking for good, so please don't ever ask me to have a drink with you again").

Training consists in teaching these skills one at a time via modeling and specific instruction. Two alcoholic patients who received this treatment were reevaluated at monthly follow-ups with a videotaped posttest being administered at the 3-month visit. Both reported using their skills effectively in their community environments. In addition, both patients expressed increased feelings of confidence and self-esteem each time they were able to handle their "drinking buddies" so well. Miller[2] also reports the use of this technique with a young problem drinker whose goal was moderate drinking, not abstinence. With this goal the object of skills training is to teach the ability to refuse additional drinks after the first one or two.

Behavioral marital counseling (207), relaxation training (157,

---

[2] MILLER, P. M. Training responsible drinking with veterans. Presented at the meeting of the American Psychological Association, Chicago, September 1975.

282), self-management training (274)[3] and vocational skills training (136) have also been used effectively to teach more adaptive skills to alcoholics. For example, Miller and Hersen (207) reported a case in which marital skills training was a major aspect of an alcoholic's treatment. Specific goals of social skills training for the couple included (1) increasing the couple's ability to express themselves more directly and to solve mutual problems more efficiently; (2) increasing positive interactional patterns; (3) decreasing the number of conversations regarding negative incidents in the past; and (4) providing each partner with positive skills needed to increase more desirable behavior in the other. These skills were taught via modeling by a man and a woman counselor, videotape feedback, behavioral rehearsal and social reinforcement. Initially, training focused on rather simple behaviors, e.g., eye contact, smiling and attentive listening. In subsequent sessions, more complex problem-solving and assertiveness skills were role-played and rehearsed. The couple were eventually given "homework assignments" geared toward practicing these new skills in everyday problem situations.

A number of specific therapeutic packages have been devised to initiate these new coping skills and to maintain them over a short time. However, a major problem that remains to be resolved involves the most efficacious way to teach alcoholics to recognize and label functional relationships between their drinking and specific antecedent and consequent events. Alcoholics frequently refer to their "urges" or "cravings" when explaining the precipitants of drinking episodes. They perceive little relationship between drinking and other problem events. In fact, they often refer to specific problematic events (e.g., marital conflict) as being "excuses" for their drinking and not really causative factors. Although a number of behavioral clinicians have taught alcoholics to analyze their behaviors within a social learning framework (274), no one has yet formulated the most efficient means of accomplishing this goal. This skill appears to be essential in ensuring continued cooperation with behavioral treatment and the generalization of treatment effects to a wide variety of problem situations.

Maintenance of the effects of skills training over long periods is also essential. One major method for accomplishing this goal is to rearrange social consequences in the natural environment so that new patterns of behavior are more frequently reinforced.

---

[3] Also, MILLER, P. M. and EPSTEIN, L. H. An experimental analysis of the effects of self-management procedures on the drinking behavior of chronic alcoholics. [Unpublished data, University of Mississippi Medical Center, 1975.]

MODIFICATION OF CONSEQUENT EVENTS

Modification of consequent events usually involves the use of operant conditioning principles whereby the alcoholic is provided with maximum social–environmental reinforcement for abstinence and punishment or withdrawal of reinforcement for heavy drinking. Most of the work in this area has been undertaken in hospitals or research centers in which an alcoholic's activities are rather confined. For example, Cohen et al. (66) successfully decreased the drinking of a 39-year-old alcoholic by making access to an enriched ward environment contingent on the consumption of less than 5 oz of alcohol per day. Consumption of more than this amount resulted in a loss of privileges for the rest of the day.

With outpatient Skid Row alcoholics, Miller and colleagues (201, 213) used a variety of reinforcers to reduce alcohol consumption. One 49-year-old subject was provided with coupons (exchangeable for a variety of goods from the hospital commissary) contingent on zero blood alcohol concentrations (BACs) assessed via random Breathalyzer measures. In a subsequent study Skid Row alcoholics were provided with a variety of goods and services (e.g., clothing, cigarettes) through community agencies contingent on their abstinence. As a result of this rather simple program, participants decreased drinking, decreased number of public drunkenness arrests and increased number of days employed. No such changes were observed in a control group receiving services on a noncontingent basis.

Hunt and Azrin (136) successfully instituted a comprehensive operant program with eight alcoholics. In addition to individual social skills training for the patients, relatives and friends were trained to provide pleasurable marital, family and social activities only during periods of abstinence. At a 6-month follow-up, patients receiving this treatment were compared with eight patients receiving traditional hospital care. Patients in the behavioral treatment spent significantly less time drinking, unemployed and away from home than did control subjects. Patients in the operant treatment group also earned higher salaries and engaged in structured social activities more frequently than did patients in the control group.

Modification of these naturally occurring marital and peer reinforcers is essential in dealing with many alcoholics in outpatient settings. One method of facilitating new interpersonal interactions is through behavioral or contingency contracting (199, 207). Essentially, the contract is a written agreement between an alcoholic and another individual (often the spouse or employer) that specifies the behaviors each agrees to change. Positive and negative consequences are then associated with either compliance or noncompliance with the agreement. Although the over-all goals of marital therapy, for example, might be broad (e.g., to increase the couple's ability to express themselves more directly and to solve mutual problems more efficiently), goals of contracting are highly specific. Such goals as specified by the couple might include the following.

Wife's requests: (1) Husband should completely abstain from alcoholic beverages. (2) Husband should increase "feeling" talk. (3) Husband should increase mutual outings (e.g., dinner, movies).

Husband's requests: (1) Wife should decrease alcohol-related nagging. (2) Wife should increase mutual home activities (e.g., watching television together). (3) Wife should increase positive and complimentary comments.

Contracts, usually kept simple, are renegotiated from time to time. For example, a wife may agree not to mention any of her husband's past drinking episodes or the possibility of future drinking in return for the husband's taking her out to dinner or on a shopping trip. While these agreements seem a bit artificial at first, they quickly lead to more spontaneous, habitual behavior patterns. Contracts between alcoholics and employers with respect to disulfiram intake were used by Bigelow et al.[4] Typically an alcoholic agrees to take disulfiram daily in the presence of his employer in return for the opportunity to work each day. Bonuses might also be provided for continuous disulfiram intake over a period of weeks or months.

Finally, operant conditioning procedures in the form of token economy programs have been used on inpatient alcoholism units. These programs consist of a system in which patients earn points or credits for appropriate behaviors and lose credits or fail to earn them for inappropriate or maladaptive behaviors. Credits are then used to purchase reinforcers (e.g., hospital privileges and passes). Token economics have been used to reinforce a variety of adaptive behavior patterns in alcoholics such as work-related activities (221) and social skills (214). These programs also function to demonstrate to alcoholics the relationship between specific behaviors and their social–environmental consequences.

---

[4] BIGELOW, G., LIEBSON, I. and LAWRENCE, C. Prevention of alcohol abuse by reinforcement of incompatible behavior. Presented at the meeting of the Association for the Advancement of Behavior Therapy, Miami, December 1973.

MODIFICATION IN THE DRINKING RESPONSE:
CONTROLLED DRINKING SKILLS

Along with evidence from recent clinical (78, 232, 260) and experimental (74, 114, 183) studies that controlled, moderate drinking is a viable therapeutic goal for some alcoholics, behavior therapists have attempted to devise treatment strategies to teach controlled drinking skills. Mills and co-workers (217) used aversive conditioning procedures to teach alcoholics the components of social drinking (i.e., ordering mixed rather than straight drinks, sipping instead of gulping drinks, and limiting the total amount of alcohol consumed). In an experimental bar situation, electric shock was delivered to an alcoholic's hand contingent on "alcoholic" as opposed to "social" drinking. Results of this procedure, when used as part of a total treatment program, are discussed later in the chapter (274).

Miller et al. (204) used a simpler procedure in which alcoholics were sequentially instructed to initiate and practice controlled drinking skills. Patients were allowed free access to alcoholic beverages in a simulated living room setting. Drinking sessions were videotaped, and the following behavioral components were assessed following each session: (1) number of sips; (2) inter-sip interval; (3) mean sip amount; (4) potency of the beverage; and (5) total amount of alcohol consumed. The three alcoholic subjects demonstrated marked changes in their drinking—in the direction of controlled drinking—as a function of the instructions. It is interesting to note that interrelationships among components were observed in terms of a negative reactivity effect; that is, as sip amount decreased, inter-sip interval also decreased, resulting in more rapid drinking. This reciprocity demonstrates the importance of modifying all of the drinking components so that the alcoholic does not learn a new, equally inappropriate drinking pattern.

Another method to alter the drinking response is through BAC discrimination training. During this training alcoholics are provided with experience in estimating their own BACs at various stages in the drinking sequence. They then learn to associate specific "internal cues" (e.g., numbness, drowsiness, tingling sensations in the face) with varying BACs. Apparently, moderate drinkers use information of this kind to "know when to stop" (135). Alcoholics, on the other hand, appear unresponsive not only to these internal cues but also to external ones such as the rate at which they drink, number of sips or potency of their drink (274).

Silverstein and associates (264) found that alcoholics demonstrated difficulty in maintaining accurate estimates of their BACs without continuous external feedback. Lovibond and Caddy (171) produced long-term maintenance by using an aversive conditioning paradigm during training. Aversive electric shocks were repeatedly paired with BACs above 0.65%. Results with 28 alcoholics undergoing this procedure demonstrated that 21 were maintaining controlled drinking patterns at follow-up contacts ranging from 16 to 60 weeks.

Caddy concluded (Chapter 8) that within moderate drinking ranges it appears that alcoholics can learn to discriminate their BACs accurately. The most efficacious ways to maintain this ability over time and to relate this skill to controlled drinking practices are not yet clear. Apparently, comprehensive behavioral programs combining BAC discrimination with such procedures as social skills training and marital counseling seem better able to accomplish this goal. In addition, Caddy feels that this approach may be most effective with alcoholics who initiate drinking simply to "have a few drinks" and then become intoxicated, compared with those who consciously overindulge to reach a high level of intoxication quickly. In any event, BAC discrimination training deserves further utilization and evaluation as a modality of treatment and prevention.

ASSESSMENT

Unfortunately, one of the most frequently overlooked aspects of alcoholism treatment has been objective behavioral assessment for purposes of planning and evaluating therapeutic strategies. In this regard, behavior therapy, with its insistence on a scientific–evaluative approach to treatment, offers the field of alcoholism an essential assessment methodology.

Initial assessments and follow-up evaluations necessitate the systematic accumulation of data regarding drinking patterns and functionally related behaviors (e.g., social skills deficits, marital conflict). The general behavior therapy literature provides numerous examples of procedures for the objective assessment of social interaction (83), marital problems (84) and emotional behaviors (127, 304).

Behaviorists in the alcoholism field have focused on two areas of assessment: (1) the development of analogue drinking measures to allow for an assessment of drinking patterns in treatment or laboratory settings; and (2) the development of a comprehensive and objective regimen for gathering data for follow-up evaluation studies. Marlatt provides a complete examination of these two foci in Chapter 12, so activities in these areas are only briefly described here.

Recently Miller (203) reviewed the assessment of addictive behaviors, describing particular laboratory analogue measures of drinking behavior: operant measures, taste-rating tasks and ad libitum alcohol and drug use in simulated natural environments.

Within an operant analysis, alcohol serves as a reinforcer for the performance of a simple motor response (e.g., lever pressing) or for a variety of more naturalistic social behaviors within a treatment setting. Numerous investigators (136, 192, 203, 224, 225) have used operant assessment to: (1) gather baseline data on the extent and patterning of alcohol misuse; and (2) determine the reinforcement value of alcohol in relation to other potential reinforcers (e.g., money, opportunity to engage in social interactions). This information provides an empirical basis for planning behavioral treatment strategies with individual alcoholics.

Marlatt et al. (183) and Miller and Hersen (206) developed taste-rating tasks in which drinking is measured under the guise of a "taste-rating experiment." Typically, alcoholics are requested to taste and rate a number of alcoholic beverages during a specified period of time. Although the subject is not told that consumption is being evaluated, the exact amount of each beverage consumed is calculated when the task is completed. The advantage of this task as a measure of treatment effectiveness is that, due to its surreptitious nature, therapeutic demand for patients to respond in a certain way (e.g., to drink little in order to please the therapist or avoid censure) is minimized.

A number of behavioral researchers have also observed drinking behavior in simulated bar (217, 255) and living room (217) settings. Patients are usually instructed to drink as they normally do in their natural environments. Videotapes of these drinking sessions provide a detailed analysis of the components of drinking behavior (e.g., number of sips, inter-sip interval). Such analysis proved to be a valuable asset in treatment geared toward teaching controlled drinking skills.

Therapeutically, these analogue measures have been used in a variety of ways which include: (1) pre- and postevaluation of specific treatment strategies (210); (2) continuous evaluation of an individual patient's treatment via single-case design experimentation (201); and (3) prediction of therapeutic outcome in behavioral treatment programs (209).

Since these measures are analogues and are administered within a treatment setting, they have limitations for outreach follow-up evaluations in the natural environment. For follow-up purposes alcohol use and misuse are usually measured via self-reports, reports from others, breath or blood sample analyses, or all of these. Follow-up evaluations, however, involve much more information than data on alcohol use per se. Possibly the most systematic and objective approach to treatment evaluation was reported by Sobell and Sobell (274).[5] One of the most valuable aspects of their follow-up approach involved the examination of drinking as a continuous versus a discrete variable. That is, many evaluation studies view success, as far as alcohol use is concerned, as an all-or-none proposition (i.e., either complete abstinence or complete inebriety). The Sobells gathered continuous data on the number of days intoxicated (consumption of 10 oz of alcohol or more), number of days of controlled drinking (6 oz or less), number of days abstinent, and number of days abstinent because of hospital or jail incarceration. In addition, data on vocational and social status were acquired. All data were verified by other sources, e.g., relatives, friends, social agencies, law enforcement agencies and hospitals.

COMPREHENSIVE BEHAVIORAL TREATMENT PROGRAMS

Although the major components (i.e., modifications in antecedents, consequences and drinking behavior) of behavioral alcoholism treatment have been described separately, in applied clinical settings they are typically combined in a broad-spectrum program to maximize therapeutic efforts. Seldom is one aspect of treatment sufficient to deal with the social–psychological complexities of alcoholics with diverse backgrounds and problems. Certainly a "shotgun" approach in which every participant receives every behavioral technique a program offers is not advocated. Therapeutic programs must be individualized within the total behavioral framework. Ideally, a comprehensive program includes a number of treatment packages, each of which is geared to the needs of a particular subgroup, e.g., Skid Row alcoholics, individuals whose treatment goal is controlled drinking, and drinkers who are still functioning well in the community.

---

[5] Also, SOBELL, M. B. and SOBELL, L. C. Evidence of controlled drinking by former alcoholics; a second year evaluation of individualized behavior therapy. Presented at the meeting of the American Psychological Association, Montreal, August 1973.

Within a comprehensive behavioral program, the first phase of the therapeutic process is a detailed assessment of the functional relationships between an alcoholic's drinking behavior and specific social, emotional, environmental, cognitive and physiological events. Emphasis is placed on direct observational assessment of an alcoholic's behavior, utilizing role-playing, videotaping, systematic reports from "significant others" and analogue drinking tasks. As discussed earlier in the chapter, specific therapeutic goals are then established in corroboration with the patient. Goals for a particular alcoholic might include: (1) increased assertiveness with his wife; (2) development of job interview techniques; (3) decreased self-derogatory thoughts and remarks; (4) increased ability to refuse offers of alcoholic beverages.

Goal priorities are established with the individual, and no general sequence of treatment components is typical. Frequently group treatment sessions are used, particularly when teaching responsible drinking skills and interpersonal skills since these behaviors naturally occur within a social context. The group approach allows other patients to model more adaptive interpersonal skills, serve as partners in role playing, and provide the patient with performance feedback and social reinforcement for behavior change.

Assessment is frequently a continuous process so no essential distinction is made between treatment and research. The patient's progress in each treatment component can be carefully monitored via single-case experimental design research. Using this evaluation procedure the therapist can determine whether: (1) the patient is actually benefiting from the treatment procedure (based on behavioral ratings); and (2) the treatment procedure per se or some other therapeutic influence (e.g., expectancy–placebo factors) was responsible for behavioral improvement. This information is helpful not only in planning and evaluating the patient's progress but also in basing improvement in the total program on pragmatic rather than personal or theoretical issues.

As with any treatment modality, an active follow-up phase is essential. Although patients have learned new behavior patterns in the treatment setting, there is no guarantee they will continue this improvement in the natural environment. Periodic follow-up sessions and "booster" treatments are necessary. Drinking episodes during follow-up are not viewed as indicating treatment failure. Behavioral practitioners have tried to avoid the all-or-nothing perception of treatment effects whereby abstinence denotes success and drinking (to any extent) denotes failure. Drinking episodes are used in a constructive way to reevaluate the patient's responses to precipitants of the drinking episode. Emphasis is also placed on the patient's ability to discontinue a drinking episode once it begins. Relapses are considered to be an opportunity for learning or relearning a new response to a problem situation.

Unfortunately, studies designed specifically to evaluate comprehensive behavioral treatment programs for alcoholics are few. As with any treatment evaluation, these studies are not easy to conduct and are fraught with methodological, procedural and ethical problems that are often difficult to resolve. Conflicts between sound experimental methodology and the realities of dealing with individual patients in treatment and during a lengthy follow-up often lead to compromises that eventually limit the value of the study.

The two most recent comprehensive experimental evaluations of behavioral treatments were reported by Sobell and Sobell (274)[5] and Vogler et al. (294). Both studies compared behavioral with nonbehavioral treatments under conditions in which the goal of treatment was either complete abstinence or controlled, social drinking. Both used inpatient alcoholics. Sobell and Sobell (274)[4] used a variety of treatments, including behavioral self-analysis, electrical aversion therapy, self-management training and social skills training. Patients in a behavioral, controlled drinking group were taught, via a shock-avoidance paradigm, to order mixed (rather than straight) drinks, take small sips, increase the time interval between drinks and limit their intake to a total of three drinks. The nonbehavioral treatment consisted of group therapy, chemotherapy and A.A. meetings. Results indicated that the behavioral treatment group was functioning significantly better on both drinking and social adjustment measures over a 2-year follow-up period (255). In addition, patients whose goal was the controlled use of alcohol were functioning significantly better (78.9% were functioning well on more than 80% of follow-up days) than patients whose goal was abstinence (53.9% functioning well on more than 80% of the follow-up days).

Vogler et al. (294) conducted a similar study in which both of their treatment groups received forms of behavior and traditional therapy. All patients received group therapy and vocational rehabilitation, attended A.A. and alcohol-education meetings, and underwent alternatives training and behavioral counseling. One group received additional training in controlled drinking skills which consisted of BAC discrimination training, aversion therapy for overconsumption and discriminated avoidance practice. Booster treatment sessions were conducted at monthly intervals for 1 year. At a 12-month follow-up no differences were found between patients receiving the extra controlled drinking skills training and those who did not—based on rate of abstinence versus controlled drinking, preferred beverage, drinking companions, drinking environment or days lost from work. However, patients who received the training in controlled drinking skills drank significantly less alcohol (mean, 3.5 gallons per year) than the group who did not receive this additional training (mean, 6.9 gallons per year).

Certainly these positive results demonstrate the need for additional long-term controlled evaluation studies. Future investigators, however, must begin to dissect these comprehensive treatment packages to determine which of the many therapeutic procedures used contribute most to successful outcome (36). In addition, drinking behavior must be evaluated more directly to determine if patients actually use information provided during training (e.g., discrimination of BAC) to modify their drinking.

FUTURE TRENDS

If behavior therapy in the treatment of alcoholism continues on its present course, three broad treatment trends are likely to be further used and developed. First, the use of techniques which teach alcoholics behavioral patterns that serve as alternatives to excessive drinking is currently being greatly expanded. Of these procedures, self-management skills training will probably evidence the most rapid growth over the next few years. Although this training has been used successfully in the treatment of other behavioral problems (i.e., obesity and cigarette smoking), it has been applied to alcoholics only minimally.

Second, operant procedures in which consequences of drinking behavior are rearranged continue to show their usefulness. On a practical level, this involves teaching "significant others" in the community (e.g., relatives, friends, employers) to reinforce adaptive behavior patterns more systematically. Although the use of operant procedures to decrease alcohol consumption in hospital and laboratory settings has been well described, there are few community reinforcement programs (66, 136). The latter involve a number of practical problems that deserve more intensive study, e.g., coordinating all or a majority of the alcoholic's community contacts so that he does not receive reinforcement—attention, assistance with problems—for inappropriate behavior (i.e., intoxication).

Third, controlled, social drinking appears to be a viable treatment goal for some alcoholics. On the basis of current experimentation (294),[5] treatment efforts geared toward this goal are likely to be expanded. Procedures developed in this area will also have significance for the prevention of alcoholism. Behaviorists are already beginning to intervene with high-risk youths, using controlled drinking skills training as a preventive strategy.[6] A major unanswered question is which types of alcoholics are most likely to benefit from training in controlled drinking.

Finally, behavior therapists have been criticized, and rightly so, for avoiding some of the more difficult problems encountered in alcoholism treatment. For example, although the therapist's and patient's positive or negative expectations of treatment success may influence treatment outcome (36), behaviorists have not systematically dealt with this issue. In addition, "motivation" or lack of it is frequently mentioned by clinicians as being a particularly difficult problem with alcoholics. Basically, this refers to the reluctance of alcoholics to admit their problem, request treatment for it, cooperate with the treatment provider, or all three. Practical questions regarding motivation refer to its definition, assessment and modification. Although behavior therapists are experienced in assessing complex behavior patterns, for the most part they avoid dealing with the motivational problems of alcoholics. A beginning point in the analysis of motivation might well consist of a behavioral definition of its components. Two of these elements might include: (1) number of outpatient treatment sessions missed; and (2) frequency of compliance with therapeutic instructions (e.g., "Please arrange for your wife to come with you for your next visit" or "Count the number of times you become angry during the next week and write down the circumstances in each case"). This type of definition, which is far from complete, enables the clinicians to increase motivational behaviors more easily. For example, Bigelow and associates[4] devised an operant strategy to increase the outpatient clinic attendance of alcoholics. Each patient was required to make a financial security deposit at the beginning of treatment that could be earned back, a little at a time, at each outpatient visit. Failure to attend an appointment resulted in a loss of part of this money. Six of seven patients treated under this motivational system maintained continued contact with the treatment agency. Gradually, such external

[6] MARLATT, G. A. Training responsible drinking with college students. Presented at the meeting of the American Psychological Association, Chicago, September 1975.

motivational procedures could be replaced by self-initiated ones via self-management training. In this way the patient learns to regulate his own behavior with minimal external incentives from the therapist.

10

Empirically Derived Components of Treatment for Alcohol Problems: Some Issues and Extensions

Mark B. Sobell

THE 2-YEAR MATURATIONAL development of a broad-spectrum treatment approach for persons with drinking problems is the first of two themes addressed in this chapter. Crucial but often unstated interactions between the empirical research and conceptual developmental aspects of behavioral research are illustrated. The second theme is an extension of that work, dealing with a broader range of patients and services, particularly outpatients and their care.

THE PATTON ALCOHOL STUDIES: A BRIEF HISTORICAL REVIEW

Alcohol research was conducted at Patton (California) State Hospital from 1969 through 1971. All of the studies used men inpatient volunteer alcoholics as subjects; all were performed in two specially designed research environments located in an alcoholism treatment unit. One of these environments was a simulated bar and lounge, including a full length mirror behind the bar, a glass and bottle display, dim lighting and piped-in music. The second, a simulated home environment, included comfortable furniture, carpeting and a television set. Each environment could be remotely monitored via closed-circuit television. These simulated environments, established within the constraints of an inpatient hospital setting, were an attempt to structure the experimental environment for increased generalization of treatment effects to the subjects' usual living environment.

The development of any behavioral modification paradigm should begin with a precise definition of the target behaviors involved.

Since drinking behavior, by definition, is a vital component of drinking problems, we initially presumed that we could obtain information about differences in drinking behavior between patients and social drinkers simply by reviewing data available in the professional literature. Much to our surprise, we were unable to find any empirical data describing drinking behavior, although speculation about the drinking of alcoholics was plentiful and conclusive (e.g., "an alcoholic drinks in a manner so as to become drunk"). Although the import of such deductive logic did not escape us, it could hardly be considered a sufficient foundation for further experimental studies. We were thus faced with the initial task of determining how social drinkers and our alcoholic patients typically consumed alcoholic beverages within the experimental environment in which we planned to investigate their drinking behavior. Prior to 1969 only a few studies involving the actual observation of drinking behavior had been reported—by Mendelson (194), for example. As a result, skepticism abounded concerning whether the drinking behavior of alcoholics was vulnerable to manipulation using only environmental variables.

This line of research evolved into two baseline drinking studies (255, 271), which were not designed, however, around epidemiological descriptions of drinking practices of social drinkers and alcoholics; nor were they designed to constitute an analogue of barroom drinking. They were intended instead to assess drinking behavior as it occurred within a specific experimental environment. The measures used to assess drinking behavior were more precise than those that had been used up to that time (194); our interest was primarily in drinking behaviors related to the act of becoming drunk, rather than behaviors involved in maintaining drinking over a number of days.

Each of the two baseline studies included a group of inpatient alcoholics (each of whom had a history of serious alcohol problems and had previously demonstrated physical dependence on alcohol) and a group of social drinkers recruited from the local community. In the first study (194), subjects were allowed to consume up to six drinks during a 3-hr period, whereas in the second study (255) this limit was increased to 16 drinks within a 4-hr interval. Each drink was 1 oz of 86-proof whisky (43% alcohol) or its equivalent in alcohol content. Results of both studies indicated that the alcoholic subjects (1) generally ordered straight drinks, whereas social drinkers preferred mixed drinks; (2) generally gulped their drinks regardless of the type of drink being consumed; (3) drank much faster than the social drinkers; (4) almost always drank more than 12 drinks during the 4-hr period, whereas such consumption was highly atypical for social drinkers; and (5) surprisingly, sipped less frequently than social drinkers, but took larger sips.

Interestingly, an apparent instructional artifact occurred in the 6-oz baseline study, a phenomenon which highlights the importance of environmental control over drinking, as was further documented later at Patton and elsewhere. In the 6-oz study, subjects were told they could drink "only 6 oz" during the 3-hr drinking session. Interviews conducted with subjects in both groups several days after their participation in the experiment revealed that these instructions probably acted as a confounding variable: The alcoholic patients, knowing that they would have to spend the remainder of the day in the hospital with no further access to alcoholic beverages, typically reported that they purposely "savored" their last two or three drinks in order to make them last longer, whereas social drinkers typically reported that because they were uncertain about whether they could consume six drinks during the allotted time tended to drink either their first or last two drinks very rapidly; in other words, they interpreted the experimental instructions as a challenge.

As a consequence, the replication study, with a 16-oz limit, proceeded with the following instructions: "Drink as much as you want; we'll stop you after 16 oz or 4 hr, whichever comes first. You may stop sooner if you wish." Figures 1 and 2 display the mean time per drink obtained in the two studies for alcoholics and normal drinkers for all drinks combined as well as for specific types of drinks. Differences between studies in the time spent to consume early drinks are obvious, with alcoholics typically consuming their first four drinks in the 16-oz study in less than half the time they spent consuming the same number of drinks in the 6-oz study. Thus even our initial investigation hinted at the great complexity of the simple act of drinking alcoholic beverages and the circumstances that control drinking behavior.

Before leaving consideration of these studies, two postscripts are relevant. First, a general replication of these baseline procedures using New Zealanders as subjects was recently reported by Williams and Brown (306). Except that the New Zealand alcoholics and social drinkers tended to prefer weaker drinks than their American counterparts, Williams and Brown found that "differences between alcoholics and normal drinkers on measures of total alcohol consumed, sip size and speed of drinking amongst New Zealand drinkers were found to be of the same order as similar differences when

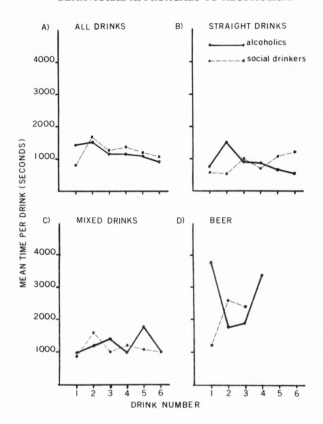

FIGURE 1.—*Mean Time per Drink by Number and Type of Drink Ordered by Alcoholics (N = 16) and Social Drinkers (N = 15) in a Baseline Study Having a Consumption Limit of Six Drinks per Subject.*

American alcoholics and normal drinkers were studied" (306, *pp. 293–294*). Considering that inherent cultural differences separate Americans and New Zealanders along a variety of other dimensions, this comparability of drinking behaviors is striking. Similar comparability recently emerged in the context of obesity research. Gaul et al. (103) reported a study in which the eating behaviors of obese and nonobese subjects were unobtrusively monitored in a naturalistic setting, a hamburger stand. They found that "obese subjects took more bites, performed fewer chews per bite, and spent less time chewing than did non-obese subjects" (103, *p. 123*). The

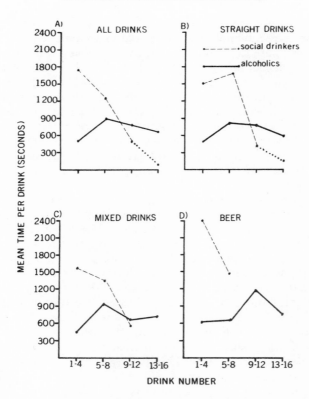

FIGURE 2.—*Mean Time per Drink by Number and Type of Drink Ordered by Alcoholics (N = 26) and Social Drinkers (N = 23) in a Second Baseline Study Having a Consumption Limit of 16 Drinks per Subject.*

finding that obese subjects took more bites than the nonobese seems to fly in the face of popular behavioral recommendations to obese individuals that they increase the number of bites they take while eating (283). This finding may well be analogous to the baseline drinking finding that alcoholics in fact sip more slowly than social drinkers. Without such data, one would be tempted to include sipping more slowly among modification procedures intended to change deviant drinking patterns to normal ones.

The next study involved unobtrusive monitoring and videotape recording of events that occurred in the simulated environments via a closed-circuit television system. The study examined the impact on sober alcoholics of self-confrontation with their own videotaped drunken behavior. In the study (256), 26 alcoholic inpatients received the experimental self-confrontation treatment. Assigned to small groups, subjects were videotaped while they consumed up to 16 standard drinks in the simulated bar; they then viewed the videotape of their drunken behavior after they had sobered up on the day subsequent to the taping session. Depending on the experimental procedure in effect, this 2-day cycle was repeated for some subjects as often as five times. A control group of 10 patients participated in drinking sessions but did not view videotapes of their drunken behavior; another control group of 10 alcoholic patients who had volunteered for the experiment did not actually participate in drinking sessions.

At the time this study was performed, self-confrontation procedures, based primarily on clinical observations rather than empirical findings (9, 76), were strongly endorsed in the literature. Clinically speaking, it was obvious to the research staff which conducted the videotape replay sessions that the tapes were having a considerable impact on the subjects. One such effect was an extreme state of stress apparently induced by the replays. To this end, it was not uncommon for subjects to chain smoke, sweat profusely and exhibit many other signs of agitation when viewing a replay. However, beyond the immediate impact of any alcoholism treatment procedure, the final evaluation of its efficiency depends on whether it yields beneficial change in drinking or associated behaviors. In this case the absence of a positive effect was clear shortly after discharge: All 26 experimental subjects resumed drinking within 6 weeks of discharge from the hospital, and 14 of these became intoxicated within 24 hr of discharge; 80% of the control subjects drank within 6 weeks of discharge. The finding of no significant differences between the groups was similarly maintained during a 1-year follow-up evaluation (257).

This study influenced our further research in two important ways. First, it gave strong support to our commitment to seek empirically based answers to clinical questions. Second, these empirical results once again broadened our thinking regarding the nature of the drinking behavior of "alcoholics." At about the same time, Bandura (12) presented a cogent operant description of excessive drinking, reinforcing our increasing interest in the antecedents and consequences of drinking problems.

The next major study conducted at Patton State Hospital has subsequently been viewed erroneously by many as a treatment study. Our basic objective in initially designing the study, however, was to determine the extent to which the drinking behavior of alcoholics was modifiable—in light of traditional concepts of alcoholism (which concluded it was not) and a few empirical studies (which suggested it was). This study, reported by Mills et al. (217), involved training social drinking as an alternative to abstinence for a small group of alcoholics. Thirteen volunteer alcoholics were allowed to order drinks in the simulated bar environment, albeit with electric shock avoidance contingencies in effect. These contingencies, based on earlier baseline data (194, 255), were intended to investigate whether alcoholics' drinking patterns could be shaped to approximate normal drinking patterns more closely. Accordingly, behaviors we had found typical of alcoholic drinking (e.g., gulping, drinking straight drinks or drinking excessively) were punished on an avoidance schedule of shock reinforcement, while criterion behaviors of sipping drinks, drinking mixed drinks and ordering limited amounts of alcohol constituted successful means for avoiding shock delivery. We have since lost confidence in aversive schedules for the treatment of alcohol problems, except under certain special circumstances. As a result, we agree with Hallam and Rachman (122) that whatever effectiveness electrical aversive conditioning might have is mediated by factors other than conditioned fear of the painful stimulus. At the time of this 1971 study, however, we believed we were dealing with a behavior likely to be so highly resistant to modification that we were not at all certain the shaping we sought was even possible. The results of that study clearly demonstrated, however, that within a controlled environment, alcoholics will engage in drinking behavior not discriminably different from that of social drinkers—given an appropriate arrangement of contingencies for doing so. Although treatment outcome results reported for that study were positive, its primary importance was in the demonstrated modifiability of the drinking behavior of alcoholics who had previously demonstrated physical dependence on alcohol.

One other study (270) of that period by the Patton group deserves mention before discussion of how these studies led to implementation of a broad-spectrum behavioral treatment approach for alcoholism. It had seemed reasonable for us to assume that alcoholics, of all people, possess an adequate knowledge of various types of alcoholic beverages and drinks. However, we conducted a pilot investigation which suggested just the opposite—that alcoholics might actually be deficient in basic knowledge about certain types of popular mixed drinks. In the baseline studies (194,

255) we found that the alcoholics demonstrated a substantial preference for straight drinks. Originally we assumed that this preference stemmed from an informed choice among alternatives. In a formal investigation of this matter, 35 alcoholics, of whom 10 had previously worked as bartenders, volunteered as subjects. Another 25 social drinkers were also recruited. All the subjects were asked to name as many mixed drinks as they could and the type of beverage alcohol used in each type of drink, to a maximum of 15 drinks identified. Whereas the social drinkers and the alcoholics who had worked as bartenders named approximately 8.5 mixed drinks, alcoholics who had not worked as bartenders could name an average of only 3.1 mixed drinks, a statistically significant difference. As with the baseline drinking data, this finding was also replicated by Williams and Brown (307) in New Zealand.

At this stage of the Patton research program, we incorporated the findings into a working hypothesis: the excessive drinking of alcoholics can be appropriately viewed as an operant behavior. Well aware that the long-term consequences of alcoholism often require medical management and that someday genetic or biochemical factors of some substantial importance to the etiology of alcohol problems might well be delineated, we were nonetheless concerned with developing an effective treatment paradigm rather than searching for "true" or ultimate etiologies. To this end, substantial data had accumulated indicating that regardless of whether the origin of alcohol problems would eventually be limited to environmental factors, these factors clearly played powerful roles in the maintenance of alcoholic drinking, and that drinking behavior itself was definitely subject to modification. On this basis we evolved a broad-spectrum behavioral treatment approach we called "individualized behavior therapy for alcoholics" (272, 273, 274, 278). The broad-spectrum treatment study is so complex it cannot be fully communicated here.

When we first began research at Patton, serious consideration of a large-scale treatment study, such as Individualized Behavior Therapy for Alcoholics (IBTA), would have been inconceivable. We were guided to the formulation of that study by the results of our empirical research and those of others. In contrast to previous Patton studies, which had all had limited objectives, we now chose to implement a multiple-component treatment evaluation study; we were well aware that studies that combine a variety of treatment methods, if successful at all, are fraught with problems in interpretation. For instance, how does one determine which components were effective, which unnecessary, and which, if any, actually detracted from the treatment effect? Or was there synergism among the various components? However, in view of the dismal history of treatment innovation and treatment outcome research in alcohol studies, we were willing to take a deductive approach to developing a treatment program. If it worked, attempts at streamlining and improving the treatment package could be the target of future research. If it clearly did not work, then we would have to consider the whole matter again.

Seventy men gamma-alcoholic inpatients served voluntarily in the study. Each had experienced physical dependence on alcohol, and each typically had had multiple alcohol-related arrests and hospitalizations. Since the assignment of subjects to groups is important for the interpretation of data, Figure 3 outlines the IBTA experimental design.

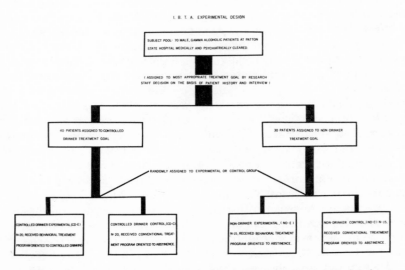

FIGURE 3.—*Experimental Design Used in Study of Individualized Behavior Therapy for Alcoholics.* From Sobell and Sobell (273).

Before being accepted for the study, subjects were screened for medical and psychiatric problems, after which a thorough social and drinking history was obtained via an intensive interview. Subjects were then assigned to a treatment goal of either controlled drinking or nondrinking (abstinence) on the basis of a majority staff decision. Choice of the controlled drinking goal was a radical departure from traditional treatment methods. The treatment goal decision of controlled drinking was based on the following criteria: that some form of nonproblem, limited drinking was desired by the subject; that the subject could reasonably be expected to learn new drinking behaviors; and that the environment to which the subject would return after hospitalization would be supportive of controlled drinking. No subject's request for a treatment goal of abstinence was denied. Within each of the two treatment-goal groups, subjects were then randomly assigned to a control group, which received only the conventional state hospital treatment oriented toward abstinence, or to an experimental group, which underwent 17 experimental treatment sessions in addition to the conventional treatment. In other words, only the controlled drinker experimental subjects received treatment oriented specifically toward the goal of controlled drinking. Their respective control subjects were strongly advised that posttreatment abstinence would be in their best interest.

Irrespective of a subject's assigned treatment goal, all experimental treatment sessions focused directly on drinking behavior, tailoring the treatment as specifically as possible to meet the individual's needs, and emphasizing helping the subject to identify the functions of excessive drinking and to develop alternative, more beneficial ways of dealing with those situations. A problem-solving, rule-learning procedure was a central element of the experimental treatment in all instances. The only explicit difference in treatment between the nondrinker and the controlled drinker experimental groups was that the controlled drinker subjects were trained in methods of nonproblem drinking and allowed to practice these behaviors during sessions. On the other hand, although nondrinker subjects were allowed to consume drinks if they wished, they were told that this was inappropriate and that certain aversive contingencies might sometimes be applied. The remainder of the treatment program involved, among other procedures, videotape self-confrontation; this time, however, the procedure took advantage of the subjects' sedation and familiarity with the drunken situation to probe for stimulus materials that would be useful during later treatment sessions. These drinking sessions were structured in such a way as to aid in the identification of specific events likely to serve as events that initiate drinking. Each subject was also given practice in methods of resisting social pressure to drink; controlled drinker experimental subjects were familiarized with a variety of popular mixed drinks.

The vast majority of IBTA treatment sessions can accurately be termed behavioral change training sessions. The sequence of these sessions incorporated a four-stage process: (1) Problem identificacation—subjects were trained to identify the specific circumstances which had in the past and were likely in the future to result in drinking that would have adverse consequences. (2) Identification of alternative responses to drinking—subjects were assisted in generating a series of behavioral options to be used when confronted with problem situations. (3) Evaluation of alternatives—subjects were taught how to evaluate each of the behavioral options in terms of their short-term and, especially, long-term effects. (4) Preparation to engage in the best behavioral alternative—subjects practiced the alternative responses which could reasonably be expected to incur the least self-damaging long-term consequences in each instance. Various procedures and behavioral techniques, specific to the case, were used to accomplish this objective. Other elements of the experimental treatment procedures are discussed in earlier publications (272, 273, 274, 278).

First-year outcome data were first published in 1973 (273). The task of gathering complete 2-year follow-up data on 69 of the 70 subjects was recently completed (278). This follow-up information was obtained from subjects and corroborative information sources (i.e., family, employer) at 3- to 4-week intervals. A variety of official records (i.e., arrest and hospital records, drivers' records) were also used routinely as data sources. A number of adjunctive measures of life functioning were also employed. To this end we used a new drinking disposition measure that was designed to categorize the drinking behavior of a subject on any given day into one of five mutually exclusive categories: (1) abstinent—no alcohol consumed; (2) controlled drinking—typically consumption of 6 oz or less of 86-proof beverage alcohol (43% alcohol) or its equivalent in alcohol content; (3) drunk—typically consumption of more than 6 oz of 86-proof whisky (43% alcohol) or its equivalent in alcohol content; (4) hospital incarceration for alcohol-related health problems, usually for detoxication; (5) jail incarceration for alcohol-related arrests.

An overview of the results of the IBTA study indicates that during the first year of follow-up both experimental groups achieved over-all functioning superior to that of their respective control groups. During the second year of follow-up controlled drinker experimental subjects continued to function significantly better than their respective controls whereas differences between the nondrinker groups were somewhat reduced, just failing to retain statistical significance. However, in this instance multiple sources of treatment outcome data proved especially helpful. The significant difference in functioning between the controlled-drinker groups was corroborated by a number of adjunctive measures of treatment outcome. By contrast, no adjunctive measures of treatment outcome revealed significant differences between the nondrinker groups. Figure 4 summarizes first- and second-year daily drinking disposition data for the study. The percentage of days functioning well was defined operationally as the sum of the abstinent and controlled drinking days.

Before concluding consideration of this study, a few additional comments are in order. First, it should be noted that the controlled drinker experimental subjects experienced far more abstinent days than those in the other three groups. This is an important point because it is easy to become confused between actual outcome and the arbitrary objective criterion of six standard drinks or less per day defined as controlled drinking. Controlled drinking, as it was practiced by the subjects of the study, was explicitly not daily drinking; more typically it was a pattern of drinking characterized by one to four drinks on two or three occasions per week to one or two such occasions per month. Our 2-year report (278) presents detailed drinking profiles for each of the 69 subjects followed. These profiles suggest that subjects who successfully engaged in controlled drinking typically did not initiate extended periods of drunk days as a result of this type of drinking. Furthermore, they indicate that only controlled drinker experimental subjects displayed a high incidence of isolated drunk days, compared with the predominant pattern exhibited by other subjects of extended periods of continuous drunk days. Finally, a third-year, double-blind, follow-up evaluation of subjects has now been completed by independent investigators, and the results should be available soon.

EXPANDING HORIZONS

In 1971 the alcoholism services of the Orange County (California) Department of Mental Health began providing the only public services for alcoholism and problem drinking for the 1.6 million residents. The significance of this fact for our discussion is the con-

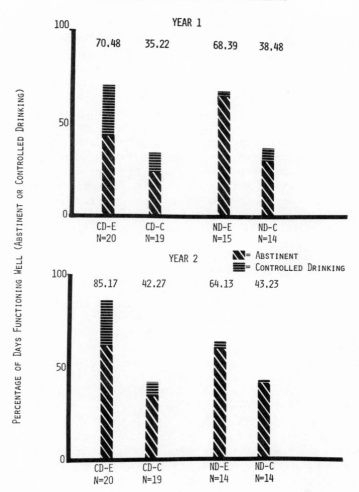

FIGURE 4.—*Summary of First and Second Year Daily Drinking Disposition Outcome Data for Four Groups of Subjects in IBTA Treatment Experiment.*

trast between the Orange County and Patton patient populations and the services appropriate to these respective groups.

To this end, the Orange County program was almost totally restricted to outpatient services; the treatment program at Patton was for inpatients. Orange County could operate on this basis because it had no identifiable Skid Row and the average annual income of its residents was among the highest for all counties in California. Similarly, many of the patients served by the program tended to be less advanced in their drinking problems, often not yet having experienced physical dependence on alcohol. Besides being less deteriorated physically than the Patton inpatients, the Orange County patients also tended to be more intact socially and economically. This more diverse population quite naturally required a broader range of services than the typical state hospital patient; this provided a stimulus at Orange County for development of more comprehensive approaches to a broad range of alcohol problems.

We are convinced that dealing with alcohol problems on an outpatient basis is compatible with a treatment orientation emphasizing a behavioral view of drinking problems. Further, the outpatient context makes it possible to identify real-life events that induce drinking as they actually occur, rather than having to depend on retrospective analyses. Further, in an outpatient setting patients can monitor—and report on—all their drinking.

Drinking by the patients is a likely event during treatment. The therapist can respond to it in a variety of ways. Unfortunately, an all too common response of alcoholism treatment personnel to such events is the intentional or unintentional punishment of the patient. Although empirical studies have not been performed to investigate systematically how such responses influence the course of treatment, we believe that punishing patients when they mention drinking instances (by issuing prophesies of impending doom or chiding them for not having acted differently) likely causes the patient to omit mention of such instances in the future. Although we lack empirical evidence for this belief, let us suppose for the moment that it is valid. How then should one react to the mention of a drinking experience? From the behavioral point of view, the therapist can be certain of one thing: the circumstances surrounding the drinking instance, its antecedents and its consequences, are likely to provide valuable information regarding environmental influences on that individual's drinking. We suggest, therefore, that mention of such events by patients should be neither punished nor ignored by therapists, but should be used for the valuable information they provide. This is not to say that patients should be encouraged to have unplanned drinking experiences but merely that therapists should encourage the patients to report accurately whatever drinking does occur during treatment.

In this regard, we have given drinking logs to patients in treatment for the past few years (267). The technique is very simple. The patient is asked to monitor and record his own daily alcohol consumption and the circumstances associated with it. The use of such logs encourages the patient to analyze the specific behavioral pattern of his drinking. It compels him to be constantly aware of that drinking and, we hope, to learn to be aware of situations which might lead to damaging drinking. A second value of the self-feedback provided by these logs is that they legitimize and so encourage discussion of situations in which drinking has occurred. Finally, the use of the logs can also facilitate early treatment intervention by immediately signaling the onset of heavy drinking.

Although use of drinking logs might appear deceptively uncomplicated, in practice they must be skillfully integrated into an overall treatment plan. We found the following guidelines helpful: Should drinking be reported, it is important first to reinforce the patient for accurately recording that drinking. The drinking should then be analyzed in terms of the consequences it incurred or could have incurred. Simply because individuals are being treated for alcohol problems, there is no reason to assume they will readily recognize the long-term consequences of their drinking. Instead, this association can be made clear by making such a functional analysis of drinking an explicit part of the treatment regimen (280).

A few examples illustrate some of the other lessons learned from 3 years of experience with an outpatient program. When public alcoholism treatment services were first made available in Orange County, the clinical judgment of the medical and treatment staff served as the only basis for determining whether a patient had a positive blood alcohol concentration (BAC) at any given time. In this regard our clinic operated no differently from most programs throughout the country: We recorded some vital signs (e.g., blood pressure); attended to clients' breath, speech and gait; and then formulated our treatment decisions based on these inadequate data. Basing decisions of immediate importance such as those involving medical management of alcohol withdrawal on clinical judgment alone seemed to be a weak procedure, especially since a large number of our patients had clearly acquired a tolerance for alcohol. Research on available apparatus quickly made it clear that reliance on clinical judgment was largely unnecessary. For a rather modest sum, we purchased a gas chromatography breath analyzer capable of performing rapid breath analyses of the concentration in blood of ethyl and other alcohols. A study describing the routine use of this instrument (95) summarizes our successful use of outpatient medical management procedures to detoxify our patients. A major component of these procedures involved relating the patients' behavior with their actual BACs, thus allowing a rough estimate of when serious withdrawal symptoms might occur. This estimate was also valuable in deciding if a patient could be safely detoxified on an outpatient basis. This type of breath analysis was also evaluated for use in therapy, and we found a portable breath screening test to be useful in outpatient treatment (276).

Other assessment and treatment procedures based on experimentally derived principles of learning and behavior, although not yet empirically validated, nevertheless appear promising. For example, most treatment programs, including those with a strong behavioral orientation, program a specific time for termination of treatment. Those familiar with shaping principles recognize that such a procedure makes being in treatment highly discriminable from nontreatment for the patient. As a consequence, we favor the systematic application of shaping principles to effect termination of treatment. That is, rather than abrupt termination, appointments are spaced further and further apart as long as the patient continues to function satisfactorily during the lengthening intervals. This allows us to check that the patient's environment is supporting the behavioral changes which occurred during treatment as well as enabling early intervention if such is not the case. Although such procedures may be unnecessary, they do constitute an effective form of aftercare. As before, this is a case where speculation abounds and only empirical testing will ultimately be decisive.

CONCLUSION

The term "behavioral" was purposely excluded from the title of this chapter in favor of the phrase "empirically derived." That substitution was made because one cannot be so certain of the value of the behavioral approach as to exclude from consideration the role of biological, genetic and sociocultural factors in alcohol problems. However, knowledge of experimentally derived principles of behavior and the application of those principles to human behavior in naturalistic settings is clearly of value in understanding the evolution of alcohol problems as well as developing appropriate treatment strategies for them. Whatever the "true" etiology, those problems, once established, typically involve biological and sociocultural as well as behavioral components. Accordingly, although knowledge of behavioral principles is helpful in dealing with alcohol problems, one also needs to be knowledgeable about biological and sociocultural factors as they relate to these problems.

Finally, it is important that a sophisticated application of behavioral principles to alcohol problems be distinguished from a simple-minded conception which deals simply with drinking responses, rewards and punishments. To apply a behavioral approach effectively to the treatment of drinking problems, one should have a firm grounding in experimental psychology, sufficient to ensure familiarity with phenomena such as scheduling effects, shaping, discrimination learning, variables affecting instrumental and classic conditioning, and so on. Furthermore, because each patient has a unique learning history, it makes behavioral sense that interventions be tailored as much as possible to the individual's unique drinking history. A sound experimental grounding can aid in choosing among alternative treatment strategies as well as recognizing unintended deleterious long-term consequences of treatment.

Throughout this chapter I attempted to show that the conduct of behavioral research in alcohol studies involves much more than first meets the eye. Furthermore, as in most behavioral research, benefits that have accrued to date do not derive simply from the application of behavioral analysis but also from the empirical scientific method, which continues to be a keystone of behavioral research. A commitment to empirical investigation guarantees a dynamic, flexible approach to our consideration of alcohol problems. Likewise, such an orientation can be expected to increase our knowledge continually about the nature of alcohol problems and thus result in the development of more effective and efficient treatment methods.

11

Critique of Alcoholism Treatment Evaluation

Linda C. Sobell

THROUGHOUT HISTORY, scientific fact and theory have ultimately taken precedence over traditional beliefs, especially those lacking a strong evidential base. However, the emergence of empirically based views has often encountered strong resistance from the general populace as well as men of science. Kuhn (159) suggests that such skepticism and intolerance exist because the evolution of a new theory is "seldom or never just an increment to what is already known. Its assimilation requires the reconstruction of prior theory and the re-evaluation of prior fact, an intrinsically revolutionary process that is seldom completed by a single man and never overnight" (159, *p.* 7).

A well-known example of resistance to empirical findings is the scientific controversy that surrounded the theory of evolution. Over a century ago men such as Charles Darwin and Thomas Huxley found themselves in the vortex of a raging scientific revolution because of evidence they offered regarding man's place in nature. When the data were first presented, such tremendous furor was raised by the general public that Thomas Huxley felt compelled to address the reaction in the following way:

"Science has fulfilled her function when she has ascertained and enunciated truth, and were these pages addressed to men of science only, I should now close this Essay, knowing that my colleagues have learned to respect nothing but evidence, and to believe that their highest duty lies in submitting to it, however it may jar against their inclinations.

"But, desiring as I do, to reach the wider circle of the intelligent public, it would be unworthy cowardice were I to ignore the repugnance with which the majority of my readers are likely to meet the conclusion to which the most careful and conscientious study I have been able to give the matter, has led me" (266, *pp.* 372–373).

Interestingly, this quotation in many ways reflects the prevailing state of the alcoholism field. For example, a new paradigm recently emerged which not only challenges traditional concepts but threatens their extirpation. This paradigm consists of several new concepts of alcohol dependence (e.g., viewing drinking problems as lying along a continuum rather than as a single entity—"alcoholism"; multivariant treatment strategies; individualized treatment goals; challenges to the notions of loss of control and irreversibility; new ways of evaluating treatment outcome). Many existing traditional beliefs in the alcoholism field lack supporting evidence (236). Moreover, some have been directly contradicted by empirical research. Interestingly, most challenges to traditional concepts have arisen during the last 5–10 years. One of the reasons for the sudden, radical proliferation of inquiry and evidence in this field is the departure of alcoholism from the legal arena and its subsequent recognition by the medical community as a treatable illness (3). Prior to that recognition, only a handful of physicians, scientists and other professionals were involved in the alcoholism field. Thus until the last decade scientific and professional involvement in this area was scarce. Of course the scientific community's entry into the field has been accompanied by an emphasis on research and empirically based findings.

Traditional ideas about the nature of alcoholism have in large part dictated that certain criteria be used in evaluating treatment outcome. This chapter addresses the fact that radical departures from tradition have now affected the evaluation of alcoholism treatment outcome, and it explores the types of outcome evaluation needed to be consistent with recent evidence.

HISTORICAL OVERVIEW

One of the most important yet neglected research areas of relevance to alcoholism is evaluation of treatment outcome. This is not to suggest, however, that the general topic has been ignored by alcohol researchers. In fact, four excellent reviews have addressed the lack of adequate treatment evaluation measures and techniques in the alcoholism field. The first of these, published in 1942 by Voegtlin and Lemere (292), evaluated more than 100 alcoholism treatment outcome studies published between 1909 and 1940. Originally the authors had not intended their review to be an assessment of evaluation procedures but rather a survey of the literature so they could "compare our [their] results with those obtained by diverse methods of therapy" (292, *p. 717*). Much to their surprise, the intended comparison was rendered virtually impossible because the studies they reviewed reported a paucity of statistical data. From their analyses Voegtlin and Lemere concluded that English-speaking professionals seemed reluctant to report statistics on the efficacy of their treatment. This absence of outcome data was not restricted to psychological treatment methods but included somatic and chemical approaches as well. Another major problem noted by these authors was the lack of "a uniform criterion of cure." In this regard, they found no consistent criteria which specified either the goals or the desired outcome of therapy. In summary, until 1940 it was very difficult to evaluate the various treatment approaches with alcoholics because of a dearth of available data.

In 1967, 25 years after Voegtlin and Lemere's review, Hill and Blane (132) surveyed 49 studies, published from 1952 through 1963, that evaluated psychotherapy with alcoholics. These studies were evaluated along two specific dimensions: (*1*) methodological standards for conducting such investigations; and (*2*) reporting standards for publishing such studies. The survey's findings were extremely disappointing: Few of the studies reviewed reported their findings in ways that permitted unambiguous conclusions. As a result, Hill and Blane concluded that these studies, individually and collectively, "fail to live up to their potential for contributing to knowledge in the field because of a failure to meet many methodological requirements for the conduct of evaluative research" (132, *p. 104*). Contrasting their findings with Voegtlin and Lemere's, Hill and Blane reported that "any 'apparent reticence' in presentation of statistical data is gone. . . . We can still agree with Voegtlin and Lemere, however, that 'we are unable to form any conclusive opinion as to the value of psychotherapeutic methods in the treatment of alcoholism' " (132, *p. 76*).

In 1970 Miller et al. (197) evaluated 34 representative alcoholism treatment studies using 12 types of sampling bias. They noted that a large proportion of the studies evinced a serious lack of attention to the numerous sources of sampling bias, either by ignoring or failing to report on types of case loss; they concluded that sampling problems are particularly evident in evaluating alcoholism treatment studies. As a consequence, these authors believe that "if a study is incompletely or misleadingly reported, its implications are of little value" (197, *p. 104*).

Crawford et al. (72) prepared the most critical review of alcoholism treatment evaluation to date. In their review of 40 articles published from 1968 through 1971, each designed to evaluate a particular psychological treatment approach with problem drinkers and alcoholics, the authors analyzed each study along several relevant methodological dimensions. Their analysis revealed that the majority of the 40 studies contained enough methodological inadequacies to "cast doubt on the integrity of the reported results. The concomitant presence of a set of such inadequacies calls to question whether perhaps half or more of these studies should have been undertaken, let alone reported" (72, *p. 26*). In other words, even though more than 30 years have passed since Voegtlin and Lemere's report first appeared, Crawford and his colleagues paint a picture of the current state of the art of alcoholism treatment evaluation that is at least as dismal as it was 30 years ago.

Given these critiques of alcoholism treatment evaluation, one might surmise that no methodological progress has occurred during the last 30–40 years. Crawford and his colleagues share this concern: "The problem is not that the field lacks an occasional investigation adequately coping with one or more aspects of evaluation problems, but rather that the median level of effort remains at such a relatively unsophisticated level that it is probably both scientifically and practically unproductive" (72, *p. 30*). The reviews, evaluating more than 200 articles spanning a period of 63 years, cast serious doubt on the value of most published studies of alcoholism treatment effectiveness. Since one must also recognize that these reviews evaluated only published treatment studies, it is certain that many more treatment "studies" failed to reach the stage of a published report.

In other health and mental health care programs treatment evaluation also met with similar subtle resistance and is characterized by comparable unsophistication (318, 319). Although reasons for such resistance are plentiful, they often lack plausibility. For instance, it is frequently argued that since evaluation is costly, it is a diversion of human resources from direct clinical services. Another source of resistance springs from the professional treatment providers. This resistance is multifaceted and stems from: (*1*) an attitude that the sacrosanct therapeutic setting is too delicate and sensitive for the probings of the indifferent researcher; (*2*) fears of unjust or negative criticism of existing therapeutic activities; (*3*) confidentiality and ethical concerns associated with the collection of information on patients; and (*4*) beliefs that evaluations are political in origin rather than part of a scientific venture (319). Finally, even though evaluation data can lead to systematic modification of treatment programs, Zusman and Bissonette caution that "with all other obstacles removed, availability of research data will lag behind the exigencies of decision-making" (319, *p. 123*). Thus immediate program change cannot be a direct consequence of a treatment evaluation project.

In the alcoholism field in particular, treatment evaluation has been a peripheral program element in all but research-oriented treatment programs. In a field where treatment success is poor and difficult to interpret (72, 132), it is hard to understand why there is such strong resistance to treatment evaluation. Furthermore, along with resistance by service providers, treatment evaluation with alcoholics has been difficult to implement because of the following special problems: (*1*) alcoholics are purported to lie about their drinking (132, 177, 268); (*2*) they are very difficult to locate for follow-up (72, 132, 197); and (*3*) appropriate follow-up procedures and treatment measures with which to evaluate alcoholism treatment programs are scarce (275).

EMERGENCE OF CURRENT TECHNIQUES AND MEASURES

The development of more adequate evaluation techniques and measures can be attributed in large part to two major influences: (*1*) the recent development and evaluation of an alternative treatment goal to abstinence—controlled drinking; and (*2*) examination and evaluation of the shortcomings of traditional concepts of alcohol dependence.

Traditional concepts of alcohol dependence convey specific implications for treatment goals and for ways of measuring treatment outcome. For example, since these concepts usually portray an alcoholic as unable to control his drinking, the drinking behavior of a treated alcoholic on follow-up must be dichotomously portrayed as abstinent or drunk. As a consequence, this nearly universal dichotomous representation of drinking behavior typically characterizes the nature of follow-up data in most alcoholism treatment outcome studies (72, 132, 275). Furthermore, treatment programs have generally chosen but one goal—abstinence (275). In other words, a necessary corollary of abstinence as the sole treatment goal is the concordant selection of abstinence as the sole criterion of therapeutic success.

Recently abstinence as the only criterion for successful treatment has been questioned by several investigators (47, 72, 132, 233, 234,

235, 275) on the following grounds: (*1*) It excludes the possibility of partial improvements. (*2*) Abstinence has not been consistently related to marked improvements in other areas of life functioning. (*3*) Changes in or cessations of drinking behavior are not easily measured because there are no readily available ways to validate this measure. (*4*) Drinking is a multifaceted behavior; to use a single dichotomous index (sober or drunk) to reflect drinking behavior prohibits evaluation of multiple components of drinking patterns and the relationship of drinking behavior to other outcome variables.

The drunk–abstinent representation of drinking behavior is often accepted uncritically as axiomatic. For example, many studies do not define what is meant by "drunk" except by using other nonprecise labels such as "heavy drinking," "occasional slips," "improved drinking" or "relapses" (150, 296, 298). It is thus an obvious and disturbing conclusion that a highly neglected area of alcoholism treatment evaluation concerns the readily observable and quantifiable behavior of drinking alcohol.

A recent review of the alcoholism treatment literature revealed a large body of data which until recently has been neglected by many researchers and clinicians (236). This literature consists of 74 studies reporting that some former identified alcoholics were successfully practicing "controlled drinking," also referred to as "social," "limited," "moderate," "nonproblem" and sometimes "normal" drinking. This chapter does not deal with those studies. That such a voluminous literature does exist, however, is germane to the present discussion in that it suggests that drinking outcomes demonstrating various degrees of "control" over drinking are a consistent finding in many well-designed alcoholism treatment evaluation studies.

PROTOTYPE FOR TREATMENT EVALUATION

The remainder of this chapter focuses on a suggested prototype for adequate treatment evaluation research in the alcoholism field. A summary of the prototype of suggested evaluation measures and procedures appears in Chart 1.

Pretreatment Measures

In order to measure and interpret treatment outcome data adequately, it is necessary to collect baseline or pretreatment measures. These measures are indicators of the patient's behavior prior to entering a treatment program. Pretreatment baseline measures provide

CHART 1.—*Prototype for Alcoholism Treatment Evaluation*

PRETREATMENT MEASURES

1. *Baseline (pretreatment) measures* are needed in order to measure and interpret treatment outcome data adequately.
2. *Measurement before and after treatment* should cover the same time interval and be designed for comparability.
3. *Follow-up tracking data:* information necessary for contacting and following subjects and their respective collaterals over a long period should be obtained prior to the subjects' discharge from a treatment program.
4. *Evaluation should be planned* prior to the actual treatment stage rather than being a retrospective venture.

TREATMENT EVALUATION MEASURES

5. *Adequate definition* of criterion variables.
6. *Measures* should be continuous and quantifiable (i.e., number of work days missed rather than majority of the interval employed).
7. *Multiple measures of treatment outcome* should be used (drinking behavior as well as other measures of life–health functioning).
8. *Data* should be presented for individual subjects as well as groups.
9. *Predictors of treatment outcome* should be developed for different treatment modalities and service providers.
10. *In-field breath tests* should be used to verify drinking behavior.

FOLLOW-UP PROCEDURES

11. *Subjects should be briefed prior to discharge* about the nature of the follow-up to be conducted—reasons for; type, frequency and duration of interviews; type of questions asked; and how the information will be used.
12. *Follow-up intervals* for all subjects should be equal.
13. *Frequent follow-up contacts* are desirable. Such contacts can gather sensitive outcome data and ensure a high follow-up rate.
14. *Multiple collateral information sources* should be used to verify self-reports.
15. *Record data* should be used to verify all quantifiable self-reports (i.e., incarcerations, days of work missed).
16. *Data from different sources* should not be combined (i.e., combining subject data with collateral data).
17. *Interviewers* should be trained in skillful interviewing techniques.

for comparative evaluation of individual change. Measurement before and after treatment should cover equal time intervals and be designed for comparability of measures. Thus if there is a 2-year follow-up interval, pretreatment measures should cover the 2-year interval prior to the onset of treatment. Questions used in follow-up interviews should also be included among pretreatment measures.

One requisite condition to treatment evaluation is planning for the evaluation prior to implementing the actual treatment program. If the evaluation is a planned rather than a retrospective venture, the difficulty in locating and tracking subjects for follow-up can be minimized by obtaining careful follow-up tracking data prior to the subjects' discharge from treatment. Follow-up tracking data consist of information (addresses, phone numbers, places of employment, residences, etc.) needed to contact and follow subjects and their respective collaterals over an extended period. This information should be gathered at the same time pretreatment measures are obtained.

Treatment Evaluation Measures

A multivariant approach to the treatment of alcoholics has recently received increasing attention (106, 233, 236, 299, 300).[1] Such an orientation emphasizes the importance of deciding prior to treatment the services most appropriate for the individual. Unfortunately, at the present time, predictors of treatment outcome are severely lacking in this field. Thus in order to know which methods work best with which patients, it is important to be able to assess individual subject change. Furthermore, it is unfortunate that most studies in the alcoholism treatment literature summarize treatment evaluation results in terms of descriptive summaries of group data. Moreover, few studies report pre- and posttreatment drinking and other behavioral data, thereby precluding a presentation of true individual change. The value of pre- and posttreatment individual subject data lies in the ability to portray each subject's change in functioning more completely with respect to a particular component of treatment.

Changes in drinking behavior do not necessarily indicate that an individual has thereby improved his life functioning in other re-

---

[1] Also, WANBERG, K. W., HORN, J. L. and FOSTER, F. M. A differential assessment model for alcoholism; the scales of the alcohol use questionnaire. J. Stud. Alc. 38: 512-543, 1977.

spects (22, 89, 104, 235), although these variables are often highly correlated, especially when group data are considered. Although attainment of total abstinence often yields improvement in other areas of life, Pattison[2] and his colleagues (232, 233, 235) presented and reviewed empirical and clinical data demonstrating that abstinent alcoholics may not exhibit positive changes in other areas of life functioning and may in fact experience marked behavioral deterioration. Thus it is important that treatment programs elicit multiple measures of treatment evaluation. Unfortunately, few have yet done so.

As mentioned earlier, reports of drinking behavior are often seen as extremely difficult to quantify and validate. Typically, drinking behavior is assessed dichotomously—the individual is either abstinent (no alcohol ingested) or drunk (varying amounts of alcohol ingested). One suggested alternative dependent variable measure for evaluating drinking behavior is daily drinking disposition. To employ such a measure, data on specific quantities and types of alcoholic beverage consumed are gathered each day of the followup interval. To minimize the demand characteristics of this paradigm, subjects are not told how the investigators plan to encode drinking behavior data. One way to summarize daily drinking disposition outcome data is to code it into five exclusive categories: (1) abstinent days (no alcohol ingested); (2) nonproblem drinking days (the specific definition of such drinking is currently unresolved); (3) drunk days (consumption of any amount exceeding the agreed-on definition of nonproblem drinking); (4) incarcerated days—jail (alcohol-related arrests); and (5) incarcerated days—hospital (hospitalized for an alcohol-related health problem, usually detoxication). To date, only the Sobells (272, 273, 274, 278) have reported daily drinking disposition data. Choice of daily drinking dispositions as the evaluation format in their study represented an attempt to develop a more sensitive quantifiable evaluation measure of drinking behavior. Another reason was to evaluate the nontraditional treatment goal of controlled drinking. Clearly, the traditional evaluation format of drunk–abstinent could not have reflected varying degrees of control over drinking.

Although daily drinking disposition data can provide more sensitive and valid measures of drinking behavior than the traditional

---

[2] PATTISON, E. M. Rationale and classification of alcoholism treatment drinking outcomes. Presented at the 1st International Medical Conference on Alcoholism, 1973.

formats of "abstinent–drunk" or "improved, same, or worse," the only available verifiable indicant of an individual's blood alcohol concentration (BAC) is a blood, breath or urine test. Recently, in-field breath testers have been used on a probe-day basis to assess drinking (213, 276).

Like drinking behavior, most other evaluation measures of life functioning have been poorly defined. Measures such as vocational, health, and interpersonal relationship status, for example, have been addressed using vague evaluative criteria such as "improved, same, or worse." Clearly, all treatment outcome measures must be adequately and unambiguously defined. Furthermore, all measures of treatment outcome should be continuous and quantifiable (e.g., "number of days missed from work" is preferred to "majority of the interval employed"). To this end, Hunt and Azrin (136) evaluated treatment outcome with alcoholics using percentage of time subjects were employed and percentage of time subjects were away from home as outcome measures. Such continuous, quantifiable parameters are preferable to probe-day measures (data are reported for a randomly selected day of the follow-up interval) or majority disposition measures (data are reported for outcome, which represents a simple majority of the follow-up interval) because they more adequately reflect behavior throughout the entire follow-up interval. However, in this regard a caveat is in order: The use of more sensitive outcome measures might make it necessary to follow subjects more frequently than has been the case in the past (278).[3]

Finally, a broader range of measures to deal with critical areas of life functioning still needs to be developed, refined and evaluated. These areas include daily drinking behavior; vocational assessment (number of days employed, type of employment, number of days missed work, amount of money earned); physical health (liver dysfunction and other types of physical impairment or problems resulting from drinking alcohol); time incarcerated as a result of alcohol use (jail and hospital); use of therapeutic supports after a treatment program; residential status and stability (how long one has lived at a residence, the type of residential facility, time spent away from home); social and familial adjustments (time spent with spouse and children or other relatives, types of social and recreational activities

---

[3] Also, SOBELL, L. C. and SOBELL, M. B. Frequent follow-up interviews as a dual process; data gathering and "continued care." Presented at the Southeastern Psychological Association meeting, Atlanta, March 1975.

engaged in); legal problems resulting from alcohol use (incarcerations, divorce, loss of driver's license); financial (losses as a result of excessive drinking, gains as a result of not misusing alcohol).

Follow-Up Procedures

It is patent that the usefulness of all treatment evaluation is highly dependent on the success of the search (follow-up) procedures used. Typically, studies in the alcoholism literature report complete outcome data for only 30–75% of all subjects in a study (72, 132, 197). What of the 25–70% of subjects not found? Are they functioning better or worse than those subjects who were located? Although arguments have been advanced favoring each position, recent evidence[3,4] suggests that unless outcome data are gathered for a large proportion of subjects in a given study, the results might be biased in a positive direction.

In a treatment follow-up study conducted at Eagleville (Pennsylvania) State Hospital,[4] researchers obtained some level of information for 81% (407) of all subjects. Unsatisfied with this retrieval rate, the investigators then implemented a second follow-up to obtain a more complete sample. This second effort located an additional 10% of the subjects for whom no data had previously been collected; hardly any of these patients were doing well. Bowen and Androes (34) draw similar conclusions. Recent data reported by Sobell and Sobell (278) also suggest that subjects who are difficult to locate are typically functioning less well than subjects found on initial contact. Of the 69 subjects found in the study 5 were extremely difficult to locate for follow-up. Final data on these subjects were collected long after their designated follow-up intervals had expired. Two of the 5 were found to be functioning worse than all other subjects in their respective treatment groups during the second year of follow-up, 2 functioned considerably below their respective group averages, and the remaining subject functioned slightly below his group average. This kind of evidence stands in direct contradiction to investigators who use the criterion of "no news is good news" as evidence of successful posttreatment adjustment (151, *p. 108*).

As noted above, an adequate assessment of any treatment pro-

[4] BARR, H. L., ROSEN, A., ANTES, D. E. and OTTENBERG, D. J. Two year follow-up study of 724 drug and alcohol addicts treated together in an abstinence therapeutic community. Presented at the 81st American Psychological Association meeting, Montreal, August 1973.

gram requires that data be gathered on a sufficiently representative sample of treated patients evaluated for postdischarge functioning. Yet many investigators, including Rhodes and Hudson (244), experienced extreme difficulty locating and then maintaining contact with subjects for an extended period. This difficulty is reflected in a low percentage of subjects for whom outcome data are reported. By contrast, Pittman and Tate (238) report follow-up (median interval was 12.9 months) data on 94.8% of all subjects, and Sobell and Sobell (278) report a follow-up rate of 98.6% (69 of 70 subjects) during a 2-year follow-up period. Unfortunately, the number of published studies with retrieval rates greater than 90% is extremely limited even though, as Pittman and Tate suggest, "considerable skepticism should be attached to any follow-up study with a retrieval rate of less than 90 percent" (238, *p. 185*).

Anyone having experience with alcoholics knows that tracking subjects and their collaterals to collect adequate follow-up data often seems like an impossible task. In this regard, Hill and Blane (132) attribute low follow-up rates to faulty follow-up techniques, which often stem from a lack of personnel or funds or simply "on the widely held conviction that alcoholics are more difficult to follow than other groups" (132, *p. 94*). Realistically, follow-up on all subjects takes time and persistence. However, if a certain amount of planning takes place before subjects are discharged from treatment, the chances of locating them—and their being cooperative with interviewers—can be increased. First, it is advisable to brief subjects on the reasons for the follow-up and the nature of the contacts to be made—how and when they can expect to be contacted, the kinds of questions they can expect to be asked, and how this information will be used. Further, to assure that a minimum number of subjects are lost to follow-up, as many collateral sources of information (friends, relatives, employers who might have knowledge of the subject's whereabouts and functioning) as possible are secured prior to the subject's discharge. In other words, if care and caution are exercised prior to a subject's discharge, more complete and reliable follow-up results are ensured (57, 272, 273, 274, 278).

Another reason why many subjects are lost to follow-up may well be a direct function of certain follow-up procedures themselves. Thus maintaining continuity of contact with subjects in a longitudinal study requires that: (1) the evaluation component be planned prior to the actual treatment stage rather than as a retrospective venture; and (2) periodic application of search techniques be used. In most studies follow-up contacts are typically impersonal, of limited duration and programmed months or years after subjects were first discharged from treatment programs. Prior to an initial follow-up contact, the subjects have little reason to keep in touch with the investigators or to monitor their own level of functioning. The method of follow-up predominant in the alcoholism field is a "shotgun" type follow-up contact, in which subjects are sought for follow-up at the end of predetermined posttreatment intervals, ranging anywhere from 6 months to 5 years (78, 105, 226, 235). As a consequence, when subjects are finally contacted, comprehensive information regarding the entire preceding interval must be obtained. This involves asking subjects about events that happened over a span of as much as 1800 days. Such an inordinate interval between discharge and follow-up has several obvious disadvantages, including (1) difficulty in locating subjects; (2) subjects' memory deficits due to the long time interval; (3) omission by the subject of events that occurred at such an early date in the follow-up interval they are perceived as no longer relevant; and (4) the opportunity for selective reporting by subjects who want to represent themselves in a "good light" and therefore report information not representative of the entire follow-up interval.

As an alternative to "shotgun" follow-up contacts Sobell and Sobell developed a follow-up procedure which required that frequent contact with subjects and their collaterals be maintained. Before describing the use and implications of these follow-up contacts, it is of interest why they were developed. Briefly, a study described in detail elsewhere (272, 273, 274, 278) was conducted at Patton State Hospital in which 70 men, all of whom had been voluntarily admitted to the hospital for treatment of alcoholism, served as subjects. Thirty-five were treated by the method of individualized behavior therapy, and the remaining 35 subjects received conventional state hospital treatment. Since some of the subjects in the experimental group had a treatment goal of controlled drinking, it was necessary to develop the more sensitive evaluation measures of drinking behavior discussed above, termed daily drinking dispositions. Using this more detailed measure, in turn, required that subjects could accurately recall the amount of drinking they had engaged in over a 6-month interval. Accordingly, in the effort to help all subjects recall events more accurately, a 3- to 4-week follow-up interval was selected. Follow-up contacts as frequent as these may also have aided in the successful tracking of these subjects as complete follow-up data were obtained on 69 of the 70 subjects (98.6%).

The initial rationale for the frequent follow-up contacts was to maximize the opportunity to gather precise and valid data. However, early during the follow-up period it became apparent that these frequent contacts not only permitted reliable data collection but also seemed to represent important "continuing care" for many subjects. In an effort to document the therapeutic effects of these follow-up contacts systematically, subjects in the study were interviewed at the end of their 2-year follow-up interval to elicit their reactions to the intensive follow-up.[3] Data from these interviews suggest that the frequent, continued follow-up contacts were perceived by the majority of subjects, both experimental and control, as beneficial and desirable. The authors conclude that such frequent follow-up contacts have several advantages over one-time follow-up contacts: (1) They provide extremely low-cost continuing care after formal treatment which may reduce the likelihood of recidivism. (2) Follow-up as a continuing care process may help consolidate gains first made in the treatment program. (3) Frequent contacts aid significantly in tracking subjects. (4) Such contacts may provide for increasingly valid self-reports by subjects because of the rapport and mutual trust that develops between the interviewer and the subject.

Two additional methodological problems concerning treatment evaluation are the necessity at times to combine data from various sources and the need to have equal follow-up intervals across subjects. When subjects are not located for follow-up, data from other sources—collaterals, records, or both—are frequently combined with or substituted for subject data. A preferred procedure would be to present data derived from different sources separately. Concerning the second problem, in order to compare treatment effects across subjects systematically, it is important that follow-up data be reported for equal time intervals.

A final concern is the validity and reliability of subjects' self-reports. Most of the descriptive, comparative and evaluative data published about alcoholics are taken from self-reports (11, 106, 278).[4] These data are frequently the basis for diagnoses as well as treatment decisions and evaluations. Unfortunately, despite the frequent and extensive use of self-reports in the alcoholism field, only a few studies have actually investigated the reliability and validity of such reports (82, 119, 120, 268, 279, 284). In this regard, it is curious that for years drinking behavior has been evaluated almost solely via self-reports, yet it has been only with the recent emergence of nontraditional treatment goals (controlled drinking) that the reliability and validity of data thus obtained have been seriously examined.

Regardless of the outcome measures used, self-reports by subjects and their collaterals have been and will probably continue to be the major source of data on drinking behavior and adjunctive measures of outcome. Given the alcoholism field's overwhelming dependence on retrospective self-reports, it is surprising that a major study systematically investigating their reliability and validity has not been reported. As a result, when self-reported data are presented it is often with the implication that they are underreported. This kind of directional bias could be tolerated if evidence existed to support such an assumption. Unfortunately, such data do not exist. Interestingly, the existing limited evidence on the reliability and validity of self-reports suggests that they are surprisingly accurate and acceptable for use as outcome data, at least concerning alcohol-related events corroborated by official record information and collateral interviews (268, 279).

Self-reports of alcoholics can be investigated for their validity and reliability in the following ways: (1) Multiple collateral sources of information (friends, relatives, employers, neighbors) can be interviewed; although this kind of validation can serve to increase confidence in treatment outcome results, many studies do not employ collateral sources of information (34, 93, 288); (2) Daily drinking can, in part, be verified on a probe-day basis by obtaining unannounced in-field breath samples of subjects' BACs (213, 276); and (3) Official records (i.e., jail, hospital, welfare, driver records) can be used to corroborate subjects' self-reports (272, 273, 274, 278). Recently, in fact, it was found that driver records in the United States and Canada are relatively easy to obtain and can be used to (1) locate subjects in follow-up studies; (2) provide objective information regarding treatment outcome; and (3) verify subjects' self-reports of motor vehicle violations (269).

FUTURE DIRECTIONS

With the inception of controlled drinking treatment goals, the validity of self-reports of drinking behavior has come under scrutiny for the first time. At the same time, issues concerning interview reactivity—experimenter bias and subject demand characteristics (177, 223)—also occasion concern. It is unfortunate that procedures for ensuring the validity of self-reports and the objectivity of interview situations have not evolved during the past 40 years; these problems burden traditional abstinence-oriented treatment programs, as well as newer treatment approaches. On the issue of interview reactivity, even conscientious experimenters unequivocally subtly and unintentionally bias their results. In fact, several investigators (15, 16, 263) recently questioned whether subtle experimenter effects occur at all. However, since no resolution of experimenter effects is imminent, the following could attenuate their possible effects: (1) use of multiple corroborating sources of information for each subject; (2) an explicit effort by experimenters to obtain objective data; (3) use of interviewers who are skilled in interviewing techniques; (4) consistent checking of public records (hospitals, jails, employers, vital statistics, etc.); and (5) ensuring that subjects are unaware of the coding categories associated with treatment outcome measures.

Attention should also be given to follow-up procedures designed to minimize the possibility of experimenter effects. In this regard, it is desirable for the interviewer to be naive about a study's experimental intent, as well as about subjects' assigned treatment groups. It is not unreasonable to assume, however, that a sophisticated observer in an experiment becomes aware of the experimental hypotheses, even though not explicitly informed of the intent (20). Furthermore, when the experimental treatments are clearly different (i.e., electromyographic biofeedback versus transcendental meditation versus conventional state hospital treatment) and frequent follow-up contacts are made with both subjects and collaterals, predictable differences among subjects would surely become apparent to relatively sophisticated observers during a few interviews. A second, costly approach to this problem is to use a series of interviewers whereby an interviewer talks with a subject only once. There are, however, two disadvantages to using either naive or one-time interviewers: (1) Establishing and maintaining rapport with subjects and their collaterals are important; interviewer-subject rapport almost certainly increases the validity of self-reported data; and (2) maintaining contact with all subjects and collaterals throughout an extended follow-up period is essential.

A final, most perplexing issue vis-à-vis evaluation of treatment outcome data is that, even if a wealth of adequate treatment outcome measures existed, it is uncertain that anyone would know how to interpret the resultant data appropriately. For example, does changed marital status (i.e., from married to divorced) reflect increased success or failure in life? Does one pattern of drinking more closely approximate "normal drinking" than another? In this regard, it becomes difficult to draw other than arbitrary and conservative inferences as few population norms have been reported. Does continued use of therapeutic supports after treatment indicate successful or unsuccessful functioning (273, 278)? Clearly, further research is needed to determine the meaning of these variables and their relationship to treatment outcome.

CONCLUSIONS

Like the other four reviews of treatment evaluation studies cited above, this review of the "state of the evaluation art" has identified problem areas that continue to plague all evaluations of alcoholism treatment. In an effort to confront some of these problems, a suggested prototype for more adequate treatment evaluations was presented. Quite obviously alcoholism treatment evaluation remains in its infancy.

Throughout this chapter the development of more adequate treatment evaluation measures and techniques was attributed in part to recent consideration of an alternative treatment goal to abstinence. At this juncture we are reminded that during the last 30 years of alcohol treatment, evaluation has either not existed or been so unsophisticated that most of the treatment research efforts are not interpretable. In this regard treatment outcome evaluation must be undertaken by all investigators in the alcoholism field, whether their treatment goals involve controlled drinking or abstinence. If evaluations and critiques are to be sound, they should be applied equally to all alcoholism treatment studies.

Lastly, although treatment evaluation can provide information to improve treatment approaches and their outcome rates, it must also be recognized that major errors in the design of treatment evaluation, the collection of outcome data, the interpretation of that data, or all of these can destroy good programs and perpetuate bad ones. Treatment evaluation, an extremely important instrument for social good, nonetheless may do more harm than good if used carelessly.

12

Behavioral Approaches to Alcoholism: A Look to the Future

G. Alan Marlatt

THIS BOOK PROVIDES an overview of the "state of the art" of behavioral approaches to the assessment and treatment of alcoholism. A wealth of material has been covered in this survey, much of it deriving from experimental work undertaken during the past 10 years. It seems fitting at this point to pause and reflect a bit on current developments in the field and to speculate about possible directions for future work. From where have we come and where are we going in the behavioral approach to drinking behavior and alcohol problems?

It is clear from the foregoing chapters that we have made tremendous advances in extending our knowledge of the behavioral parameters of social drinking and alcoholism within a relatively short time. These advances parallel the recent growth and development of behavior therapy and behavior modification approaches to a wide variety of clinical problems. We are beginning to amass a great deal of data on assessment and treatment of alcoholism, much of it stemming from controlled laboratory investigations and carefully designed evaluation studies. This emphasis on methodology and experimentation, of course, is the outstanding characteristic of the behavioral approach. At the same time, however, advances in empirical knowledge of these clinical issues have not yet led to the development of fully integrated theoretical models to account for the development—the etiology—of alcoholism. This gap is due in part to the fact that our theoretical underpinnings are founded in general learning theory, particularly in the principles of classic and operant conditioning. These theories of learning, however, are not "theories" in the usual sense; most, notably the operant position, have been described as basically atheoretical in nature. So, rather

183

than talking about behavioral theories of alcoholism, we speak of behavioral approaches: methods of studying social drinking and alcoholism which focus on the observable parameters of drinking behavior. In the absence of a consolidating theoretical network, it becomes difficult to predict the course of future developments in this field. A behaviorist would say that the best predictors of future behavior can be found in the study of past behavior. Perhaps by looking backward over what we have accomplished to date, we will be able to discern the threads of future developments.

The development of behavioral approaches to alcoholism seems to have passed through a number of stages, although the distinctions I make here are somewhat arbitrary. The first stage was characterized by an emphasis on the application of classic conditioning procedures to treat alcoholism. In 1929 a Russian investigator, Kantorovich (143), published the first account of Pavlovian aversive conditioning techniques applied with alcoholics, using electric shock as the unconditioned stimulus. Much research continued to investigate aversive conditioning treatment methods during the 1940s and 1950s, pioneered by the work of Lemere and Voegtlin (166), who evaluated the emetic aversion procedures employed at the Shadel hospital in Seattle. As Wilson reported in Chapter 7, the effectiveness of electrical aversion therapy with alcoholics has been seriously challenged on the basis of recent outcome research. Emetic aversion techniques, on the other hand, may prove to be more efficacious. Research in the near future should tell us just how effective the chemical aversion method is based on well-controlled outcome studies. With the exception of emetic conditioning procedures, however, interest in aversion therapy as a treatment method for alcoholism seems to be on the wane.

The second stage of the behavioral approach was stimulated by the development of Hullian learning theory and the drive-reduction explanation of reinforcement advocated by such theorists as Dollard and Miller (81). Behavioral investigators interested in alcoholism began to apply this theory to provide a theoretical account of the reinforcing effects of alcohol. Several reports appeared during the 1950s which advanced the hypothesis that alcohol consumption is reinforced by its tension-reducing properties. This position was first stated by Conger in 1956 (69) based on his studies on the effects of alcohol on conflict behavior in rats (68). Other reports began to appear about this time (e.g., 149, 262) supporting the view that alcoholism could be viewed as a learned disorder, reinforced through the tension-reduction effects of alcohol. Recently the tension-reduction hypothesis, at least in its simplest form, has fallen into disrepute. Reviews by Cappell and Herman (49, 50) and Marlatt (182) show that the research findings on the tension-reducing properties of alcohol are often contradictory and inconclusive. The tension-reduction hypothesis has had considerable heuristic value, however, and the chances are good that research in this area will continue for some time to come. We still have much to learn about the effects of alcohol on various emotional or affective states. A recent study by Russell and Mehrabian (248) highlights some of the unanswered questions in this area. In addition, much research has yet to be done on the related issue of stress-induced drinking: Will people drink more alcohol when faced with a tension-producing situation (e.g., 130, 212)? How will such factors as expectation and prior experience with alcohol affect this relationship? Will training in various methods of relaxation (e.g., progressive muscle relaxation, biofeedback, meditation) lead to a reduction in drinking behavior (282)? In the absence of a viable alternative theory, the tension-reduction hypothesis will continue to serve as an impetus for behavioral research in the years ahead.

The third phase of development was ushered in by Mello and Mendelson in 1965 (190). In contrast to the research stemming from the tension-reduction theory, the third phase is characterized by an emphasis on assessment and the topographical description of drinking behavior. For the first time, alcoholics and social drinkers were observed in controlled laboratory settings where they had continual access to alcohol for prolonged periods. Operant procedures were employed to compare the relative effectiveness of alcohol with other reinforcers and to investigate the effects of a variety of reinforcement contingencies on drinking rates and patterns. This phase of research, still actively ongoing, has yielded a wealth of information on the determinants and effects of alcohol consumption. Nathan, a pioneer in this area, reviewed many of these findings (Chapter 3). Treatment procedures deriving from the operant approach are also described by Miller (Chapter 9).

The emphasis on behavioral assessment in this third stage of development has led to a number of related assessment procedures, which I reviewed in Chapter 4. Unobtrusive assessment techniques (e.g., the taste-rating task) have been increasingly used in studies that investigated potential determinants of drinking behavior. Self-report measures, including continuous self-monitoring of alcohol consumption, have been refined and improved in recent years. Observation of drinking behavior in the natural environment has recently emerged as a promising assessment strategy, as indicated by Reid in Chapter 5. Cahalan (Chapter 2) presented us with extensive survey data on drinking rates and patterns in American society. Future research will tell us more about the reliability, validity and interrelationship of these various assessment procedures. The use of behavioral assessment methods as predictors of response to treatment intervention (in addition to their use in evaluating treatment outcome) should also receive increasing attention. Most importantly, future research should tell us much about the relationship between laboratory measures of alcohol consumption and drinking behavior in the real world. In the years to come, behavioral researchers may well be spending more time in bars than in their laboratories.

The increasing focus on assessment methods speaks to a central issue in the alcoholism field: Despite the burgeoning literature on alcoholism and the physical effects of alcohol, the fact remains that we know comparatively little about the parameters of drinking behavior in the drinker's own environment. Many authors have described loss-of-control drinking as a pathognomonic symptom of alcoholism, for example, but few if any studies have provided direct observations or descriptions of this behavior. Part of this problem stems from the fact that most investigations have been conducted with alcoholics after they have been admitted for treatment, with little direct knowledge of how their drinking problems developed in the first place. Only by studying the natural occurrence of drinking behavior in social drinkers and alcoholics can we begin to formulate theoretical models of the etiology of alcoholism. If drinking behavior is learned, and if alcoholism represents an extreme condition on the learning continuum, then future research must address itself to the development of drinking problems in the general population. To understand alcoholism and how it develops fully, we must direct our attention to the study of nonalcoholics to establish the parameters of social drinking. How can we teach an alcoholic to drink in a responsible manner (if this is one of our goals) unless we know more about how social drinkers have learned to drink? How can we prevent a social drinker from becoming a problem drinker unless we discover how the majority of social drinkers remain nonalcoholics? Longitudinal studies will tell us a great deal in this area, as will cross-cultural investigations of various ethnic groups who differ widely in their propensity to develop drinking problems.

The fourth stage of development has extended our knowledge of behavioral treatment methods for problem drinking and alcoholism.

This stage paralleled developments in the assessment phase described above. New behavioral treatment methods, other than those based on aversion therapy, began to be introduced during the 1960s. At first these investigations reported the use of single-treatment techniques applied to the alcoholic population, e.g., desensitization (158), covert sensitization (53) and the token economy (221). Although many of these individual techniques were found to be effective to some degree, they did not conceptualize alcoholism as a multidetermined complex of associated behaviors. The need for a comprehensive combination of behavioral procedures in the treatment of alcoholism was first reported by Lazarus in 1965 (164). As noted by Nathan (Chapter 6), Lazarus advocated a multifaceted broad-spectrum approach to treatment, including such components as aversion therapy, systematic desensitization, assertiveness training and marital counseling. Perhaps the most well-known broad-spectrum treatment program is the Sobells' individualized behavior therapy procedure described elsewhere in this volume. Other such programs have been described by Vogler and his colleagues (294) and Hunt and Azrin (136). Hamburg (124) and Briddell and Nathan (36, 223) have recently published critical reviews. Comparative "dismantling" outcome studies should eventually identify the most effective components of these multimodal programs.

One of the most important guiding principles common to the broad-spectrum programs is the assumption that treatment must include the development of alternative behaviors to replace (or facilitate the control of) drinking. Whereas the early aversive conditioning approach attempted to suppress or eliminate drinking behavior by creating a conditioned aversion to alcohol, contemporary behavioral approaches often employ such methods as social skill training to teach the patient alternative coping abilities in situations previously associated with drinking. It is likely that research in this area will adopt a self-control model of behavioral treatment, in which patients are taught a number of assessment and intervention techniques they can apply to modify and maintain changes in their own behavior (179, 287). In this manner an alcoholic can be taught to become his own therapist or behavior modifier, thereby increasing the generalizability and maintenance of treatment benefits. In a self-control treatment program patients can learn to apply self-monitoring techniques to assess the determinants and consequences of their own drinking behavior in order to identify "high-risk" situations in which the probability of drinking or increased intake is high. Once these situations are clearly defined and recognized, the patient can be taught to engage in alternative coping behaviors (e.g., assertiveness training to resist social pressures). In line with this increasing emphasis on self-control procedures, we can expect to see self-help manuals and other educational resources which individuals can use to learn about and control their own drinking behavior. One such manual is already available (216).

As our knowledge gained through assessment and treatment research increases, a fifth stage of development is beginning to emerge. This stage represents a shift in emphasis from the treatment of alcoholism toward the prevention of problem drinking. As we know more about the development of alcoholism and the effectiveness of behavioral treatment methods with alcoholics, we are realizing that this knowledge can be put to work in establishing effective educational and prevention programs for people who otherwise might develop serious drinking problems. In particular, the promising results found during recent controlled drinking treatment programs with alcoholics suggest that these techniques could also be used to teach social drinkers how to drink in a responsible manner. A number of already established behavioral procedures could be incorporated into a comprehensive prevention program. Blood alcohol concentration (BAC) discrimination training methods, reviewed by Caddy (Chapter 8), could be employed to teach social drinkers how to recognize and control their alcohol consumption. Some of the Sobells' procedures, including videotape feedback showing how a drinker behaves under the influence of alcohol, could also be employed as part of a prevention program. Behavioral contracting and limit-setting procedures, described by Miller (Chapter 9), have important implications for prevention. Much recent work in the self-control field, including Meichenbaum's studies in self-instructional training (187), could also be included in future prevention programs.

During the next few years we may begin to see the application of such prevention programs in the educational setting. The public today is up in arms about increasing levels of drinking by adolescents and young adults. Newspaper headlines cry out about the growing menace of the "teen-age alcoholic." Concern is expressed about recent laws that have lowered the legal alcohol-purchasing age in many states. Instead of reacting to this alarm with educational and media programs that stress the harmful effects of drinking and the evils of alcoholism, why not support the establishment of training programs in our schools which teach the basic elements of responsible drinking behavior? We already have similar classes which teach students how to drive safely and responsibly. Why not a similar program for high-school students of legal drinking age who have chosen to drink? I have described a prevention program of this type that was successfully applied with college students.[1] In response to the criticism that we are teaching students to drink (thereby encouraging or facilitating the use of alcohol), my response has been that we are teaching people who have chosen to drink how to drink in a responsible manner. Similar prevention programs could be established with other high-risk populations such as military personnel or persons arrested for driving while under the influence of alcohol. Behavioral approaches with an emphasis on teaching new behaviors within a self-control perspective have much to offer educational and prevention programs.

At the start of this chapter, I stated that empirical knowledge in the behavioral field has developed at a faster pace than our theoretical conceptualizations. To date, these theories have been limited largely to a discussion of the tension-reduction hypothesis and its implications for understanding the reinforcing effects of alcohol. However, there is now increasing recognition that drinking is a social behavior. The use of the term "social drinking" illustrates the importance of social factors in drinking behavior. Drinking is typically learned in social settings, with the family environment and peer relations playing dominant roles. Drinking occurs most often in social situations: in bars and taverns, at cocktail parties and social receptions, in restaurants and airplanes. Recent research showing the importance of modeling and other sources of interpersonal influence which affect drinking behavior suggests the potency of social factors. The theoretical framework most compatible with this emphasis on social factors is the social learning theory, as developed by such theorists as Bandura (12) and Mischel (218). It seems likely that behaviorists interested in drinking behavior and alcoholism will turn increasingly to social learning theory as a guide to future work (2, 214). In our own research program, for example, we are beginning to study the effects of alcohol on social behaviors such as aggression (161) and to assess the effects of social determinants such as anger and interpersonal evaluation on alcohol consumption (131, 184).

Along with an increasing awareness of the importance of social factors, future research within a social-learning theory framework

[1] MARLATT, G. A. Training responsible drinking with college students. Presented at the American Psychological Association meeting, Chicago, 1975.

will focus more on the mediating role of cognitive factors as they relate to drinking behavior. Many behavioral theorists are now investigating the importance of cognitive factors in the behavior modification field (178). In alcoholism research, studies have already demonstrated that cognitive expectations may play an important role in the determination of drinking behavior. In our own laboratory, for example, two studies demonstrated that the subject's expectation that a drink contains alcohol is a more significant determinant of over-all consumption (183) or of associated social behaviors (161) than is the actual alcoholic content of the drink. Expectation or placebo factors may play a more important role in mediating alcohol consumption than has been previously recognized.

A crucial phenomenon in the alcoholism field which may eventually be explained in terms of cognitive factors is the "control paradox." The term "control" looms large in any account of problem drinking or alcoholism. One of the key symptoms of alcoholism, from a disease model perspective, is loss of control drinking. Recent behavioral experiments have attempted to inculcate controlled drinking in alcoholics. McClelland and his colleagues (174) claim that the consumption of alcohol by human subjects may elicit increased fantasies of personal power or control. A number of recent reports have attempted to show that alcoholics differ from nonalcoholics in terms of their scores on Rotter's Internal-External Locus of Control Scale (237, 245). One of the central assumptions of Alcoholics Anonymous is that alcoholics must learn to accept the belief that they have no control over alcohol. The first of the Twelve Steps an alcoholic learns in A.A. is to give up the notion of personal control and to develop the acceptance of a higher being who is in ultimate control of his life. Many alcoholics pursuing the goal of abstinence relapse because they are testing their own ability to control their drinking.

The control paradox can be stated as follows. Alcoholics (and to some extent nonalcoholics as well) come to believe that they can control their own emotional states through drinking. By drinking alcohol, they expect a certain effect, whether it is to feel happy or less anxious or depressed, or to relieve the symptoms of withdrawal, etc. In common terms, the alcoholic drinks to get "high," or "stoned," or "wiped out"—to obtain a "buzz" from "booze." On one level he chooses to self-administer a drug—alcohol—to control or change his cognitive–emotional state. As his reliance on alcohol as a self-medicating drug increases, however, and his tolerance to the physical effects of alcohol develops, it becomes more difficult for him to maintain voluntary "control" over alcohol use. Alcohol begins to exert a control of its own as it becomes more and more a part of the drinker's life. Where once alcohol was the drinker's slave—under his control—it becomes the master of the alcoholic's behavior. In common parlance an alcoholic becomes "addicted" at this stage, and "loss of control" over drinking occurs. He is now caught in the middle—between a desire to control his own behavior, including his drinking, and an increasing awareness that he is controlled by the very substance he onced used to control his moods and thoughts. This paradox has been described in a provocative article by Bateson (19), who proposes a cybernetic model of alcoholism based on an analysis of the control phenomenon.

Any treatment program for alcoholism that is to be ultimately effective must take this "control paradox" into account. An alcoholic's expectations about the effects of alcohol are central to understanding this issue. An effective treatment program must include some attempt to alter an alcoholic's expectations or attitudes about the effects of alcohol, perhaps by applying the attribution theory (140) or some other cognitive change procedure. At the same time, we must try to develop alternatives to alcohol which are equally attractive and meet alcoholics' expectations of effectiveness. A.A., perhaps in part because of its spiritual underpinnings, seems to provide an effective alternative for many alcoholics. Another promising approach, based on preliminary research findings (23, 261), is the use of meditation as an alternative to drinking. Both alcohol and meditation produce "altered states of consciousness" which seem to act as powerful reinforcements for many individuals. Meditation may offer the alcoholic an alternative method of increasing his sense of personal control, and it has none of the drawbacks of alcohol.[2] Research will one day tell us whether this is a viable alternative to drinking.

The foregoing predictions highlight some of the important trends for future research as I see them. It should be noted, of course, that these speculations reflect my own background and biases, and may not reflect the views of other authors of this volume. One thing is certain, however: behavioral research on alcoholism and drinking behavior will continue to grow at an exponential rate. More research has been conducted in this field during the past 10

[2] MARLATT, G. A. and MARQUES, J. K. Meditation, self-control and alcohol use. Presented at the Eighth International Conference on Behavior Modification, Banff, Alberta, 1976.

years than in any previous period. This sudden growth of interest in alcoholism is not limited to the behavioral approach alone. Research on the physiological, biochemical and genetic determinants of alcoholism is also growing at a rapid pace. As developments in these related fields continue, behavioral research will increase in complexity and significance. It is hoped that the material presented in this book will promote an interdisciplinary approach to the understanding of alcoholism.

BIBLIOGRAPHY

1. AGRAS, W. S. Behavior modification; principles and clinical applications. Boston; Little, Brown; 1972.
2. ALBRECHT, G. L. The alcoholism process; a social learning viewpoint. Pp. 11-42. In: BOURNE, P. G. and FOX, R., eds. Alcoholism; progress in research and treatment. New York; Academic; 1973.
3. AMERICAN MEDICAL ASSOCIATION. COMMITTEE ON ALCOHOLISM. Hospitalization of patients with alcoholism. (Reports of officers.) J. Amer. med. Ass. 162: 750, 1956.
4. ANANT, S. S. A note on the treatment of alcoholics by a verbal aversion technique. Canad. J. Psychol. 8: 19-22, 1967.
5. ANANT, S. S. Treatment of alcoholics and drug addicts by verbal aversion techniques. Int. J. Addict. 3: 381-388, 1968.
6. ARMSTRONG, J. D. The search for the alcoholic personality. Ann. Acad. polit. social Sci. 315: 40-47, 1958.
7. ASHEM, B. and DONNER, L. Covert sensitization with alcoholics; a controlled replication. Behav. Res. Ther., Oxford 6: 7-12, 1968.
8. BACON, S. D. Alcohol and complex society. Pp. 79-94. In: PITTMAN, D. J. and SNYDER, C. R., eds. Society, culture, and drinking patterns. New York; Wiley; 1962.
9. BAILEY, K. G. and SOWDER, W. T., JR. Audiotape and videotape self-confrontation in psychotherapy. Psychol. Bull. 74: 127-137, 1970.
10. BAILEY, M. B., HABERMAN, P. W. and ALKSNE, H. The epidemiology of alcoholism in an urban residential area. Quart. J. Stud. Alc. 26: 19-40, 1965.
11. BAILEY, M. B., HABERMAN, P. W. and SHEINBERG, J. Identifying alcoholics in population surveys; a report on reliability. Quart. J. Stud. Alc. 27: 300-315, 1966.
12. BANDURA, A. Principles of behavior modification. New York; Holt, Rinehart & Winston; 1969.
13. BANDURA, A. Behavior theory and the models of man. Amer. Psychol. 29: 859-869, 1974.
14. BANDURA, A. The ethics and social purposes of behavior modification. Pp. 13-20. In: FRANKS, C. M. and WILSON, G. T., eds. Annual review of behavior therapy; theory and practice. Vol. 3. New York; Brunner-Mazel; 1975.
15. BARBER, T. X. and SILVER, M. J. Fact, fiction, and the experimenter bias effect. Psychol. Bull. Monogr. 70 (Part 2): 1-29, 1968.
16. BARBER, T. X. and SILVER, M. J. Pitfalls in data analysis and interpretation; a reply to Rosenthal. Psychol. Bull. Monogr. 70 (Part 2): 48-62, 1968.
17. BARKER, R. G., ed. The stream of behavior. New York; Appleton-Century-Crofts; 1963.
18. BARLOW, D. H., LEITENBERG, H., AGRAS, W. S., CALLAHAN, E. J. and MOORE, R. C. The contribution of therapeutic instructions to covert sensitization. Behav. Res. Ther., Oxford 10: 411-415, 1972.
19. BATESON, G. The cybernetics of "self"; a theory of alcoholism. Psychiatry 34: 1-18, 1971.

20. BEATTY, W. W. How blind is blind? A simple procedure for estimating observer naivete. Psychol. Bull. 78: 70-71, 1972.
21. BEGELMAN, D. A. Ethical issues in behavioral control. J. nerv. ment. Dis. 156: 412-419, 1971.
22. BELASCO, J. A. The criterion question revisited. Brit. J. Addict. 66: 39-44, 1971.
23. BENSON, H. Decreased alcohol intake associated with the practice of meditation; a retrospective investigation. Ann. N.Y. Acad. Sci. 233: 174-177, 1974.
24. BERNSTEIN, D. A. and PAUL, G. L. Some comments on therapy analogue research with small animal "phobias." J. Behav. ther. Psychiat. 2: 225-237, 1971.
25. BERSOFF, D. N. Silk purses into sows' ears; the decline of psychological testing and a suggestion for its redemption. Amer. Psychol. 28: 892-899, 1973.
26. BIGELOW, G. E., LIEBSON, I. A. and GRIFFITHS, R. R. Alcoholic drinking; suppression by a brief time-out procedure. Behav. Res. Ther., Oxford 12: 107-115, 1974.
27. BIJOU, S. W. and PETERSON, R. F. The psychological assessment of children; a functional analysis. In: MCREYNOLDS, P., ed. Advances in psychological assessment. Vol. 2. Palo Alto, CA; Science & Behavior; 1971.
28. BILLINGS, A. G., WEINER, S., KESSLER, M. and GOMBERG, C. A. Drinking behavior in laboratory and barroom settings. J. Stud. Alc. 37: 85-89, 1976.
29. BLAKE, B. G. The application of behaviour therapy to the treatment of alcoholism. Behav. Res. Ther., Oxford 3: 75-85, 1965.
30. BLAKE, B. G. A follow-up of alcoholics treated by behaviour therapy. Behav. Res. Ther., Oxford 5: 89-94, 1967.
31. BOIS, C. and VOGEL-SPROTT, M. Discrimination of low blood alcohol levels and self-titration skills in social drinkers. Quart. J. Stud. Alc. 35: 86-97, 1974.
32. BOLMAN, W. M. Abstinence versus permissiveness in the psychotherapy of alcoholism; a pilot study and review of some relevant literature. Arch. gen. Psychiat. 12: 456-463, 1965.
33. BORKENSTEIN, R. F. Breathalyzer, Model 900. Breath tests to determine alcoholic influence; instruction manual. Red Bank, NJ; Stephenson Corporation; 1963.
34. BOWEN, W. T. and ANDROES, L. A follow-up study of 79 alcoholic patients: 1963–1965. Bull. Menninger Clin. 32: 26-34, 1968.
35. BOWMAN, R. S., STEIN, L. I. and NEWTON, J. R. Measurement and interpretation of drinking behavior. I. On measuring patterns of alcohol consumption. II. Relationships between drinking behavior and social adjustment in a sample of problem drinkers. J. Stud. Alc. 36: 1154-1172, 1975.
36. BRIDDELL, D. W. and NATHAN, P. E. Behavior assessment and modification with alcoholics; current status and future trends. In: HERSEN, M., EISLER, R. M. and MILLER, P. M., eds. Progress in behavior modification. Vol. 2. New York; Academic; 1975.
37. BURT, D. W. Characteristics of the relapse situation of alcoholics treated with aversive conditioning. Behav. Res. Ther., Oxford 12: 121-123; 1974.

38. CADDY, G. R. Behaviour modification in the management of alcoholism. Ph.D. dissertation, University of New South Wales; 1972.
39. CADDY, G. R. and LOVIBOND, S. H. Self-regulation and discriminated aversive conditioning in the modification of alcoholics' drinking behavior. Behav. Ther., N.Y. 7: 223-230, 1976.
40. CADDY, G. R., SUTTON, M. and LEWIS, J. The role of feedback and internal cues in blood alcohol concentration estimation. [In press.]
41. CAHALAN, D. Problem drinkers; a national survey. San Francisco; Jossey-Bass; 1970.
42. CAHALAN, D. and CISIN, I. H. Final report on a service-wide survey of attitudes and behavior of naval personnel concerning alcohol and problem drinking. (Rep. No. AD-AO 13-236; NIAAA/NCALI-75/15.) Springfield, VA; U.S. Nat. Tech. Inform. Serv.; 1975.
43. CAHALAN, D., CISIN, I. H. and CROSSLEY, H. M. American drinking practices; a national survey of drinking behavior and attitudes. (Rutgers Center of Alcohol Studies, Monogr. No. 6.) New Brunswick, NJ; 1969.
44. CAHALAN, D., CISIN, I. H., GARDNER, G. L. and SMITH, G. C. Drinking practices and problems in the U.S. Army, 1972. Final Report. (Information Concepts Inc.; Rep. No. 73-6.) Pp. 364-638. In: U. S. CONGRESS. SUB-COMMITTEE ON DRUG ABUSE IN THE MILITARY. Review of military drug and alcohol programs. Hearings, 93d Congress, 1st session, 18, 19 and 20 September 1973. Washington, DC; U.S. Govt Print. Off.; 1973.
45. CAHALAN, D. and ROOM, R. Problem drinking among American men aged 21-59. Amer. J. publ. Hlth 62: 1473-1482, 1972.
46. CAHALAN, D. and ROOM, R. Problem drinking among American men. (Rutgers Center of Alcohol Studies, Monogr. No. 7.) New Brunswick, NJ; 1974.
47. CALIFORNIA. DEPARTMENT OF PUBLIC HEALTH. Alcoholism and California; follow-up studies of treated alcoholics; description of studies. (Publ. No. 5.) Berkeley; 1961.
48. CALLAHAN, E. J. and LEITENBERG, H. Aversion therapy for sexual deviation; contingent shock and covert sensitization. J. abnorm. Psychol. 81: 60-73, 1973.
49. CAPPELL, H. An evaluation of tension models of alcohol consumption. Pp. 177-209. In: GIBBONS, R. J., ISRAEL, Y., KALANT, H., POPHAM, R. E., SCHMIDT, W. and SMART, R. G., eds. Research advances in alcohol and drug problems. Vol. 2. New York; Wiley; 1975.
50. CAPPELL, H. and HERMAN, C. P. Alcohol and tension reduction; a review. Quart. J. Stud. Alc. 33: 33-64, 1972.
51. CAUDILL, B. D. and MARLATT, G. A. Modeling influences in social drinking; an experimental analogue. J. cons. clin. Psychol. 43: 405-415, 1975.
52. CAUTELA, J. R. Treatment of compulsive behavior by covert sensitization. Psychol. Rec. 16: 33-41, 1966.
53. CAUTELA, J. R. Covert sensitization. Psychol. Rep. 20: 459-468, 1967.
54. CAUTELA, J. R. The treatment of alcoholism by covert sensitization. Psychotherapy, Chicago 7: 86-90, 1970.
55. CAUTELA, J. R. The treatment of overeating by covert conditioning. Psychotherapy, Chicago 9: 211-216, 1972.

56. CAVAN, S. Liquor license; an ethnography of bar behavior. Chicago; Aldine; 1966.

57. CHAFETZ, M. E., BLANE, H. T., ABRAM, H. S., GOLNER, J., LACY, E., McCOURT, W. F., CLARK, E. and MEYERS, W. Establishing treatment relations with alcoholics. J. nerv. ment. Dis. 134: 395-409, 1962.

58. CHASE, A. The great pellagra cover-up. Psychol. Today 8: 83-86, 1975.

59. CHATTERJEE, B. and ERIKSON, C. Cognitive factors in heart rate conditioning. J. exp. Psychol. 64: 272-279, 1962.

60. CIMINERO, A. R., CALHOUN, K. S. and ADAMS, H. E., eds. Handbook of behavioral assessment. New York; Wiley; 1977.

61. CISIN, I. H. Community studies of drinking behavior. Ann. N.Y. Acad. Sci. 107: 607-612, 1963.

62. CLAESON, L. E. and MALM, U. Electro-aversion therapy of chronic alcoholism. Behav. Res. Ther., Oxford 11: 663-665, 1973.

63. CLARK, W. [B.] Operational definitions of drinking problems and associated prevalence rates. Quart. J. Stud. Alc. 27: 648-668, 1966.

64. CLARK, W. B. and CAHALAN, D. Changes in problem drinking over a four-year span. Addict. Behav., Oxford 1: 251-259, 1976.

65. COHEN, M., LIEBSON, I. A. and FAILLACE, L. A. The modification of drinking in chronic alcoholics. Pp. 745-766. In: MELLO, N. K. and MENDELSON, J. H., eds. Recent advances in studies on alcoholism; an interdisciplinary approach. Washington, DC; U.S. Govt Print. Off.; 1971.

66. COHEN, M., LIEBSON, I. A. and FAILLACE, L. A. The role of reinforcement contingencies in chronic alcoholism; an experimental analysis of one case. Behav. Res. Ther., Oxford 9: 375-379, 1971.

67. COHEN, M., LIEBSON, I. A., FAILLACE, L. A. and ALLEN, R. P. Moderate drinking by chronic alcoholics; a schedule-dependent phenomenon. J. nerv. ment. Dis. 153: 434-444, 1971.

68. CONGER, J. J. The effects of alcohol on conflict behavior in the albino rat. Quart. J. Stud. Alc. 12: 1-29, 1951.

69. CONGER, J. J. Alcoholism; theory, problem and challenge. II. Reinforcement theory and the dynamics of alcoholism. Quart. J. Stud. Alc. 17: 296-305, 1956.

70. COOPERATIVE COMMISSION ON THE STUDY OF ALCOHOLSM. Alcohol problems; a report to the nation. (Prepared by PLAUT, T. F. A.) New York; Oxford University Press; 1967.

71. CRAVEY, R. H. and JAIN, N. C. Current status of blood alcohol methods. J. chromat. Sci. 12: 209-213, 1974.

72. CRAWFORD, J. J., CHALUPSKY, A. B. and HURLEY, M. M. The evaluation of psychological approaches to alcoholism treatments; a methodological review. Palo Alto, CA; American Institutes for Research; 1973.

73. CUTLER, R. E. and STORM, T. Observational study of alcohol consumption in natural settings; the Vancouver beer parlor. J. Stud. Alc. 36: 1173-1183, 1975.

74. CUTTER, H. S. G., SCHWAB, E. L. and NATHAN, P. E. Effects of alcohol on its utility for alcoholics. Quart. J. Stud. Alc. 31: 369-378, 1970.

75. DANAHER, B. G. and LICHTENSTEIN, E. Aversion therapy issues; a note of clarification. Behav. Ther., N.Y. 5: 112-116, 1974.

76. DANET, B. N. Self-confrontation in psychotherapy reviewed; videotape playback as a clinical and research tool. Amer. J. Psychother. 22: 245-257, 1968.

77. DAVIDSON, W. S., 2d. Studies of aversive conditioning for alcoholics; a critical review of theory and research methodology. Psychol. Bull. 81: 571-581, 1974.

78. DAVIES, D. L. Normal drinking in recovered alcohol addicts. Quart. J. Stud. Alc. 23: 94-104, 1962.

79. DAVISON, G. C. Counter-control 'in behavior modification. Pp. 153-167. In: HAMERLYNCK, L. A., HANDY, L. C. and MASH, E. J., eds. Behavior change; methodology, concepts and practice. Champaign, IL; Research Press; 1973.

80. DAVISON, G. C. and WILSON, G. T. Attitudes of behavior therapists towards homosexuality. Behav. Ther., N.Y. 4: 686-696, 1973.

81. DOLLARD, J. and MILLER, N. E. Personality and psychotherapy; an analysis in terms of learning, thinking and culture. New York; McGraw-Hill; 1950.

82. EDWARDS, G., HENSMAN, C. and PETO, J. Drinking in a London suburb; reinterview of a subsample and assessment of response consistency. Quart. J. Stud. Alc. 34: 1244-1254, 1973.

83. EISLER, R. M. Assessment of social skills deficits. In: HERSEN, M. and BEL-LACK, A. S., eds. Behavioral assessment; a practical handbook. New York; Pergamon: 1976.

84. EISLER, R. M., HERSEN, M. and AGRAS, W. S. Videotape; a method for the controlled observation of nonverbal interpersonal behavior. Behav. Ther., N.Y. 4: 420-425, 1973.

85. EISLER, R. M., MILLER, P. M., HERSEN, M. and ALFORD, H. Effects of assertive training on marital interaction. Arch. gen. Psychiat. 30: 643-649, 1974.

86. EKMAN, G., FRANKENHAEUSER, M., GOLDBERG, L., BJERVER, K., JAȒPE, G. and MYRSTEN, A.-L. Effects of alcohol intake on subjective and objective variables over a five-hour period. Psychopharmacologia, Berl. 4: 28-38, 1963.

87. ELKINS, R. L. Conditioned flavor aversions to familiar tap water in rats; an adjustment with implications for aversion therapy treatment of alcoholism and obesity. J. abnorm. Psychol. 83: 411-417, 1974.

88. ELKINS, R. L. Aversion therapy for alcoholism: chemical, electrical or verbal imaginary? Int. J. Addict. 10: 157-209, 1975.

89. EMRICK, C. D. A review of psychologically oriented treatment of alcoholism. I. The use and interrelationships of outcome criteria and drinking behavior following treatment. Quart. J. Stud. Alc. 35: 523-549, 1974.

90. EVANS, I. M. Classial conditioning. In: FELDMAN, M. P. and BROADHURST, A., eds. The theoretical and experimental bases of behavior therapy. London; Wiley. [In press.]

91. EYSENCK, H. J. and BEECH, H. R. Counter conditioning and related methods. Pp. 543-611. In: BERGIN, A. E. and GARFIELD, S. L., eds. Handbook of psychotherapy and behavior change; an empirical analysis. New York; Wiley; 1971.

92. EYSENCK, H. J. and RACHMAN, S. Causes and cures of neurosis. San Diego, CA; Knapp; 1965.

93. FAILLACE, L. A., FLAMER, R. N., IMBER, S. D. and WARD, R. F. Giving

alcohol to alcoholics; an evaluation. Quart. J. Stud. Alc. 33: 85-90, 1972.

94. FARRAR, C. H., POWELL, B. J. and MARTIN, K. L. Punishment of alcohol consumption by apneic paralysis. Behav. Res. Ther., Oxford 6: 13-16, 1968.

95. FELDMAN, D. J., PATTISON, E. M., SOBELL, L. C., GRAHAM, T. and SOBELL, M. B. Outpatient alcohol detoxification; initial findings on 564 patients. Amer. J. Psychiat. 132: 407-412, 1975.

96. FELDMAN, M. P. and MacCULLOCH, M. J. Homosexual behavior; therapy and assessment. New York; Pergamon; 1971.

97. FOY, D. W., MILLER, P. M., EISLER, R. M. and O'TOOLE, D. H. Social skills trainings to teach alcoholics to refuse drinks effectively. J. Stud. Alc. 37: 1340-1345, 1976.

98. FRANKS, C. M. Conditioning and conditioned aversion therapies in the treatment of the alcoholic. Int. J. Addict. 1: 61-98, 1966.

99. FRANKS, C. M. Reflections upon the treatment of sexual disorders by the behavioral clinician; an historical comparison with the treatment of the alcoholic. J. Sex Res. 3: 212-222, 1967.

100. FRANKS, C. M. Alcoholism. Pp. 448-480. In: COSTELLO, C. G., ed. Symptoms of psychopathology; a handbook. New York; Wiley; 1970.

101. FRANKS, C. M. and WILSON, G. T., eds. Annual review of behavior therapy; theory and practice. Vol. 3. New York; Brunner-Mazel; 1975.

102. FRIEDMAN, P. R. Legal regulation of applied behavior analysis in mental institutions and prisons. Arizona Law Rev. 17: 39-104, 1975.

103. GAUL, D. J., CRAIGHEAD, W. E. and MAHONEY, M. J. Relationship between eating rates and obesity. J. cons. clin. Psychol. 43: 123-125, 1975.

104. GERARD, D. L. and SAENGER, G. Out-patient treatment of alcoholism; a study of outcome and its determinants. (Brookside Monogr., No. 4.) Toronto; University of Toronto Press; 1966.

105. GERARD, D. L., SAENGER, G. and WILE, R. The abstinent alcoholic. A.M.A. Arch. gen. Psychiat. 6: 83-95, 1962.

106. GILLIS, L. S. and KEET, M. Prognostic factors and treatment results in hospitalized alcoholics. Quart. J Stud. Alc. 30: 426-437, 1969.

107. GLATT, M. M. The question of moderate drinking despite "loss of control." Brit. J. Addict. 62: 267-274, 1967.

108. GOLDBERG, L. Behavioral and physiological effects of alcohol on man. Psychosom. Med. 28: 570-595, 1966.

109. GOLDFRIED, M. R. and SPRAFKIN, J. Behavioral personality assessment. Morristown, NJ; General Learning Press; 1974.

110. GOLDIAMOND, I. Toward a constructional approach to social problems; ethical and constitutional issues raised by applied behavior analysis. Behaviorism 2: 1-84, 1974.

111. GOLDMAN, M. S., TAYLOR, H. A., CARRUTH, M. L. and NATHAN, P. E. Effects of group decision-making on group drinking by alcoholics. Quart. J. Stud. Alc. 34: 807-822, 1973.

112. GOTTHEIL, E., ALTERMAN, A. I., SKOLODA, T. E. and MURPHY, B. F. Alcoholics' patterns of controlled drinking. Amer. J. Psychiat. 130: 418-422, 1973.

113. GOTTHEIL, E., CORBETT, L. O., GRASBERGER, J. C. and CORNELISON, F. S., JR. Treating the alcoholic in the presence of alcohol. Amer. J. Psychiat. 128: 475-480, 1971.

114. GOTTHEIL, E., CORBETT, L. O., GRASBERGER, J. C. and CORNELISON, F. S., JR. Fixed interval drinking decisions. *I*. A research and treatment model. Quart. J. Stud. Alc. 33: 311-324, 1972.

115. GOTTHEIL, E., CRAWFORD, H. D. and CORNELISON, F. S., JR. The alcoholic's ability to resist available alcohol. Dis. nerv. Syst. 34: 80-84, 1973.

116. GREENBERG, L. A. Intoxication and alcoholism; physiological factors. Ann. Amer. Acad. polit. social Sci. 315: 22-30, 1958.

117. GRIFFITHS, R. R., BIGELOW, G. E. and LIEBSON, I. A. Suppression of ethanol self-administration in alcoholics by contingent time-out from social interactions. Behav. Res. Ther., Oxford 12: 327-334, 1974.

118. GUSFIELD, J. R. Status conflicts and the changing ideologies of the American temperance movement. Pp. 101-120. In: PITTMAN, D. J. and SNYDER, C. R., eds. Society, culture, and drinking patterns. New York; Wiley; 1962.

119. GUZE, S. B. and GOODWIN, D. W. Consistency of drinking history and diagnosis of alcoholism. Quart. J. Stud. Alc. 33: 111-116, 1972.

120. GUZE, S. B., TUASON, V. B., STEWART, M. A. and PICKEN, B. The drinking history; a comparison of reports by subjects and their relatives. Quart. J. Stud. Alc. 24: 249-260, 1963.

121. HABERMAN, P. W. and SCHEINBERG, J. Public attitudes toward alcoholism as an illness. Amer. J. publ. Hlth 59: 1209-1216, 1969.

122. HALLAM, R. and RACHMAN, S. Theoretical problems of aversion therapy. Behav. Res. Ther., Oxford 10: 341-353, 1972.

123. HALLAM, R., RACHMAN S. and FALKOWSKI, W. Subjective, attitudinal, and physiological effects of electrical aversion therapy. Behav. Res. Ther., Oxford 10: 1-13, 1972.

124. HAMBURG, S. Behavior therapy in alcoholism; a critical review of broad-spectrum approaches. J. Stud. Alc. 36: 69-87, 1975.

125. HARTE, R. A. An instrument for the determination of ethanol in breath in law-enforcement practice. J. forens. Sci. 16: 493-510, 1971.

126. HEDBERG, A. G. and CAMPBELL, L., 3d. A comparison of four behavioral treatments of alcoholism. J. Behav. Ther., Elmsford, NY 5: 251-256, 1974.

127. HERSEN, M. Self-assessment of fear. Behav. Ther., N.Y. 4: 241-257, 1973.

128. HERSEN, M., MILLER, P. M. and EISLER, R. M. Interactions between alcoholics and their wives; a descriptive analysis of verbal and nonverbal behavior. Quart. J. Stud. Alc. 34: 516-520, 1973.

129. HETHERINGTON, E. M. and FRANKIE, G. Effects of parental dominance, warmth and conflict on imitation in children. J. Person. social Psychol. 6: 119-125, 1967.

130. HIGGINS, R. L. and MARLATT, G. A. Effects of anxiety arousal on the consumption of alcohol by alcoholics and social drinkers. J. cons. clin. Psychol. 41: 426-433, 1973.

131. HIGGINS, R. L. and MARLATT, G. A. Fear of interpersonal evaluation as a determinant of alcohol consumption in male social drinkers. J. abnorm. Psychol. 84: 644-651, 1975.

132. HILL, M. J. and BLANE, H. T. Evaluation of psychotherapy with alcoholics; a critical review. Quart. J. Stud. Alc. 28: 76-104, 1967.

133. HOLZINGER, R., MORTIMER, R. and VAN DUSEN, W. Aversion conditioning treatment of alcoholism. Amer. J. Psychiat. 124: 246-247, 1967.

134. HORN, J. L. and WANBERG, K. W. Symptom patterns related to the excessive

use of alcohol. Quart. J. Stud. Alc. **30:** 35-58, 1969.

135. HUBER, H., KARLIN, R. and NATHAN, P. E. Blood alcohol level discrimination by nonalcoholics; the role of internal and external cues. J. Stud. Alc. **37:** 27-39, 1976.

136. HUNT, G. M. and AZRIN, N. H. A community-reinforcement approach to alcoholism. Behav. Res. Ther., Oxford **11:** 91-104, 1973.

137. JAIN, N. C. and CRAVEY, R. H. A review of breath alcohol methods. J. chromat. Sci. **12:** 214-218, 1974.

138. JELLINEK, E. M. The disease concept of alcoholism. Highland Park, NJ; Hillhouse Press; 1960.

139. JOHNSON, S. M. and BOLSTAD, O. D. Methodological issues in naturalistic observation; some problems and solutions for field research. Pp. 7-68. In: HAMERLYNCK, L. A., HANDY, L. C. and MASH, E. J., eds. Behavior change; methodology, concepts and practice. Champaign, IL; Research Press; 1973.

140. JONES, E. E., KANHOUSE, D. E., KELLEY, H. H., NISBETT, R. E., VALINS, S. and WEINER, B. Attribution; perceiving the causes of behavior. Morristown, NJ; General Learning Press; 1972.

141. JONES, R. R., REID, J. B. and PATTERSON, G. R. Naturalistic observation in clinical assessment. Pp. 42-95. In: MCREYNOLDS, P., ed. Advances in psychological assessment. Vol. 3. San Francisco; Jossey-Bass; 1974.

142. KANFER, F. H. and SASLOW, G. Behavioral diagnosis. Pp. 417-444. In: FRANKS, C. M., ed. Behavior therapy; appraisal and status. New York; McGraw-Hill; 1969.

143. KANTOROVICH, N. V. An attempt at associative reflex therapy in alcoholism. Nov. Refleksol. Fizl. nerv. Sist. **3:** 436-447, 1929.

144. KATZ, R. C. and ZLUTNICK, S., eds. Behavior therapy and health care; principles and applications. New York; Pergamon; 1975.

145. KAZDIN, A. E. Self-monitoring and behavior change. In: MAHONEY, M. J. and THORESEN, C. E., eds. Self-control; power to the person. Monterey, CA; Brooks-Cole; 1974.

146. KELLER, M. The definition of alcoholism and the estimation of its prevalence. Pp. 310-329. In: PITTMAN, D. J. and SNYDER, C. R., eds. Society, culture, and drinking patterns. New York; Wiley; 1962.

147. KENDALL, R. E. Normal drinking by former alcohol addicts. Quart. J. Stud. Alc. **26:** 247-257, 1965.

148. KESSLER, M. and GOMBERG, C. Observations of barroom drinking; methodology and preliminary results. Quart. J. Stud. Alc. **35:** 1392-1396, 1974.

149. KINGHAM, R. J. Alcoholism and the reinforcement theory of learning. Quart. J. Stud. Alc. **19:** 320-330, 1958.

150. KISH, G. B. and HERMANN, H. T. The Fort Meade alcoholism treatment program; a follow-up study. Quart. J. Stud. Alc. **32:** 628-635, 1971.

151. KNOX, W. J. Four-year follow-up of veterans treated on a small alcoholism treatment ward. Quart. J. Stud. Alc. **33:** 105-110, 1972.

152. KNUPFER, G. Epidemiology studies and control programs in alcoholism. V. The epidemiology of problem drinking. Amer. J. publ. Hlth **57:** 973-986, 1967.

153. KNUPFER, G., FINK, R., CLARK, W. and GOFFMAN, A. Factors related to amount of drinking in an urban community. (Drinking Practices Study, Rep. No. 6.) Berkeley; California State Department of Public Health; 1963.

154. KOPEL, S. The effects of self-control, booster sessions, and cognitive factors on the maintenance of smoking reduction. Ph.D. dissertation, University of Oregon; 1974.

155. KOSTURN, C. F. and MARLATT, G. A. Elicitation of anger and opportunity for retaliation as determinants of alcohol consumption. (ERIC Rep. No. ED-106-678.) Arlington, VA; Computer Microfilm International Corp.; 1974.

156. KRAFT, T. Alcoholism treated by systematic desensitization; a follow-up of eight cases. J. roy. Coll. gen. Practit. 18: 336-340, 1969.

157. KRAFT, T. and AL-ISSA, I. Alcoholism treated by desensitization; a case report. Behav. Res. Ther., Oxford 5: 69-70, 1967.

158. KRAFT, T. and AL-ISSA, I. Desensitization and the treatment of alcoholic addiction. Brit. J. Addict. 63: 19-23, 1968.

159. KUHN, T. S. The structure of scientific revolutions. 2d ed. (Foundations of the Unity of Science Ser., Vol. 2, No. 2.) Chicago; University of Chicago Press; 1970.

160. LAIN, M. E. and SCHOENFELD, L. S. Effects of three conditioning paradigms on visual attention to alcoholic stimuli. Percept. motor Skills 38: 409-410, 1974.

161. LANG, A. R., GOECKNER, D. J., ADESSO, V. J. and MARLATT, G. A. Effects of alcohol on aggression in male social drinkers. J. abnorm. Psychol. 84: 508-518, 1975.

162. LANG, P. J. Fear reduction and fear behavior; problems in treating a construct. In: SHLIEN, J. M., ed. Research in psychotherapy. Vol. 3. Washington, DC; American Psychological Association; 1968.

163. LAWSON, D. M., WILSON, G. T., BRIDDELL, D. W. and IVES, C. C. Assessment and modification of alcoholics' drinking behavior in controlled laboratory settings; a cautionary note. Addict. Behav., Oxford 1: 299-303, 1976.

164. LAZARUS, A. A. Towards the understanding and effective treatment of alcoholism. South Afr. med. J. 39: 736-741, 1965.

165. LEMASTERS, E. E. Blue collar aristocrats; life-styles at a working class tavern. Madison; University of Wisconsin Press; 1975.

166. LEMERE, F. and VOEGTLIN, W. L. An evaluation of the aversion treatment of alcoholism. Quart. J. Stud. Alc. 11: 199-204, 1950.

167. LICHTENSTEIN, E., HARRIS, D. E., BIRCHLER, G., WAHL, J. M. and SCHMAHL, D. P. Comparison of rapid smoking, warm, smoky air, and attention placebo in the modification of smoking behavior. J. cons. clin. Psychol. 40: 92-98, 1973.

168. LIEBSON, I. A. and BIGELOW, G. E. A behavioural-pharmacological treatment of dually addicted patients. Behav. Res. Ther., Oxford 10: 403-405, 1972.

169. LIEBSON, I. A., BIGELOW, G. E. and FLAME, R. Alcoholism among methadone patients; a specific treatment method. Amer. J. Psychiat. 130: 483-485, 1973.

170. LOUIS HARRIS and ASSOCIATES, INC. American attitudes toward alcohol and alcoholics. Prepared for the U.S. National Institute on Alcohol Abuse and Alcoholism. New York; 1971.

171. LOVIBOND, S. H. and CADDY, G. Discriminated aversive control in the moderation of alcoholics' drinking behavior. Behav. Ther., N.Y. 1: 437-444, 1970.

172. LUDWIG, A. M. On and off the wagon; reasons for drinking and abstaining by alcoholics. Quart. J. Stud. Alc. **33**: 91-96, 1972.

173. MACANDREW, C. The differentiation of male alcoholic outpatients from nonalcoholic psychiatric outpatients by means of the MMPI. Quart. J. Stud. Alc. **26**: 238-246, 1965.

174. MACCULLOCH, M. J., FELDMAN, M. P., ORFORD, J. F. and MACCULLOCH, M. L. Anticipatory avoidance learning in the treatment of alcoholism; a record of therapeutic failure. Behav. Res. Ther., Oxford **4**: 187-196, 1966.

175. MCCLELLAND, D. C., DAVIS, W. N., KALIN, R. and WANNER, E. The drinking man. New York; Free Press; 1972.

176. MCNAMEE, H. B., MELLO, N. K. and MENDELSON, J. H. Experimental analysis of drinking patterns of alcoholics; concurrent psychiatric observations. Amer. J. Psychiat. **124**: 1063-1069, 1968.

177. MADSEN, W. The American alcoholic; the nature–nurture controversy in alcoholic research and therapy. Springfield, IL; Thomas; 1974.

178. MAHONEY, M. J. Cognition and behavior modification. Cambridge, Mass.; Ballinger; 1974.

179. MAHONEY, M. J. and THORESON, C. E. Self-control; power to the person. Monterey, CA; Brooks-Cole; 1974.

180. MALETZKY, B. M. "Assisted" covert sensitization in the treatment of exhibitionism. J. cons. clin. Psychol. **42**: 34-40, 1974.

181. MARLATT, G. A. The drinking profile; a questionnaire for the behavioral assessment of alcoholism. In: MASH, E. J. and TERDAL, L. G., eds. Behavior therapy assessment; diagnosis, design and evaluation. New York; Springer; 1976.

182. MARLATT, G. A. Alcohol, stress and cognitive control. In: SARASON, I. G. and SPIELBERGER, C. D., eds. Stress and anxiety. Vol. 3. Washington, DC; Hemisphere; 1976.

183. MARLATT, G. A., DEMMING, B. and REID, J. B. Loss of control drinking in alcoholics; an experimental analogue. J. abnorm. Psychol. **81**: 233-241, 1973.

184. MARLATT, G. A., KOSTURN, C. F. and LANG, A. R. Provocation to anger and opportunity for retaliation as determinants of alcohol consumption in social drinkers. J. abnorm. Psychol. **84**: 652-659, 1975.

185. MASH, E. J. and TERDAL, L. G., eds. Behavior therapy assessment; diagnosis, design and evaluation. New York; Springer; 1976.

186. MAXWELL, W. A., BAIRD, R. L., WEZL, T. and FERGUSON, L. Discriminated aversion conditioning within an alcoholic treatment program in the training of controlled drinking. Behav. Engng **2**: 17-19, 1974.

187. MEICHENBAUM, D. Self-instructional methods. In: KANFER, F. H. and GOLDSTEIN, A. P., eds. Helping people change. New York; Pergamon; 1975.

188. MELLO, N. K. Psychopharmacology; some aspects of the behavioral pharmacology of alcohol. Pp. 787-809. In: EFRON, D., ed. Psychopharmacology; a review of progress, 1957-1967. (U.S. Public Health Service Publ. No. 1836.) Washington, DC; U.S. Govt Print. Off.; 1968.

189. MELLO, N. K. Behavioral studies of alcoholism. In: KISSIN, B. and BEGLEITER, H., eds. The biology of alcoholism. Vol. 2. Physiology and behavior. New York; Plenum; 1972.

190. MELLO, N. K. and MENDELSON, J. H. Operant analysis of drinking patterns of chronic alcoholics. Nature, Lond. **206**: 43-46, 1965.
191. MELLO, N. K. and MENDELSON, J. H. Experimentally induced intoxication in alcoholics; a comparison between programmed and spontaneous drinking. J. Pharmacol. exp. Ther. **173**: 101-116, 1970.
192. MELLO, N. K. and MENDELSON, J. H. A quantitative analysis of drinking patterns in alcoholics. Arch. gen. Psychiat. **25**: 527-539, 1971.
193. MELLO, N. K. and MENDELSON, J. H. Drinking patterns during work contingent and noncontingent alcohol acquisition. Psychosom. Med. **34**: 139-164, 1972.
194. MENDELSON, J. H., ed. Experimentally induced chronic intoxication and withdrawal in alcoholics. Quart. J. Stud. Alc., Suppl. No. 2, 1964.
195. MENDELSON, J. H. and MELLO, N. K. Experimental analysis of drinking behavior of chronic alcoholics. Ann. N.Y. Acad. Sci. **133**: 828-845, 1966.
196. MERRY, J. The "loss of control" myth. Lancet **1**: 1257-1258, 1966.
197. MILLER, B. A., POKORNY, A. D., VALLES, J. and CLEVELAND, S. E. Biased sampling in alcoholism treatment research. Quart. J. Stud. Alc. **31**: 97-107, 1970.
198. MILLER, M. M. Treatment of chronic alcoholism by hypnotic aversion. J. Amer. med. Ass. **171**: 1492-1495, 1959.
199. MILLER, P. M. The use of behavioral contracting in the treatment of alcoholism; a case report. Behav. Ther., N.Y. **3**: 592-596, 1972.
200. MILLER, P. M. Behavioral assessment in alcoholism research and treatment; current techniques. Int. J. Addict. **8**: 831-837, 1973.
201. MILLER, P. M. A behavioral intervention program for chronic public drunkenness offenders. Arch. gen. Psychiat. **32**: 915-918, 1975.
202. MILLER, P. M. Behavioral treatment of alcoholism. New York; Pergamon; 1976.
203. MILLER, P. M. Assessment of addictive behaviors. In: CIMINERO, A. R., CALHOUN, K. S. and ADAMS, H. E., eds. Handbook of behavioral assessment. New York; Wiley; 1977.
204. MILLER, P. M., BECKER, J. V., FOY, D. W. and WOOTEN, L. S. Instructional control of the components of alcoholic drinking behavior. Behav. Ther., N.Y. **7**: 472-480, 1976.
205. MILLER, P. M. and EISLER, R. M. Alcohol and drug abuse. In: CRAIGHEAD, W. E., KAZDIN, A. E. and MAHONEY, M. J., eds. Behavioral modification; principles, issues, and applications. Boston; Houghton Mifflin; 1975.
206. MILLER, P. M. and HERSEN, M. Quantitative changes in alcohol consumption as a function of electrical aversive conditioning. J. clin. Psychol. **28**: 590-593, 1972.
207. MILLER, P. M. and HERSEN, M. Modification of marital interaction patterns between an alcoholic and his wife. In: KRUMBOLTZ, J. D. and THORESON, C. E., eds. Counseling methods. New York; Holt, Rinehart & Winston; 1976.
208. MILLER, P. M., HERSEN, M. and EISLER, R. M. Relative effectiveness of instructions, agreements, and reinforcement in behavioral contracts with alcoholics. J. abnorm. Psychol. **83**: 548-553, 1974.
209. MILLER, P. M., HERSEN, M., EISLER, R. M. and ELKIN, T. E. A retrospective

analysis of alcohol consumption on laboratory tasks as related to therapeutic outcome. Behav. Res. Ther., Oxford 12: 73-76, 1974.

210. MILLER, P. M., HERSEN, M., EISLER, R. M. and HEMPHILL, D. P. Electrical aversion therapy with alcoholics; an analogue study. Behav. Res. Ther., Oxford 11: 491-497, 1973.

211. MILLER, P. M., HERSEN, M., EISLER, R. M., EPSTEIN, L. H. and WOOTEN, L. S. Relationship of alcohol cues to the drinking behavior of alcoholics and social drinkers; an analogue study. Psychol. Rec. 24: 61-66, 1974.

212. MILLER, P. M., HERSEN, M., EISLER, R. M. and HILSMAN, G. Effects of social stress on operant drinking of alcoholics and social drinkers. Behav. Res. Ther., Oxford 12: 67-72, 1974.

213. MILLER, P. M., HERSEN, M., EISLER, R. M. and WATTS, J. G. Contingent reinforcement of lowered blood/alcohol levels in an outpatient chronic alcoholic. Behav. Res. Ther., Oxford 12: 261-263, 1974.

214. MILLER, P. M., STANFORD, A. G. and HEMPHILL, D. P. A social-learning approach to alcoholism treatment. Social Casework 55: 279-284, 1974.

215. MILLER, W. R. Alcoholism scales and objective assessment methods; a review. Psychol. Bull. 83: 649-674, 1976.

216. MILLER, W. R. and MUÑOZ, R. F. How to control your drinking. Englewood Cliffs, NJ; Prentice-Hall; 1976.

217. MILLS, K. C., SOBELL, M. B. and SCHAEFER, H. H. Training social drinking as an alternative to abstinence for alcoholics. Behav. Ther., N.Y. 2: 18-27, 1971.

218. MISCHEL, W. Personality and assessment. New York; Wiley; 1968.

219. MULFORD, H. A. and MILLER, D. E. Drinking in Iowa. IV. Preoccupation with alcohol and definitions of alcohol, heavy drinking, and trouble due to drinking. Quart. J. Stud. Alc. 21: 279-291, 1960.

220. MULFORD, H. A. and MILLER, D. E. Public definitions of the alcoholic. Quart. J. Stud. Alc. 22: 312-320, 1961.

221. NARROL, H. G. Experimental application of reinforcement principles to the analysis and treatment of hospitalized alcoholics. Quart. J. Stud. Alc. 28: 105-115, 1967.

222. NATHAN, P. E. Alcoholism. In: LEITENBERG, H., ed. Handbook of behavior modification. New York; Appleton-Century-Crofts; 1976.

223. NATHAN, P. E. and BRIDDELL, D. W. Behavioral assessment and treatment of alcoholism. Pp. 301-349. In: KISSIN, B. and BEGLEITER, H., eds. The biology of alcoholism. Vol. 5. Treatment and rehabilitation of the chronic alcoholic. New York; Plenum; 1977.

224. NATHAN, P. E. and O'BRIEN, J. S. An experimental analysis of the behavior of alcoholics and nonalcoholics during prolonged experimental drinking; a necessary precursor of behavior therapy. Behav. Ther., N.Y. 2: 455-476, 1971.

225. NATHAN, P. E., TITLER, N. A., LOWENSTEIN, L. M., SOLOMON, P. and ROSSI, A. M. Behavioral analysis of chronic alcoholism. Arch. gen. Psychiat. 22: 419-430, 1970.

226. NØRVIG, J. and NIELSEN, B. A follow-up study of 221 alcohol addicts in Denmark. Quart. J. Stud. Alc. 17: 633-642, 1956.

227. NOTTERMAN, J., SHOENFELD, W. and BERSH, P. Conditioned heart rate re-

sponses in human beings during experimental anxiety. J. comp. physiol. Psychol. 45: 1-8, 1952.

228. O'LEARY, K. D. and WILSON, G. T. Behavior therapy; application and outcome. Englewood Cliffs, NJ; Prentice-Hall; 1975.

229. ORNE, M. T. On the social psychology of the psychological experiment; with particular reference to the demand characteristics and their implications. Amer. Psychol. 17: 776-783, 1962.

230. PAREDES, A., JONES, B. and GREGORY, D. An exercise to assist alcoholics to maintain prescribed levels of intoxication. Alc. tech. Rep., Okla. City 2: 34-36, 1974.

231. PATTERSON, G. R. and REID, J. B. Intervention for families of aggressive boys; a replication study. Behav. Res. Ther., Oxford 11: 383-394, 1974.

232. PATTISON, E. M. A critique of abstinence criteria in the treatment of alcoholism. Int. social Psychiat. 14: 268-276, 1968.

233. PATTISON, E. M. A critique of alcoholism treatment concepts; with special reference to abstinence. Quart. J. Stud. Alc. 27: 49-71, 1966.

234. PATTISON, E. M. Nonabstinent drinking goals in the treatment of alcoholics. Pp. 401-455. In: GIBBINS, R. J., ISRAEL, Y., KALANT, H., POPHAM, R. E., SCHMIDT, W. and SMART, R. G., eds. Research advances in alcohol and drug problems. Vol. 3. New York; Wiley; 1976.

235. PATTISON, E. M., HEADLEY, E. B., GLESER, G. C. and GOTTSCHALK, L. A. Abstinence and normal drinking; an assessment of changes in drinking patterns in alcoholics after treatment. Quart. J. Stud. Alc. 29: 610-633, 1968.

236. PATTISON, E. M., SOBELL, M. B. and SOBELL, L. C., eds. Emerging concepts of alcohol dependence. New York; Springer; 1977.

237. PHARES, E. J. Locus of control in personality. Morristown, NJ; General Learning Press; 1974.

238. PITTMAN, D. J. and TATE, R. L. A comparison of two treatment programs for alcoholics. Int. J. social Psychiat. 18: 183-193, 1972.

239. POMERLEAU, O. F. and BRADY, J. P. Behavior modification in medical practice. Penn. med. J. 78: 49-53, 1975.

240. RACHMAN, S. and TEASDALE, J. Aversion therapy and behavior disorders; an analysis. London; Routledge & Kegan Paul; 1969.

241. REGESTER, D. C. Change in autonomic responsivity and drinking behavior of alcoholics as a function of aversion therapy. Ph.D. dissertation, University of Nebraska; 1971.

242. REID, J. B. and PATTERSON, G. R. The modification of aggression and stealing behavior of boys in the home setting. In: BANDURA, A. and RIBES, E., eds. Behavior modification; experimental analysis of aggression and delinquency. Hillsdale, NJ; Lawrence Erlbaum Associates. [In press.]

243. REINERT, R. E. and BOWEN, W. T. Social drinking following treatment for alcoholism. Bull. Menninger Clin. 32: 280-290, 1968.

244. RHODES, R. J. and HUDSON, R. M. A follow-up of tuberculous Skid Row alcoholics. I. Social adjustment and drinking behavior. Quart. J. Stud. Alc. 30: 119-128, 1969.

245. ROHSENOW, D. J. and O'LEARY, M. R. Locus of control research on alcoholic populations; a review. I. Development, scales and treatment. Int. J. Addict. [In press.]

246. ROSEN, A. C. A comparative study of alcoholic and psychiatric patients with the MMPI. Quart. J. Stud. Alc. 21: 253-266, 1960.
247. RUGGELS, W. L., ARMOR, D. J., POLICH, J. M., MOTHERSHEAD, A. and STEPHEN, M. A follow-up study of clients at selected alcoholism treatment centers funded by NIAAA; final report. Prepared for U.S. National Institute on Alcohol Abuse and Alcoholism. Menlo Park, CA; Stanford Research Institute; 1976.
248. RUSSELL, J. A. and MEHRABIAN, A. The mediating role of emotions in alcohol use. J. Stud. Alc. 36: 1508-1536, 1975.
249. SANDERSON, R. E., CAMPBELL, D. and LAVERTY, S. G. An investigation of a new aversive conditioning treatment for alcoholism. Quart. J. Stud. Alc. 24: 261-275, 1963.
250. SANSWEET, S. J. Aversion therapy. The Wall Street Journal, 2 January 1974.
251. SCHACHTER, S. Obesity and eating; internal and external cues differentially affect the eating behavior of obese and normal subjects. Science 161: 751-756, 1968.
252. SCHACHTER, S. Some extraordinary facts about obese humans and rats. Amer. Psychol. 26: 129-144, 1971.
253. SCHACHTER, S., GOLDMAN, R. and GORDON, A. Effects of fear, food deprivation and obesity on eating. J. Person. social Psychol. 10: 91-97, 1968.
254. SCHAEFER, H. H. Twelve-month follow-up of behaviorally trained ex-alcoholic social drinkers. Behav. Ther., N.Y. 3: 286-289, 1972.
255. SCHAEFER, H. H., SOBELL, M. B. and MILLS, K. S. Baseline drinking behavior in alcoholics and social drinkers; kinds of drinks and sip magnitude. Behav. Res. Ther., Oxford 9: 23-27, 1971.
256. SCHAEFER, H. H., SOBELL, M. B. and MILLS, K. C. Some sobering data on the use of self-confrontation with alcoholics. Behav. Ther., N.Y. 2: 28-39, 1971.
257. SCHAEFER, H. H., SOBELL, M. B. and SOBELL, L. C. Twelve month follow-up of hospitalized alcoholics given self-confrontation experiences by videotape. Behav. Ther., N.Y. 3: 282-285, 1972.
258. SELIGMAN, M. P. and HAGER, J. L. Biological boundaries of learning. New York; Appleton-Century-Crofts; 1972.
259. SELZER, M. L. The Michigan Alcoholism Screening Test; the quest for a new diagnostic instrument. Amer. J. Psychiat. 127: 1653-1658, 1971.
260. SELZER, M. L. and HOLLOWAY, W. H. A follow-up of alcoholics committed to a state hospital. Quart. J. Stud. Alc. 18: 98-120, 1957.
261. SHAFII, M., LAVELY, R. and JAFFE, R. Meditation and the prevention of alcohol abuse. Amer. J. Psychiat. 132: 942-945, 1975
262. SHOBEN, E. J., JR. Views on the etiology of alcoholism. III. The behavioristic view. Pp. 47-55. In: KRUSE, H. D., ed. Alcoholism as a medical problem. New York; Hoeber-Harper; 1956.
263. SILVER, M. J. Investigator effects, experimenter effects and experimenter bias; a taxonomy and a clarification. J. Supp. Abst. Serv. 3 (Ms. no. 335); 1973.
264. SILVERSTEIN, S. J., NATHAN, P. E. and TAYLOR, H. A. Blood alcohol level estimation and controlled drinking by chronic alcoholics. Behav. Ther., N.Y. 5: 1-15, 1974.
265. SKOLODA, T. E., ALTERMAN, A. I., CORNELISON, F. S., JR. and GOTTHEIL,

E. Treatment outcome in a drinking-decisions program. J. Stud. Alc. 36: 365-380, 1975.

266. SMITH, H. W. Man and his gods. New York; Grosset & Dunlop; 1956.

267. SOBELL, L. C. and SOBELL, M. B. A self-feedback technique to monitor drinking behavior in alcoholics. Behav. Res. Ther., Oxford 11: 237-238, 1973.

268. SOBELL, L. C. and SOBELL, M. B. Outpatient alcoholics give valid self-reports. J. nerv. ment. Dis. 161: 32-42, 1975.

269. SOBELL, L. C. and SOBELL, M. B. Driver records; an aid in follow-up tracking and verification of self-reports of alcoholics. Int. J. Addict. [In press.]

270. SOBELL, L. C., SOBELL, M. B. and SCHAEFER, H. H. Alcoholics name fewer mixed drinks than social drinkers. Psychol. Rep. 28: 493-494, 1971.

271. SOBELL, M. B., SCHAEFER, H. H. and MILLS, K. C. Differences in baseline drinking behavior between alcoholics and normal drinkers. Behav. Res. Ther., Oxford 10: 257-267, 1972.

272. SOBELL, M. B. and SOBELL, L. C. Individualized behavior therapy for alcoholics; rationale, procedures, preliminary results and appendix. (California Mental Health Research Monogr. No. 13.) Sacramento; California Department of Mental Hygiene; 1972.

273. SOBELL, M. B. and SOBELL, L. C. Alcoholics treated by individualized behavior therapy; one year treatment outcome. Behav. Res. Ther., Oxford 11: 599-618, 1973.

274. SOBELL, M. B. and SOBELL, L. C. Individualized behavior therapy for alcoholics. Behav. Ther., N.Y. 4: 49-72, 1973.

275. SOBELL, M. B. and SOBELL, L. C. The need for realism, relevance and operational assumptions in the study of substance dependence. Pp. 133-167. In: CAPPELL, H. D. and LeBLANC, A. E., eds. Biological and behavioral approaches to drug dependence. (International Symposia on Alcohol and Drug Problems Series.) Toronto; Addiction Research Foundation; 1975.

276. SOBELL, M. B. and SOBELL, L. C. A brief technical report on the Mobat; an inexpensive portable test for determining blood alcohol concentration. J. appl. Behav. Anal., Lawrence, KS 8: 117-120, 1975.

278. SOBELL, M. B. and SOBELL, L. C. Second year treatment outcome of alcoholics treated by individualized behavior therapy; results. Behav. Res. Ther., Oxford 14: 195-215, 1976.

279. SOBELL, M. B., SOBELL, L. C. and SAMUELS, F. H. The validity of self-reports of alcohol-related arrests by alcoholics. Quart. J. Stud. Alc. 35: 276-280, 1974.

280. SOBELL, M. B., SOBELL, L. C. and SHEAHAN, D. B. Functional analysis of drinking problems as an aid in developing individual treatment strategies. Addict. Behav., Elmsford, NY 1: 127-132, 1976.

281. SOMMER, R. The isolated drinker in the Edmonton beer parlor. Quart. J. Stud. Alc. 26: 95-110, 1965.

282. STEFFEN, J. J., NATHAN, P. E. and TAYLOR, H. A. Tension-reducing effects of alcohol; further evidence and some methodological considerations. J. abnorm. Psychol. 83: 542-547, 1974.

283. STUART, R. B. and DAVIS, B. Slim chance in a fat world. Champaign, IL; Research Press; 1972.

284. SUMMERS, T. Validity of alcoholics' self-reported drinking history. Quart. J.

Stud. Alc. **31:** 972-974, 1970.
285. SYME, L. Personality characteristics of the alcoholic; a critique of current studies. Quart. J. Stud. Alc. **18:** 288-302, 1957.
286. SYTINSKY, I. A. and GUREVITCH, Z. P. Modern methods in treatment of chronic alcoholism; a review of the Soviet literature. Addict. Behav., Oxford **1:** 269-279, 1976.
287. THORESON, C. E. and MAHONEY, M. J. Behavioral self-control. New York; Holt, Rinehart & Winston; 1974.
288. TOMSOVIC, M. A follow-up study of discharged alcoholics. Hosp. Community Psychiat. **21:** 94-97, 1970.
289. TRACEY, D. A. and NATHAN, P. E. Behavioral analysis of chronic alcoholism in four women. J. cons. clin. Psychol. **44:** 832-842, 1976.
290. U.S. NATIONAL INSTITUTE ON ALCOHOL ABUSE AND ALCOHOLISM. First special report to the U.S. Congress on alcohol and health. (DHEW Publ. No. HSM 72-9099.) Washington, DC; U.S. Govt Print. Off.; 1971.
291. VOEGTLIN, W. L. Conditioned reflex therapy of chronic alcoholism; ten years' experience with the method. Rocky Mtn med. J. **44:** 807-811, 1947.
292. VOEGTLIN, W. L. and LEMERE, F. The treatment of alcohol addiction; a review of the literature. Quart. J. Stud. Alc. **2:** 717-803, 1942.
293. VOEGTLIN, W. L., LEMERE, F., BROZ, W. R. and O'HOLLAREN, P. Conditioned reflex therapy of chronic alcoholism. *IV.* A preliminary report on the value of reinforcement. Quart. J. Stud. Alc. **2:** 505-511, 1941.
294. VOGLER, R. E., COMPTON, J. V. and WEISSBACH, T. A. Integrated behavior change techniques for alcoholics. J. cons. clin. Psychol. **43:** 233-243, 1975.
295. VOGLER, R. E., FERSTL, R., KRAEMER, S. and BRENGELMANN, J. C. Electrical aversion conditioning of alcoholics; one year follow-up. J. Behav. Ther., Elmsford, NY **6:** 171-173, 1975.
296. VOGLER, R. E., LUNDE, S. E., JOHNSON, G. R. and MARTIN, P. L. Electrical aversion conditioning with chronic alcoholics. J. cons. clin. Psychol. **34:** 302-307, 1970.
297. VOGLER, R. E., LUNDE, S. E. and MARTIN, P. L. Electrical aversion conditioning with chronic alcoholics; follow-up and suggestions for research. J. cons. clin. Psychol. **36:** 450, 1971.
298. WALTON, H. J., RITSON, E. B. and KENNEDY, R. I. Response of alcoholics to clinic treatment. Brit. med. J. **2:** 1171-1174, 1966.
299. WANBERG, K. W. and HORN, J. L. Alcoholism syndromes related to sociological classifications. Int. J. Addict. **8:** 99-102, 1973.
300. WANBERG, K. W. and KNAPP, J. A multidimensional model for the research and treatment of alcoholism. Int. J. Addict. **5:** 69-98, 1970.
301. WEBB, E. J., CAMPBELL, D. T., SCHWARTZ, R. D. and SECHREST, L. Unobtrusive measures; nonreactive research in the social sciences. Chicago; Rand McNally; 1966.
302. WEINER, J. B. The morning after. New York; Dell; 1974.
303. WIENS, A. N., MONTAGUE, J. R., MANAUGH, T. S. and ENGLISH, C. J. Pharmacological aversive counterconditioning to alcohol in a private hospital; one year follow-up. J. Stud. Alc. **37:** 1320-1324, 1976.
304. WILLIAMS, J. G., BARLOW, D. H. and AGRAS, W. S. Behavioral measurement of severe depression. Arch. gen. Psychiat. **27:** 330-333, 1972.

305. WILLIAMS, R. J. Alcoholics and metabolism. Sci. Amer. 179: 50-53, 1948.
306. WILLIAMS, R. J. and BROWN, R. A. Differences in baseline drinking behavior between New Zealand alcoholics and normal drinkers. Behav. Res. Ther., Oxford 12: 287-294, 1974.
307. WILLIAMS, R. J. and BROWN, R. A. Naming mixed drinks; alcoholics vs social drinkers. Psychol. Rep. 35: 33-34, 1974.
308. WILLIAMS, T. K. The ethanol-induced loss of control concept in alcoholism. Ed.D. dissertation, Western Michigan University; 1970.
309. WILSON, G. T. and DAVISON, G. C. Aversion techniques in behavior therapy; some theoretical and metatheoretical considerations. J. cons. clin. Psychol. 33: 327-329, 1969.
310. WILSON, G. T. and DAVISON, G. C. Behavior therapy and homosexuality; a critical perspective. Behav. Ther., N.Y. 5: 16-28, 1974.
311. WILSON, G. T. and EVANS, I. M. The therapist-client relationship and behavior therapy. In: GURMAN, A. and RAZIN, A., eds. The therapist's contribution to effective psychotherapy. New York; Pergamon [In press.]
312. WILSON, G. T., LEAF, R. C. and NATHAN, P. E. The aversive control of excessive alcohol consumption by chronic alcoholics in the laboratory setting. J. appl. Behav. Anal., Lawrence, KS 8: 13-26, 1975.
313. WILSON, G. T. and ROSEN, R. C. Training controlled drinking in an alcoholic through a multifaceted behavioral treatment program; a case study. In: KRUMBOLTZ, J. D. and THORESON, C. E., eds. Counseling methods. New York; Holt, Rinehart & Winston; 1976.
314. WILSON, G. T. and TRACEY, D. A. An experimental analysis of aversive imagery versus electrical aversive conditioning in the treatment of chronic alcoholics. Behav. Res. Ther., Oxford 14: 41-51, 1976.
315. WISOCKI, P. A. The empirical evidence of covert sensitization in the treatment of alcoholism; an evaluation. Pp. 105-113. In: RUBIN, R. D., FENSTERHEIM, H., HENDERSON, J. D. and ULLMANN, L. P., eds. Advances in behavior therapy. New York; Academic Press; 1972.
316. WOLPE, J. The practice of behavior therapy. 2d ed. New York; Pergamon; 1974.
317. WRIGHT, H. F. Observational child study. In: MUSSEN, P. H., ed. Handbook of research methods in child development. New York; Wiley; 1960.
318. ZUSMAN, J. Mental health service quality control; an idea whose time has come. Comp. Psychiat. 13: 497-506, 1972.
319. ZUSMAN, J. and BISSONNETTE, R. The case against evaluation; with some suggestions for improvement. Int. J. ment. Hlth 2: 111-125, 1973.

Index of Persons

Al-Issa, I., 82
Anant, S. S., 102
Antes, D. E., 176(*n.*)
Ashem, B., 102, 103
Azrin, N. H., 86, 109, 138, 175, 187

Bacon, S. D., 7
Bailey, M. B., 10
Bandura, A., 66, 94, 99, 106, 112, 154, 189
Barker, R. G., 65
Barr, H. L., 176(*n.*)
Bateson, G., 191
Beech, H. R., 96
Begelman, D. A., 112
Bigelow, G. E., 30, 77, 79, 80, 87, 109, 139
Bissonnette, R., 170
Blake, B. G., 91, 95, 96, 130
Blane, H. T., 168, 177
Bois, C., 117, 118, 121, 122, 123
Bolstad, O. D., 65
Bowman, R. S., 42
Brady, J. P., 83
Briddell, D. W., 37, 91, 187
Brown, R. A., 31, 151, 156
Burt, D. W., 100

Caddy, G. R., 32, 47, 75, 81, 96, 97, 117, 118, 121, 122, 123, 124, 125, 128, 141, 188
Cahalan, D., 1, 9(*tab.*), 10(*n.*), 12(*tab.*), 14(*tab.*), 15(*tab.*), 16(*tab.*), 17(*tab.*), 19(*tab.*), 20(*tab.*), 21(*tab.*), 22(*n.*), 41, 42, 186

Callahan, E. J., 106
Campbell, L., 3d., 83, 84, 94, 96, 111
Cappell, H., 5, 185
Caudill, B. D., 56, 62, 66, 68, 70, 71, 72
Cautela, J. R., 102, 106
Cavan, S., 60
Cisin, I. H., 6, 7, 13
Claeson, L. E., 93
Clark, W. B., 20(*tab.*)
Cohen, M., 61, 77, 79, 138
Conger, J. J., 184
Cravey, R. H., 46
Crawford, J. J., 168, 169
Cutler, R. E., 46, 64, 65, 67, 68

Danaher, B. G., 101
Darwin, C., 166
Davidson, W. S., 96
Davison, G. C., 100, 101, 102, 110
Dollard, J., 184
Donner, L., 102, 103

Eisler, R. M., 5, 135
Elkins, R. L., 100, 101
Epstein, L. H., 137(*n.*)
Eysenck, H. J., 90, 96

Foster, F. M., 173(*n.*)
Fox, J., 7
Foy, D. W., 136
Franks, C. M., 4, 90, 98
Friedman, P. R., 111

210

Index of Subjects

213